ADVANCED BRAND MANAGEMENT

MANAGEMENT

From Vision to Valuation

ADVANCED BRAND MANAGEMENT
From Vision to Valuation

Paul Temporal

John Wiley & Sons (Asia) Pte Ltd

This publication is designed to provide accurate and authoritative information in
regard to the subject matter covered. It is sold with the understanding that the Publisher
is not engaged in rendering professional services. If professional advice or other expert
assistance is required, the services of a competent professional person should be sought.

Other Wiley Editorial Offices

John Wiley & Sons, Inc., 605 Third Avenue, New York, NY 10158-0012, USA
John Wiley & Sons Ltd, Baffins Lane, Chichester, West Sussex PO19 1UD, England
John Wiley & Sons (Canada) Ltd, 22 Worcester Road, Rexdale, Ontario M9W 1L1, Canada
John Wiley & Sons Australia Ltd, 33 Park Road (PO Box 1226), Milton, Queensland 4046,
Australia
Wiley-VCH, Pappelallee 3, 69469 Weinheim, Germany

Library of Congress Cataloging-in-Publication Data:

0-471-47925-X (Cloth)

Typeset in 11/15 point, Goudy by Linographic Services Pte Ltd
Printed in Singapore by Saik Wah Press Pte Ltd
10 9 8 7 6 5 4 3 2 1

Contents

Acknowledgments

Contrary to popular belief, writing books gets harder, not easier the more you progress. Readers have higher expectations, the number of books available increases, and pressures on time are more difficult to handle. To produce a book like this requires not just a lot of co-operation, but a lot of assistance and ideas from other people. I would like to take this opportunity to express my gratitude to some of the many people and organizations that have wholeheartedly given of their precious time and energy to help make the book what it is.

Aaron Boey
Abdullah Fazalbhoy
Bronwyn Coles
Catherine Chai
Catherine Hu
Danny Ng
David Haigh
Edward Chalk
Gary Moyer
Mark Fields
Natalie Croft
Nik Mustapha
Peter Snell
Stan Shih
Takahiro Ooi
Tom Maas
Tomomitsu Taue

Walter Cheung
Yusuke Horita
Acer
Aegis
Asia Market Intelligence
Brand Finance
Hakuhodo Inc.
Hang Seng Bank
Jim Beam
Lloyds TSB
Malaysia Airlines
Mazda
Mercedes-Benz
Oxford University Press
Phil Corporation
Philips
Unilever Malaysia

Thanks also to the ever-friendly Wiley team for their support, in particular, Janis Soo for managing the project so well, Robyn Flemming for great editing, and Nick Wallwork for the opportunity and guidance.

Preface

Brands have never been more important than they are today. The accelerating rate of turbulent change, the volatility of economies and markets, the relentless progress of technologies and innovations, and increasing market fragmentation have caused the destruction of many companies and their products that have failed to develop the lifeline of a strong brand. Though we are not far into the new century, already markets are littered with failures, physical and virtual, that could have survived had strong branding been in place.

We are in the world of parity where everything tends to be equal, and the world marketplace is a world of commodities. The availability of new technologies has enabled companies to easily replicate the products, systems, services, and processes of others, generating a huge strategic problem for businesses of differentiation. Added to this problem is the rapidly decreasing life cycle of products, in some cases now down to a matter of weeks.

Strong brands alleviate these problems. They differentiate companies and products from their competitors, make access to new markets and industries easier, provide returns on investment worth multiples of the value of the net assets of businesses through an endless stream of profits, and—best of all—have no life cycle if they are looked after and managed well.

Powerful brands, when nurtured and managed properly, give companies longevity and the potential for immortality. Coca-Cola is nearly 120 years old, and Tide washing powder is over 50 years old, but both are still leaders in their chosen markets, despite intensive competition. Powerful brands such as these wouldn't have lasted so long without careful management, and it is brand management that this book is about.

Good brand management helps make strong brands and great customer relationships, but it is surprising that many companies still pay little attention to the management of their brands, compared to the meticulous way in which they manage other aspects of their business.

One reason for this might be that in many parts of the world, brand management is still fairly new to marketers. In Asia, for example, it is only recently that the power of branding has been understood, and there are many young people who find themselves in senior positions having had little brand management experience. Not that this situation is peculiar to the Far East. Branding itself is still an evolutionary concept, and the techniques associated with managing brands are also developing and emerging.

This book is intended to help all those people who have brand-related responsibilities, from CEOs to product managers, by providing a comprehensive guide to the different elements involved in brand management, including examples of good and not-so-good practice from around the world. The management of a brand is no easy task because of the dynamic nature of the forces that impact on markets. It is not a theoretical concept one can learn quickly—it is highly practical in nature—and so the book focuses on lots of practical examples and cases so that readers can learn from the experiences of others.

It will provide you with answers to many of the main issues facing brand builders and managers, such as:

- Should the brand vision replace the corporate vision?
- Should the brand determine business strategy, or vice versa?
- What returns on investment do brands bring?
- How can the long-term and short-term demands of the business be accommodated in brand management?
- Should brands be proactive or reactive, strategic or tactical?
- How is it possible to gain a strong and sustainable brand position and differentiation in crowded markets?
- How are decisions made to reposition brands, revitalize them, or let them die?
- How are brands revitalized?
- How far can a brand be stretched, and what are the pitfalls to avoid?
- What roles do emotion and attitude play in brand management and development?
- What impact do new technologies have on brand management and consumer relationships?

- How is brand management different in the physical and virtual worlds?
- What options are available for organizing and structuring the brand management process?
- What role should the CEO play in brand building and management?
- How can we use our limited budgets to best advantage?
- What trends are taking place in brand communications?
- How can we create a brand culture so that everyone lives the brand?
- How can we measure the success of our brand(s)?
- What tools and checklists are needed in brand management?

Just to give you a flavor of what is to come in the book, here is a light-hearted, but nevertheless accurate, view of just a few of the decisions and situations that face those whose job it is to manage a brand.

A DAY IN THE LIFE OF A BRAND

I'm a quite famous brand—well, I like to think so. I'm available in most parts of the world and have pretty good market share and profitability in most markets. I've been around for quite a while (don't ask me my age), and hope that what they say about brands having no life cycles is true.

I have a brand manager (BM) who is quite senior in the company here, and he reports to a brand management committee that includes other brand managers in our product brand portfolio, plus corporate marketing, and various others who seem to be determined to influence my future in some way. People think strong brands have it easy, but that's not the case. Here's a typical day that I have to go through.

8.00 am: Agency news. The worldwide advertising agency has got the boot, and has to re-pitch against the competition next month. Well, they've not done too badly, but I never thought they understood my personality very well. I hope the top guys give the new agency a thorough briefing—I seem to remember the last one wasn't too great.

9.00 am: Panic in the camp. Europe had a quality problem in the French factory the day before yesterday that hit the press. There were actually accusations that I was poisoning people! Why do the press always report the bad news? Discussions here (most of which I can't repeat) centered around what we *might* say. They are still talking—faxes and phones are going berserk, and we still haven't replied to the public at all. This is going to get worse if Corporate Communications doesn't snap out of it. Haven't they heard of crisis management? And what about my image? People trust me; I stand for top quality! I feel a headache coming on, and I suspect others' heads will roll.

10.00 am: Good news at last. I have been valued in dollar terms and have made it into the top 20 brands in the world. I've been telling top management that I'm a strategic asset, not just a brand, but did they believe me? I restrain myself from saying, "I told you so."

11.00 am: Request from Asia to change my personality to fit the local culture. My BM said, "No way." Good for him. He said that we have to be consistent with my brand character, but we can emphasize the more appropriate aspects in campaigns, and can use market communications to localize me a bit more.

12.30 pm: Lunch and indigestion. I was asked to co-brand with a drinks brand that appeals to an entirely different audience. Thanks, but no thanks. Despite promises of more sales, which has the salesforce leaping up and down, my values just don't fit. I mean, really! Who wants to be seen arm-in-arm with a down-market product? Image is everything.

2.00 pm: My BM was put on the spot by the chief marketing officer (prompted by an outside consultant, I suspect), who has asked him what business I am in. To make it clear, he said: "Not the *company* business, the business of your *brand*." A great question, and a predictable answer from my BM of: "Let me give that some serious thought." I wonder how long he's got to come up with the answer, and where this will lead us.

2.30 pm: The rack. This is pure torture. They are having discussions about how far they can "stretch" me—or "extend the brand," as my BM puts it. Much talk of which target audience, why, will it work, what about my current positioning, etc. I feel most uncomfortable—like a patient being discussed by a group of specialists, some of whom are of doubtful origin and qualifications.

4.00 pm: Message from London asking HQ to refresh me, as I'm looking a bit old-fashioned. Thanks a lot, guys—and what about yourselves? Well, I don't mind some new packaging if my fans like it, but let's be sensible and not do anything that is out of character. Evolution is OK—revolution is out. My BM says he will take a look at this.

4.30 pm: Gloom all around. The markets have been down now for over two weeks, and recession is all the talk. People at the top want my talk time cut—"Reduce all A&P expenditure on all brands" came the imperative from on high. Argument ensues, with one camp saying "Cutting down is good if we focus a lot more," and the other saying "If our competitors are going to be quiet, now is the time to spend more, create more market share, and be remembered as the brand that was always there for people." I kind of like that last argument, but I fear the cost cutters will win.

6.00 pm: I was just about to call it a day when I heard that the proposed customer relationship management program for me has been given the go-ahead. Great! Now I can begin to get to know all my customers individually, and look after those who are high-value and have been very loyal to me. I hope the team doesn't get too caught up in technology, and that they concentrate on how better relationships can really benefit consumers.

6.30 pm: Let's go out on a high note. I have to attend an event I've sponsored tonight. See you tomorrow!

WHAT IS BRAND MANAGEMENT?

Of course, not all matters of importance hit brand managers every day, like the above suggests, but these are typical important strategic issues that brand managers have to deal with over time. They also have to involve themselves in many other things as part of their work, but put very simply, brand management is a process that tries to take control over everything a brand does and says, and the way in which it is perceived. There is a need, therefore, to influence the perceptions of various target audiences to ensure that people see what you want them to see with respect to your brand. This means identifying clearly what your brand stands for, its personality, and how to position it so that it appears different and better than competing brands. It involves integrated communications, and constant tracking of the brand and its competitors.

The overall aim of this process, naturally, is to increase the value of the brand over time, however that may be measured. Profitability will be one measure, market share another, volume of sales perhaps another, and the emotional associations of the brand with consumers yet another. These will be discussed as we go along. But one of the hardest parts of brand management is to achieve a balance between the short-term numbers given by top management to satisfy various stakeholders, and the long-term growth of the brand. For example, price cutting might buy short-term market share—but at what cost to the brand's long-term image? For listed companies there is the need to perform to stock market requirements on a quarterly basis in terms of sales and profitability while maintaining, or even increasing, investment in the brands that deliver the results. There can therefore be conflicts of interest between the needs of the business and those of the brands.

As you will now have begun to see, brand management is a difficult job. What makes it more difficult is the fact that many of the elements that influence a brand's success are often outside the control of those responsible for its management, such as competitor moves, economic factors, and consumer trends. Proactivity and reactivity live side by side in the daily work of brand managers, and this is the very reason that makes brand management so exciting—brands live in ever-changing landscapes, full of opportunities and challenges.

There are also several dimensions of a more tactical nature that have to be given meticulous attention on an everyday basis. Brand managers have to juggle constantly with many activities to ensure that they can affect the image of the brand in both the short and long term. The situation becomes more complex and difficult for those whose job it is to manage a corporate brand under which there may be several sub-brands and/or product brands, as consistency and autonomy of brands can conflict. All of these factors will be discussed in the book. Also, the subject of discussion will be the culture of the company, whether the right brand culture has been put into place, and how to do this.

But it all starts with brand strategy. Every aspect of brand management should be driven by the strategy of the brand, whether corporate or product. Unfortunately, many companies don't have a clear brand strategy and end up with confused images and consumer perceptions of the brand. They concentrate on trying to control the outside elements without having clear guidelines upon which they can do this.

So, although there are many issues that I will address, it is appropriate to start the book with a look at the changing roles of brand management, brand strategy, and how the interaction between brands and businesses has changed in recent times. I hope you enjoy the book.

1

The Changing Roles of Brand Management

There have been several developments over the last 30 years with respect to how businesses have changed their view of the customer and how consumers have reacted. These changes have led to the emergence of brand management as an important and complex role. Here is a short summary of how business relationships with consumers have evolved, and how the role of brand management has changed as a result.

BUSINESS EVOLUTION AND THE CONSUMER

The dreadful days of product focus

Some of you may remember the early days of mass production, when companies developed products that they thought the public needed and would want to buy, produced them, and then threw them into the market with the conviction that sales would result. The consumer often responded by buying these products because they were new and enhanced the quality of their lives. Consumer-durable and fast-moving goods, such as refrigerators, televisions, and cosmetics, had triggered the insatiable appetite of the consumer for branded products. However, there were as many failures as there were successes during this time, as marketers hadn't really understood what consumers wanted, because *they hadn't asked them*. This approach to marketing has largely disappeared, although when I meet with certain companies I may still have some doubts. Some Japanese companies, for instance, still have a mindset that says, "Let's develop a great product and then go out there and sell it to the consumer, who doesn't know what he wants."

The emergence of market orientation

Marketers soon learned that it was a wise move to understand a little more about what customers had in mind. Mass marketing was still predominant, but marketers began to realize that not all markets were homogenous. Within categories such as washing powders, they discovered that different people expected different types of product performance—for instance, some people wanted a heavy-duty detergent, while others wanted a product suitable for use with delicate fabrics. So, during the 1970s and early 1980s we saw the introduction of market segmentation and the growth of market research as an industry. For the brand manager, this meant the growth of product categories and many opportunities for brand extensions.

The age of the big brands

The age of the big brands dates from the late 1980s, when powerful brands, led by experienced and senior brand managers, began to dominate their chosen markets. There has been a tremendous demand for luxury brands during this time, with some brands, such as Nike, becoming global players. The whole world has now become more brand-conscious. Research studies claim that children become brand-conscious from as young as four years of age. Even in the less-developed and underdeveloped countries, the big brands have a presence and are the focus of consumer attention. However, the fragmentation of markets referred to above has led brand management into the complex world of mass customization, and there has been a strong movement away from pure, generic products manufactured to suit mass markets. Brand management has now turned its attention to customizing generic products to the needs of different market segments, and this has led to a proliferation of products available to consumers, and to tremendous profits for those companies that understand these complex markets correctly.

The realization of brand value

It is now widely acknowledged that brands, if created, developed, and managed well, can achieve spectacular financial results. If we look at the market capitalization of heavily branded companies versus unbranded companies in both the U.S. and the U.K., the S&P and FTSE markets respectively, we see that around 70% or more of the market capitalization isn't represented by the net asset value of the companies concerned. There is a huge gap between market capitalization and net tangible assets, and intangible assets represent this unexplained value, a significant part being the value of the brand itself. Other intangible items include patents, customer lists, licenses, know how, and major contracts, but the value of the brand itself is increasingly becoming the biggest item. Brand names are often worth multiples of the value of the actual business. As a result, brands are often bought and sold for considerable amounts of money, which represent not so much the tangible assets belonging to the company, but the expectation of the brand's level of sales into the foreseeable future.

A strong corporate brand name brings with it additional financial strength which can be measured and used in many ways, including:

- **Mergers and acquisitions:** Brand valuation plays a major part in these undertakings. Potential acquirers of branded goods companies, together with their investors and bankers, find comfort in the knowledge that the price being paid for a company can be substantiated by reference to the value of specific intangible as well as tangible assets being acquired.
- **External investor relations:** For some major companies, building a portfolio of world-class brands is a central objective. Brand valuation can be used to provide hard numbers in what is often a soft argument.
- **Internal communications:** Brand valuation can help explain performance and be used as a means of motivating management. The use of internal royalty rates based on brand values can also make clear to a group of companies the value of the corporate assets they are being allowed to use.

- **Marketing budget allocation:** Brand valuation can assist in budgeting decisions, providing a more systematic basis for decision making.

- **Internal marketing management:** Strategic use of brand valuation techniques allows senior management to compare the success of different brand strategies and the relative performance of particular marketing teams.

- **Balance sheet reporting:** In certain parts of the world, acquired brands are now carried as intangible assets and amortized.

- **Licensing and franchising:** Accurate brand valuation allows a realistic set of charges to be created for the licensing and franchising of brand names.

- **Securitized borrowing:** Companies such as Disney and Levi Strauss have borrowed major sums against their brand names.

- **Litigation support:** Brand valuations have been used in legal cases to defend the brand value, such as in illicit use of a brand name or receivership.

- **Fair trading investigations:** Brand valuation has been used to explain to non-marketing audiences the role of brands, and the importance their value has for the companies that spend so much to acquire and maintain them.

- **Tax planning:** More and more companies are actively planning the most effective domicile for their brand portfolios with branded royalty streams in mind.

- **New product and market development assessment:** New business strategies can be modeled using brand valuation techniques to make judgments on, for example, best brand, best market extension, and best consumer segment.

The difference between brand value and brand equity

There is a subtle difference between brand value and brand equity, and unfortunately the two are often confused. When we talk about *brand value*, we mean the actual financial worth of the brand. *Brand equity*, on the other hand, is often used in referring to the descriptive aspects of a brand, whether symbols, imagery, or consumer associations, and to reflect the strength of a brand in terms of consumer perceptions. It is a term used to represent the more subjective and intangible views of the brand as held by consumers, and is somewhat misleading, as the word "equity" has a financial origin.

There are several dimensions of brand equity, as opposed to brand value. Some of these key aspects of brand performance or strength are:

- *Price premium*—the additional price that consumers will pay for the brand compared to other offers.
- *Satisfaction/loyalty*—levels of satisfaction with the brand that help determine loyalty and prevent price sensitivity.
- *Perceived quality*—relative to other brands.
- *Leadership*—in terms of market leadership, connected to market share.
- *Perceived value*—a value-for-money concept linked not just to tangible items such as quality, but also to intangible factors.
- *Brand personality*—the characteristics of the brand's character that differentiate it from others.
- *Mental associations*—the most important one being trust.
- *Brand awareness and recognition*—key measures of brand strength concerned with how well the brand is known in the market.
- *Market share*—volume, and in some cases perceived positioning.
- *Market price*—premiums enjoyed by the brand.
- *Distribution coverage*—including percentage share.

There is no absolute score for these dimensions, but this mix of attitudinal, behavioral, and market measures of brand equity should be the focus for good brand management practice. What is interesting with this list is that it contains a mixture of what I would see as some of the drivers of both brand value and brand equity. Calculating brand value is, of course, a very specialized area, and the key drivers of brand performance are not all contained in the above list, but there is a substantial overlap. For those readers interested in establishing the financial value of brands, the methodology of Brand Finance plc is outlined in detail in Chapter 9.

So, although there is a difference in terminology, it appears that there is a connection between brand value and brand equity, because many of the components of brand equity have been found to be the drivers of brand value. While we don't need to go into detail here about the methodologies involved in calculating brand equity and brand value, the point I want to make is that companies wishing to achieve spectacular rates of return on investment should be concentrating on building up the strength of the corporate brand name in their chosen markets. Whichever list or source you look at with regard to the components of brand equity and value, it quickly becomes apparent that the only route to doing this is to concentrate on providing consumers with the best possible brand experience, and this is where strong brand management is essential.

Brands driving business strategy

Branding has been so successful that companies are now replacing corporate visions and missions with brand visions and missions. Figure 1.1 shows what I believe to be the old, 20th-century, business model. With this business strategy, companies developed corporate visions and missions that, while they looked impressive when mounted along the corridor walls, were largely ignored by anyone other than top management, who used them to drive the business forward. Branding merely provided support, usually in the form of advertising and promotion (A&P).

Figure 1.1: Brand link to corporate strategy in the 20th century

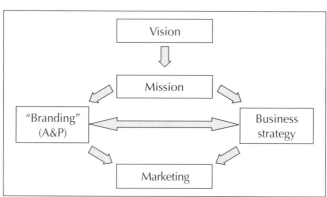

This business process has now changed. The model being used by successful brands is to develop a vision and mission for the *brand*, and to let this drive the business strategy and all related activities, as shown in Figure 1.2. You will notice that business strategy leads directly into customer relationship strategy, and then the marketing activities. This concentration on relationships is explained in further detail below.

Figure 1.2: Brand link to corporate strategy in the 21st century

Greater focus on the brand–consumer relationship

Using this view of the consumer world—that is, focusing on how brands relate to consumers—the latest and most profitable strategies are those that strengthen the relationship of the brand with consumers, and then use this as the basis to drive the business forward and build brand value. Consumer insight plays a vital role here. Examples of how branding has been affected by this new way of thinking are given later in this chapter.

Brands—fascists or friends?

A recent argument, typified in the book *No Logo* by Naomi Klein, suggests that branding is a somewhat antisocial activity. Taking an anti-globalization stance, Klein declares that brands have come to represent "a fascist state where we all salute the logo and have little opportunity for criticism because our newspapers, television stations, Internet servers, streets and retail spaces are all controlled by multinational corporations." She goes on to say that the power and presence of advertising curtails choice, that brands are symbols of American power, and that they result in environmental damage, human rights abuses, and sweat-shop labor.

In its issue dated September 8–14, 2001, *The Economist* magazine led with an article arguing why brands are good for everyone. The article, entitled "Pro Logo®, The case for brands," argues that brands are becoming more vulnerable (and thus less powerful) and consumers more promiscuous (and thus more powerful). It further argues that brands enable consumers to express themselves and to enjoy the benefits of trust, self-expression, and new ways of enjoying their lives. Rather than promoting poor environmental and working conditions, brands are held captive by public opinion and are actively encouraged to help create a better world. The article makes the point, with some force, that, "far from being instruments of oppression, they [brands] make firms accountable to consumers." To my mind, brand management is the conduit through which the psychological demands of consumers are delivered. If brand managers fail to satisfy these complex desires, then the brands they have responsibility for will cease to exist.

Brands that care

It is my belief that the great brands of the future will be brands that care. They will be able to balance profitability with social responsibility. They will balance brand spirit with human spirit. They will be less unilateral in their actions and more altruistic. They will behave not as businesses, but as living entities that care for what happens in the world and for the people who live in it. Above all, they will focus on relationship building and bringing people together.

All of the above add up to a distinct shift in the role and status of brand management in the commercial world.

THE CHANGING ROLES OF BRAND MANAGEMENT

Over the last couple of decades, there have been some discernible changes in the role of brand management and the activities of brand managers. Principally, they consist of the following changes in emphasis.

Change from an industry focus to a market focus

One of the more obvious trends in business has been the movement away from product-led marketing toward customer-led marketing. This needs little explanation, but its impact on brand management in one sense has been to force managers to get closer to, and listen to, the customer. This has brought about many initiatives in market research, customer service, and quality management, and has also meant that brand managers are increasingly getting involved in new product development.

Change from tactical thinking to strategic thinking

Another change has been the movement of corporate strategic thinking away from looking purely at how to grow the business within a specific industry, toward a mindset that looks at expansion across many industries and in multiple markets. This has led brand management to take a much more strategic view, and to become a more holistic activity, looking at how to project consistent identities and create consistent images in a variety of different situations. Brand managers still, however, have to fight the day-to-day tactical battles associated with shifting markets and competitive attacks.

Change from local market focus and analysis to global market focus and analysis

The economies of scale required to achieve world-class brands and the breakdown of market boundaries has meant that more companies are adopting a global focus, and that brand management now has to achieve the right balance between global identities and local adaptations. This trend has also led to the emergence of many more strategic alliances involving co-branding, in order to reduce the cost of global reach. In some cases, companies are now telling brand managers to tailor brand offerings specifically to local markets, as is the case with Coca-Cola's "Think Local, Act Local" global strategy.

Change from product management to category management

Vicious competition in many markets, especially in fast-moving consumer goods, has given rise to the management of categories as opposed to individual products, with the brand manager looking at a multi-product portfolio and a complex set of positioning alternatives. This has been spurred in part by the fact that consumers think in terms of categories, such as shampoos, skincare products, and so on. There has also been a shift in power, especially in fast-moving consumer goods, from the brand manager to the retailer, and so brand managers must cope with the reality that their brands have to fit in with what the retailer would like to offer to the consumer. Brand managers have to constantly assess what value their brand(s) are providing to the retailer and the consumer in the chosen category. Constant monitoring of competitive intruders is mandatory, as they may quickly erode the value a brand represents. Brand managers now have to view individual brands within a mix of several brands that satisfy both the consumer's desire for choice and the seller's need for profitability and a target audience.

As a result of this competition, the creation of new categories has now become important, as some of the power brands crowd existing categories with their product line extensions. (Brand extensions are discussed in Chapter 4.) Smart companies are changing the nature of categories, as shown in the case of Phil Corporation in Chapter 2.

Change from product branding to corporate branding

There has been a marked change in direction, by companies around the world, away from concentrating on product branding and toward focusing on the corporate brand. Even the masters of product branding, Procter & Gamble (P&G), are now putting much more strategic effort into leveraging their corporate brand name. There are many reasons for this. When a company is creating and building brands independently, with little endorsement from the parent, it is an expensive exercise. Product branding requires each brand to stand on its own and have its own investment, which in research and development (R&D) and A&P alone can be enormous. Without generous parental support, getting through the stages of brand awareness and acceptance in the marketplace can be highly resource-consuming, and this is one reason why Unilever is reducing the number of its brands from 1,600 to 400.

While product branding continues to play an important part in brand strategy, there has been a marked trend toward corporate and umbrella branding, with even the traditional die-hard product brand organizations such as Procter & Gamble bringing the corporate brand more into the spotlight. P&G has now made leveraging the corporate brand a global strategy, and throughout the world we are now seeing its initials used in support of product brands. One reason for this is that, for decades, P&G has been losing out on building the dollar value of the parent brand itself. In 2000, the market capitalization of the company sadly declined, but if we look at the stock market indices around the world, it is plain to see that heavily branded companies consistently outperformed unbranded companies in market capitalization over the last 20 years. With corporate branding, most frequently seen where the company adds its name to the product brands it launches, there is the added value of trust and the shared synergies of the other investments needed. But one of the main determinants of this trend is the fact that brands can be valued in financial terms.

Change from product responsibility to customer relationship responsibility

Another interesting development has been the move away from the management of product(s) to the management of customer relationships, signified by the fact that some companies are now giving brand managers responsibility for specific groups of customers, across an entire product range. In this respect, *brand* management is becoming *customer* management. Customer relationship management, as a discipline, is now regarded as a necessary part of the brand manager's skill repertoire. This is dealt with in detail in Chapter 6.

Change from managing the physical brand world to both physical and virtual brand worlds

The rapid rise of the Internet as an information and commercial tool has forced traditional brand companies to establish Internet branding strategies. The virtual world raises additional problems for the brand manager, especially in terms of providing consumers with a consistent brand experience. The Internet world is complex and ever-changing, and is characterized by extreme volatility. The rules of branding in the virtual world are somewhat different from those that apply in the physical world; nevertheless, it is a "must have" and will be discussed in Chapter 7.

Change from managing brand performance to managing brand value and equity

Companies have now become much more concerned with the total value of their brands, not just with profitability. The valuation of brands is by no means an exact science, but the sale of brands for prices far in excess of their asset valuation has meant that brand building has become a business in its own right. For the brand manager, this means that several measures of performance have to be taken into account simultaneously, as brand equity measurement can include a whole host of variables, including brand awareness, brand loyalty, perceived quality, price, market share and cash-flow premiums, internationality, support, protection, and many others.

Brand valuation has come into play over the last decade or so as a technique for justifying, and measuring returns on, brand investment. Brand management has now become the management of profitable strategic assets (brands) that can often be worth multiples of the net assets of the business, and so the performance of brand managers is now more closely evaluated on this basis.

Change from financial accountability to social responsibility

While those people responsible for brand management are very much judged on the financial performance of the brands under their charge, they also have to balance this with a commitment to social responsibility. Many companies are now tying their brands into the needs of communities and helping to solve societal problems, such as Hewlett-Packard is doing with its community programs. Brand management isn't just about creating profit at all costs, as Naomi Klein would have us believe; it is about encouraging people to do better, and helping them to enjoy a better quality of life.

Neither is it about capitalizing on events that are problematic to other people. The terrible events of September 11, 2001, provided some companies with the opportunity to make money out of the tragedy and human suffering. As Professor Stephen A. Greyser said, "Some of the immediate donations of goods and services presumably were driven by a clear philanthropic motivation." But other companies acted in a more socially responsible manner. Hallmark Cards Inc., which saw sales of greetings cards rise rapidly, was meticulous in its brand management by subjecting all cards to a special test so as not to offend. In fact, their first action was to search for cards among the current offerings that might be offensive. Avoiding offense was more important than boosting card sales, and Hallmark withdrew nine cards from distribution. Their second action was to create cards that fitted the changing mood of the nation. Hallmark delivered new patriotic cards in six weeks, as opposed to the 12–15 months normally required for new product development. Dan Sifter, general manager of Hallmark's seasonal card unit, said: "It's a question of finding the right balance between what consumers want to say to each other—finding warmth—and striking the right patriotic note without being jingoistic."

American Greetings took a similar stance. Within 24 hours of the attacks on New York and Washington, it posted four patriotic electronic greetings on its website (www.americangreetings.com), which offers e-cards free of charge. Visitors to the sites sent 350,000 of these greetings during the first week after the attacks.

Brand management is all about building relationships with consumers, not taking advantage of those relationships.

All in all, the above changes mean that brand management is a much more dynamic and complex function than it has ever been, and the challenge now for many companies is to develop the right blend of skills and experience in their managers. What *hasn't* changed is the unassailable fact that strong brand management creates and maintains brand excellence. What *has* changed is that we can now measure the dollar value of brands. This means that chief executive officers can now look at tangibles rather than intangibles; the brand manager's job can now be appraised more exactly; and there is a closer-than-ever focus on the consumer, the source of brand equity and value.

SO, WHO OWNS AND BUILDS BRANDS?

The movement toward a focus on the relationship between the brand and consumers has forced managers to answer the question of who actually owns and builds brands. Until recently, many companies believed that it is *they* who build brands. The correct answer to this question, now acknowledged by leading brand companies, is that it is the *consumer* who owns and builds brands. The enlightened companies have remembered that brands only exist in the minds of consumers, and without the psychological commitment from consumers they are merely companies, products, and services, and will remain so.

This undisputed fact is the rationale for replacing corporate visions with brand visions, and for allowing the brand to dictate business strategy. The fact that it is consumers who own and build brands doesn't mean that brand management has nothing to do with the brand-building process. On the contrary, brand management is the catalyst that helps consumers recognize and build relationships with brands. Brands are relationships, and brand managers have to nurture the relationships between brands and consumers. This means, of course, that they have to understand the consumer even better than before, and gain real insight into how their minds work. This only comes from outside-in thinking, as opposed to inside-out thinking—a topic that is explored in the next chapter.

2

Brand Vision, Strategy, and Consumer Insight

BRAND MANAGEMENT BEGINS WITH BRAND STRATEGY

Incoming chief operating officer of Nissan, Carlos Ghosn, said: "One of the biggest surprises is that Nissan didn't care about its brand. There is nobody really responsible for the strategy of the brand" (quoted in *Business Week,* October 1999). To my mind, this is one of the most common mistakes made by companies that would like to have a strong brand but that don't make the grade—*they don't have a brand strategy.* Without a brand strategy, brand management becomes difficult, if not impossible. Strategy gives focus and direction to brand management, and provides the platform that enables brand managers to gain consistency in all their brand-related activities.

But we all know that strategy starts with the business. And for too long, companies have refined the art of inside-out thinking, researching and developing products they think the market will want. The truth is that the most brilliant strategies come from deep consumer insight— really getting inside the minds of the consumers that you hope will build your brand (that is, outside-in thinking). It is this continual search for outside-in thinking that can lead to unusual but real insights into how people perceive things, and what "hot buttons" will switch them on to your brand.

If we use consumer insight, then, the business of the brand might be different from the business of the business, so before we remind ourselves what the key elements of brands are, let's think about the business of

15

brands. It's quite easy—all you have to do is ask yourself one important question: "What business is my brand in?" Consider the following examples.

What business is your brand in? *SAME AS VISION*

Charles Revson, of Revlon Cosmetics, when asked what business Revlon was in, famously replied: "We are not in the business of selling cosmetics, we are in the business of selling hope." He clearly saw that to think of his business as just being cosmetics would lead to non-differentiation. By saying this, he was expressing the business of the brand. Cosmetics manufacturing/selling is clearly what the business does, but the brand gives hope to those who want to be more attractive or more beautiful, perhaps like the Revlon Girl of the Year. This real consumer insight led to the company achieving great positioning and, ultimately, global success.

Whiskey is another such "commodity," but when Johnny Walker Black Label was researched by watching consumers drink it, the brand changed its business strategy. Videos of people drinking with others on different occasions led to a paradigm shift in thinking. After an 18-month boardroom "discussion," it was decided that the company was in the business not of manufacturing and selling high-quality liquor, but of marketing fashion accessories. The consumer insight was seeing people "wear" their drinks as they would a watch, bracelet, or other fashion accessory. Nike isn't in the business of marketing sports shoes and accessories; the brand wants to help athletes and ordinary people get the best out of themselves. I was engaged recently in discussions with a CEO who also had a paradigm shift in thinking. His company makes products that "make things shine," such as car polish, shoe-care products, and so on. He has now decided that his brand is in the "feelings" business, because the end-result of using his brands is that consumers feel good about themselves and their image. This paradigm shift in thinking has impacted greatly on the company and is taking it into previously unsought areas.

Perhaps one of the best examples of looking at the brand as a business is that of Hallmark Inc., detailed in the following case study.

Case Study 1

HALLMARK INC.
The business of the Hallmark brand—
a paradigm shift in thinking

If you were to ask people what business they think Hallmark is in, most of them would probably say that the company is in the business of manufacturing and selling greetings cards, and indeed, Hallmark is famous for that type of product. But this isn't what the Hallmark brand business is all about. The Hallmark brand is focused clearly on the relationships business, and the brand wants "to be the best at helping people to express their feelings and strengthen the important relationships in their lives." This is a powerful vision statement, and taking this view of the business has led Hallmark Inc. into a tremendous array of business opportunities that have proved to be highly successful and profitable.

The company has existed for over 90 years, and has around 5,000 stores that generated net sales in 1999 of US$3.9 billion. Hallmark Entertainment is now the leading producer/distributor of mini-series, TV movies, and home videos, and the *Hallmark Hall of Fame* has won more Emmy awards than any other television series. The company is also involved in cable TV, real estate, and the retailing of other relationship-building products such as Crayola Crayons, Silly Putty, party plates, gifts, wrappings, and more.

The whole of the Hallmark business is built around emotion, and it genuinely cares for its customers. Relationships aren't just the foundation for good brands; they are a powerful driver of human emotion and behavior, and by expressing the business in a brand-related way based on building relationships, Hallmark found the key to becoming one of the top privately-owned brands in the world. However, it isn't just the relationships route to branding that has made Hallmark so successful; rather, it's the way it builds emotion into every touchpoint with the consumer, and generates brand loyalty in return.

The role of consumer insight

Hallmark and the other examples referred to above indicate that brands are now driving business strategy, but *only* when they reach deeply into the psychological world of consumer insight. The really "hot buttons" that consumer insights unveil are emotional, not rational, and lead to excellent brand performance.

It is the brand manager's responsibility to work with brand strategy consultancies and other agencies to discover these insights, which are sometimes far from obvious. However, as it is consumers who create brand power, brand managers must discover the underlying motives that exist in their minds that will trigger favorable attitudes and compulsive desires toward their brands.

Living with the consumer

In the never-ending search for consumer insights that may produce a paradigm shift in thinking for brands and businesses, some companies are now hiring research crews to live for a few days with "prototype" consumers, in order to learn how they think and behave in their everyday lives (bedroom and bathroom scenes excluded!). Traditional research—both quantitative and qualitative—has the drawback of relying on what consumers *say*, which is sometimes different from what they actually *do* in real life. Brand management has to find out how to press the "hot buttons" that turn consumers on, and this means gaining a full understanding of what motivates them in real-life situations.

Companies trying to create consumer brands are waking up to the fact that the place to start understanding consumer behavior is in the home, where people's real lives are lived in a context of wide-ranging emotions, the sometimes-conflicting demands of different relationships, and relaxed, rather than ideal, personal standards, as opposed to the office or a research room. For example, Procter & Gamble have been filming homemakers going about their daily routines, and have noticed mothers multitasking. One mother was seen feeding her baby while preparing a meal and snatching glances at the television. In natural scenarios such as this, companies can see what programs and advertisements attract homemakers, and what products they use or could use. A bank in the United States has undertaken similar research to discover the process by which families at various stages of their life cycle discuss and make major financial decisions. Unilever has sent staff out into rural villages in underdeveloped areas to live with the villagers and learn more about their way of life, in order to help with brand relationships and product development (see Case Study 2).

Case Study 2
UNILEVER MALAYSIA
Romancing the consumer

One of Unilever's Path to Growth strategic agendas is "reconnecting with the consumer," with the aim of:

- focusing everyone in the company on the consumer;
- turning knowledge gained about the consumer into creative insight; and
- anticipating and responding to consumer change.

According to Unilever, the only way to achieve this is by:

- deepening their knowledge of consumers' habits and attitudes;
- having a culture of "getting close" to the consumer; and
- having the skills to tap insights into the consumer and to turn them into business opportunities.

Unilever has this strategic thrust as a global initiative, but this case shows how it has been done in this operating company in Malaysia.

In preparation for its Romancing the Consumer program:

- Managers of Unilever Malaysia visited 50 homes and held face-to-face interviews bi-monthly to gain consumer insights.
- Twenty staff brought 120 consumers to the factory quarterly for face-to-face-understanding dialogue.
- All staff were given cross-category training so that not only

could inter-brand communications be enhanced, but also staff could answer questions about any brands asked of them by consumers.

- A specific project—Project Rambo—was devised. The whole company was closed for one day, and every employee—old and young, from the tea lady to the chairman—went out to do merchandising of products in shops to ensure that the visibility of Unilever products at retail customers' premises was first class, and to get retail feedback.

Project Rambo saw high energy and a high commitment by Unilever Malaysia's entire workforce to work with trade partners to enhance product displays to better attract shoppers' attention. The experience even inspired Unilever's employees to tidy up merchandising in stores where they usually shop!

The Rural Marketing Program was another initiative aligned with reconnecting with the consumer, but primarily with those in the rural market. The idea of this program when it was conceived was to raise the awareness of Unilever products in the rural areas of the country by having rural-relevant activities, and at the same time putting products on sale. The program was also aimed at providing Unilever Malaysia with the opportunity to engage rural consumers with Unilever brands and people. The first event, held in October 2000, was a tremendous success, and similar events followed over the next year in different parts of the country.

Additional activities included marketing staff staying in villagers' homes for two days to gain a detailed insight into the usage and buying patterns of household, personal care, and food products. All such events were planned well in advance and started with a meeting with the head of the village and his committee. The team was briefed on the objectives of the event and the type of activities to be organized. These often included traditional games to enable participation by all age groups. The local villagers took charge of these activities, and

Unilever staff organized prizes and appearances by special guests. Each of the events attracted between 3,000 and 6,500 people.

With its ongoing Romancing the Consumer program, the company has been successful in developing a culture of getting consumer insights and using them to drive the business.

Moen Inc., a maker of plumbing equipment, actually videotaped American women in the shower (naturally, with their permission), and discovered that they tended to hold on to the shower unit heating control with one hand while shaving their legs with the other! This safety risk—which hadn't previously been apparent—led Moen to redesign their shower unit to prevent accidental burns.

Research of this kind underlines that brand managers must do their homework country-by-country, as cultural nuances determine consumer behavior. For instance, in the United States and in Mediterranean countries the kitchen is the central part of a family's home life, where they congregate to socialize and talk about their day; whereas in China, say, the kitchen is usually a small area designated just for cooking, and the hall or living room is the part of the home where the family gather to spend time together.

Intel has used an anthropologist to study "the minutiae of daily life" with the aim of making technology much more friendly and fun for consumers. Again, this involves making visits to people's homes and accompanying them on shopping trips and other excursions away from the home. Intel, like many other companies, has come to see that creating products and then trying to persuade consumers to buy them isn't enough; if they really want to understand what makes consumers tick, they must look closely at their behaviors. The result for Intel has been the release of new products, such as the Sound Morpher and the QX3 Computer Microscope for children. The design of these products took into account the behavior of eight- to 14-year-old youngsters, who tend to be a bit rough with the things they use and are very hands-on. The QX3, for instance, although functioning when connected to a personal computer, is detachable from its stand so that the children can share the experience with their friends.

ner insight is the gateway to an understanding of the rational ional behavior of people, and there is no doubt that brand that are built on emotion and the realism of everyday life are more successful. In the following section, you will see how powerful the world of emotion can be in building and managing strong brands.

BUILDING A BRAND STRATEGY

The rational and emotional sides of brand strategy

We must never forget that brand promises are often made in the world of commercial reality—in terms of exceptional quality, service, and, nowadays, innovation. However, this isn't where the source of success for brands lies. These elements are merely the price a company has to pay to get into the branding game, and the branding game is a mind game. As parity becomes the norm, and brands match each other feature-by-feature and attribute-by-attribute, it is becoming harder to create a brand strategy through rational means. So, while consumers screen the rational elements of quality and other compelling product attributes as part of the buying process, the real decision to buy is taken at an emotional level.

As an example of how consumers think using a bi-cameral (left and right brain) thought process, look at the following questions and statements. The *rational* thoughts tend to be analytical and steer people away from emotional buy-in. It is the *emotional* statements that brand managers need from consumers.

Rational	Emotional
Do I need it?	I want it!
What does it do?	It looks cool!
What does it cost?	I'm going to get it!
How does it compare to …?	I only want this one!

If we look at the powerful brands around the world, we can see that they swing consumers highly to the right—making their decisions very emotionally-driven. In fact, the great brands build tremendous emotional capital with their strategies.

Characteristics of power brands—emotional capital

Brand management is increasingly turning more to the emotional side of strategy in order to win and keep customers. The power brands develop emotional capital, because they:

- *Are very personal*—people choose brands for very personal reasons, whether they be self-expression, a sense of belonging, or other reasons.
- *Evoke emotion*—brands sometimes unleash unstoppable emotion, arousing passion and unquestionable excitement.
- *Live and evolve*—they are like people in that they live, grow, evolve, and mature. But luckily, if they are well managed, they have no life cycle and can live forever.
- *Communicate*—strong brands listen, receive feedback, change their behavior as they learn, and speak differently to different people, depending on the situation, just as people do. They believe in dialogue, not monologue.
- *Develop immense trust*—people trust the brands they choose, and often resist all substitutes.
- *Engender loyalty and friendship*—trust paves the way for long-lasting relationships, and brands can be friends for life.
- *Give great experiences*—like great people, great brands are nice to be with, good to have around, and are consistent in what they give to their friends.

Given these facts about the emotional capital that brands develop, we need to move on to see how they actually do it. What is the process of establishing an emotional relationship with consumers?

The emotional brand relationship process

In order to build an emotional brand strategy there are certain steps brand managers have to take, like the steps of a ladder, as shown in Figure 2.1. Let's think of it as two people, as opposed to a brand and consumers. One person sees another across a room at a particular function, and wants to meet them. Following this awareness, an opportunity to meet may arise, and although the conversation is short, it leads to the decision whether or not the interest is sufficient to carry the relationship further. Further meetings reinforce this mutual respect, and the two people become friends. If the friendship blossoms, it generates trust and loyalty between them, and it's highly likely that they will become friends for life or have a lasting relationship.

Figure 2.1: The emotional brand relationship process

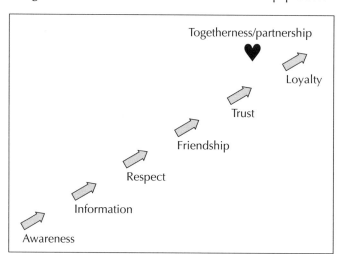

The brand–consumer relationship grows in a very similar way. Awareness comes first, followed by involvement and purchase—a few meetings—which can lead on to the friendship and trust levels, which in turn lead to brand loyalty and lifetime customer relationships. The power brands get to and past the friendship and trust levels; those that don't get that far can often get stuck at the first stage. In fact, big spending on awareness follows many brand launches, but the subsequent management of the brand doesn't take it up the ladder. For example, in 2000 Lastminute.com received an 84% brand awareness rating but only a 17% trust rating. Some brand managers spend millions on awareness—which is an essential step to achieve—but then neglect the emotional side of the brand–consumer relationship which is necessary for real long-term success.

BRAND PERSONALITY, ATTITUDE, AND TRUST

Building brand charisma

Probably one of the most successful ways to build an emotional brand strategy is to create a personality for your brand. The people in the real world that stand out from the crowd always seem to have some kind of "charisma." They have a personality and attitude that others respect and are sometimes in awe of. They have a presence that almost commands people to follow them without asking, and others always want to be around them. They aren't necessarily extroverted or introverted, but people feel good when they are around. Great brands are like great people in this respect, and the role of the brand manager is to manage the brand–consumer relationship by building a powerful and irresistible brand personality.

Like human relationships, whether they turn out right or wrong isn't usually a function of logic and rationality; rather, it is a result of emotional hits and misses. Given this reality, it seems strange that in many cases brand management continues to focus on the non-emotional side of the relationship, promoting features, attributes, price discounts, and so on, which have little impact on the growth of the brand–customer relationship. Such activities might bring in short-term sales increases, but they are open to imitation and won't attract and retain customers by developing an emotional relationship with them. In fact, they may well discourage this and "cheapen" the brand in the eyes of consumers.

Relationships thrive on emotions; they survive or perish depending on the emotional fit between people. Brands therefore have to reflect personalities that people like, and this means having an emotional basis or edge to them. Indeed, the best brands have personalities carefully crafted to suit them and their target audiences. People have a universal longing to be liked, given attention, and to be loved. But brand management often ignores this. Research clearly shows that companies lose 68% of their customers because they feel neglected or aren't given attention. (For details of this research and similar findings, see *Romancing the Customer*, by myself and Martin Trott, John Wiley &

Sons, Singapore, 2001.) This makes the emotional dimension of the brand–consumer relationship very important, and it is the personality and attitude of the brand that attracts and keeps people loyal to it. Case Study 3 shows how an established brand has taken itself to a higher level in the light of more competition, by creating an appropriate personality based on transforming rational attributes into emotional ones.

Case Study 3

LAND ROVER
Turning rational attributes into an emotional brand personality

The attraction of a strong personality is irresistible, and clever brand managers build personality into their companies, products, and services. Land Rover agrees that the brand (or marque) gives products an identity, as well as authenticity and authority. But it also agrees that the rational traits and attributes that products have aren't powerful enough discriminators in the consumers' decision to buy.

Land Rover took the rational attributes determined by research and turned them into emotional personality characteristics, emphasizing that brands have to appeal to the heart as well as the head.

The rational attributes held by Land Rover were:

- 4x4 engineering and capability;
- heritage;
- robust; and
- individualistic.

Land Rover decided that these attributes weren't enough, and that more-muscular emotional values had to be articulated and introduced into everything Land Rover did. This was especially important as competitors could copy Land Rover's rational attributes through engineering, quality, reliability, specifications, performance, and styling. So, the following emotional values were created, based on rational attributes.

- *Individualism*—as opposed to the quirkiness of "individualistic."
- *Authenticity*—as opposed to "heritage" with its museum-like, musty connotation.
- *Guts and determination*—as opposed to "robust."
- *Supremacy and leadership*—as opposed to "4x4 engineering and capability."

Land Rover then added the characteristics that its target audience could relate to, namely:

- the excitement of adventure; and
- the love of freedom.

These characteristics were felt to be much more powerful and expressive of the Land Rover marque, and differentiated Land Rover's products from the rest of the crowd.

Another of the world's most famous brands, still extremely valuable despite legal problems, has built its identity on just two personality characteristics, though they, too, are emotionally-based. The brand is Marlboro, and the characteristics are strength and independence. The projection of these characteristics has made the brand world-class, with the Marlboro cowboy (strong and independent), Marlboro country (wide-open plains and imposing mountains), packaging (strong red and white colors), and appropriate sponsorships (such as Formula 1) all symbolizing these two personality traits.

Nike is a similar brand that has risen to fame through its "Just Do It" attitude, symbolizing the urge to get the best out of oneself, to push beyond one's limits, to win—a truly heroic brand. Brands such as these manage not just to develop a personality that the target audience likes, but also have an "attitude" toward life that attracts people.

Absolut vodka is another brand with a distinctive personality and attitude made up mainly of wit and humor. The brand itself and its market communications were created before the vodka was ever made. It is Absolut's wit, rather than its taste, that is the reason for the brand's success. As the president of Absolut, Goran Lundqvist, says: "Absolut is a personality. We like certain people, but some people are just more fun and interesting."

Brand attitude

Brand attitude is a complexity of things, but for the consumer it is based largely on what the brand stands for and, in particular, how the brand personality is communicated. Brand attitude is a product of brand communications—how the brand talks to the consumer. It is contained in the visuals and the copy of advertisements, for example. If a brand has a personality constructed around the words "warm," "friendly," and "approachable," and communicates this well, it will be perceived as having a "caring" attitude. The words "knowledgeable," "trustworthy," and "professional," when brought to life through communications, suggest a more businesslike attitude.

The key to the way in which the brand should be communicated is often found in matching the attitude and personality of the brand to that of the consumer, so again I emphasize that it is important to understand what makes your target audience tick. If that understanding isn't there, then the attitude of the brand may turn off the emotional relationship process. It may either "invite" or "alienate" consumers. So, for example, if a brand's character exudes confidence, it may make some consumers feel inferior and others smart. An ambitious or sophisticated brand attitude can invite those with ambition, but turn off those who think they will never be able to climb those heights. A fun brand might make people feel their shyness or generate really good thoughts about themselves. A reliable brand could make someone feel secure or bored, and a tough brand might attract the active but turn off gentle people, and so on. Attitude is a two-way street, and brand managers have to manage these inner thoughts and self-directed feelings of consumers.

Flexing the brand values

Some brands cleverly mix the rational and emotional characteristics of their brand's personality, so that they can flex the brand character to suit the audience they are addressing. By having several brand personality characteristics, they can emphasize different aspects of their character to different target audiences. So where, for example, a telecommunications company brand has a set of characteristics such as

- friendly,
- innovative,
- trustworthy,
- understanding, and
- contemporary,

it can put across all these characteristics to each of the two main target audiences, but emphasize "friendly," "contemporary," and "trustworthy" a little more than the others for the residential consumer, and emphasize "innovative" and "understanding" more to the business community. In brand communications, the attitude of the brand personality would thus appear more emotional to the residential audience—because they are more attracted by an emotional attitude, and more rational to the business audience—because this is their attitude toward decision making. The brand–consumer relationship will still be based on emotional strategy, but the degree of emotion exhibited is controlled according to the needs of the consumer group that the brand is trying to build a relationship with, and is represented by the attitude of the brand when communicated. (Further illustrations and examples of how to build brand personality can be found in my book *Branding in Asia*, John Wiley & Sons, Singapore, 2000.)

So, brands often mirror consumers' thoughts, feelings, attitudes, behaviors, lifestyles, and personality. Several successful brands have achieved global status because of brand management's ability to relate to and keep in touch with consumer emotions, mirroring their minds. Brand managers must be specialists in "coaching"; bringing out the best in the relationship between all the players—the brand and consumers. And there is no better way to do this than by managing attitudes, feelings, and emotions. Brand management is in the reflections business, anticipating what consumers want to see reflected back at them through the brand mirror.

Brand trust

An essential part of any brand management strategy must be the establishment of trust in the brand. This is really the key to reaching the long-term emotional relationship with consumers that makes brands famous. Many writers say that trust is derived from the quality of the brand experience that the branded product or service provided. Trust in the corporate brand also derives from this. While it is true that you have to pay meticulous attention to quality, reliability, and, these days, innovation, there is much more to it than that. Trust is a very emotional issue, and not a particularly rational one, and so brands have to create personal links with consumers. If consumers own and build brands as I have stated, then there is more that can be done to catalyze this process, in addition to the development of personality and attitude as described above.

Adding romance and sensuality

If we look at some of the brands that have really captured the emotions and spirit of people, we see that they also build in a degree of romance and sensuality. Some do this on the service side, but others manage to do it on the design side. Apple's iMac is a good example of the creation of an emotional connection with consumers via design. People want to hold it, touch it, and choose from among the attractive colors of hot pink, purple, blue, orange, or green. (Steve Jobs says there will be more products coming out from Apple that "will be so gorgeous you will want to lick them.") Sensuality enhances the "wanting to own" process by touching the mind of the consumer in a highly emotional way.

Montblanc was the first company to achieve this emotional sensuality with its writing instruments. Such design features built into brands trigger passionate responses in the subconscious mind. And this is where emotions outweigh rational thoughts, making brand decisions easier. Most people don't know what an iMac can do and yet many still want one, and they may not realize that other brands have the same attributes of a good writing instrument as a Montblanc pen. The fact that a BMW bike can outperform a Harley-Davidson with ease might never enter the mind of a Harley buyer. Emotions trigger the mind 3,000 times faster than rational thoughts, so brand managers must give thought to owning the dimensions of passion, sensuality, "coolness," nostalgia, mystery, and spirit.

In the following case study you will find many of the brand ingredients mentioned in this chapter. The company—Phil Corporation—created a brand that became the business, but only after a paradigm shift in thinking about the brand vision. An emotional personality was built around the vision, and has now extended out into products and services.

Case Study 4

PHIL CORPORATION'S GOKHATAK
Building a new brand

Phil Corporation of India has been in the photographic industry for around 20 years. They found that when photographic companies were making the transition from silver halide technology to digital technology, they simply looked at "digitizing" the process. Instead of using an optical camera, companies were developing digital cameras. Instead of printing pictures in mini-labs, companies were looking at inkjet printers or laser printers. The customer was spending a lot more money but was getting a lot less, it would seem, in terms of quality and convenience. Companies seemed to be missing the real promise of being digital.

What digital technology could offer was the ability to customize and personalize pictures. In keeping with a broader trend toward mass customization, digital technology could add a new dimension to photography—the ability to create an individual experience in a low-cost, convenient manner.

Phil Corporation decided to look at the business from the point of view of the customer, rather than as a supplier of products and services. Using its own proprietary technology, the company decided to establish a chain of stores, kiosks, shop counters, and an Internet presence that would focus on giving customers the ability to make far more choices and involve themselves far more in creating pictures and memories than offered by traditional mini-lab stores. In fact, the product or service would focus on offering a wide range of services, including taking portrait pictures, adding an appropriate background, personalizing it with a message, printing and framing it—all in about 15 minutes for under US$5.

Research showed that photographs taken by consumers are often stored in shoe-boxes or in envelopes that are never opened. The main reason for this is that, very often, these photographs contain small mistakes. Digital technology makes it possible for consumers to preview pictures, make corrections and enhancements, and then print only those photographs that they want to preserve or share. By adding a range of frames, albums, mugs, greetings cards, and personal mementoes, a consumer could create a set of photographs that would be far more meaningful and personal than simply getting a roll of film developed at the neighborhood mini-lab.

Looking beyond photographs, the same outlet could also sell other items where digital technology made it possible for consumers to customize and personalize their requirements. For example, with music and CDs, instead of going to a shop and buying an album containing a set of songs, how about a place that lets you make your own album by putting all your favorite jazz songs together? What about a virtual picture gallery where you could create a picture of the size that would fit your wall, with your choice of frame and mount?

New digital technology is making the concept of mass customization possible with new digital devices that are linked to the Internet, making the sharing and storing of personal information enjoyable and effortless. New mobile phones are likely to have digital cameras and MP3 players built in. This promises to usher in new products and services based on the convergence of these technologies and industries.

Phil Corporation therefore felt that by creating a brand of consumer services that cut across traditional industries, they would open up a host of new opportunities as digital technology brought synergies and "convergence" opportunities for consumers.

GoKhatak—the brand

Phil Corporation looked for a name that was youthful, catchy, and different, that could appeal to the large Indian population. Although many of the major brand names in India were multinational brands or English-sounding brand names, Phil Corporation felt that finding a brand name that had its roots in India would convey a warmer and more emotional appeal.

The slang word "Khatak," meaning "got it right," was chosen as the root word. The word is derived from the sound of a cricket bat hitting a ball at just the right spot, making the sound "khatak." The prefix "Go" was added to give it a sense of movement and an international touch that would make it more appealing to the young Indian consumers who were in touch with the rest of the world but also felt comfortable with Indian contemporary culture.

The brand vision and personality

The GoKhatak brand vision was all about making people feel good about themselves, sharing good times and expressing themselves in special ways. The brand now became the mission for the whole company. The products and services would reflect the brand personality and business of the brand.

To bring a bold sense of style, the graphics incorporated a glamorized bright orange color and pictures of young Indian models with an international look. Phil Corporation felt that while it had an initial edge in terms of technology, it wouldn't be long before other companies would copy its concepts and services. The outcome of the discussions concerning this was that a brand personality had to be created to enhance a strong identity that would ensure long-term customer loyalty. GoKhatak needed to develop a long-term partnership with its customers, and in a workshop session the key brand values, personality, and positioning statements were finalized.

Instead of moving hastily to advertise the brand, the company decided it was more important to bring to life the brand values in all corporate activities that influenced its image. A separate company was created with the name GoKhatak Enterprises Limited. The starting point was to change the mindset of everyone working in the company. For example, the new brand had a personality that was:

- fun-loving,
- friendly, and
- innovative,

and so it wouldn't do for the staff to be rigid, beauraucratic, and stuck in tradition. As a consequence of this, a new set of human resource policies and recruitment guidelines were drawn up to attract the right people, and to train employees in what these brand values meant for their particular jobs. This was particularly important for front-line staff, but support staff were also seen as being critical to the development of a strong brand experience.

A review was made of the communication and design of product packaging, and major changes were made in line with the brand personality. Initially, the temptation had been to focus on the youth market, but it was clear that the brand had to appeal to a wide audience to be successful and have long-term sustainability.

Brand guardianship

A top management team was made responsible for managing the brand and ensuring that every aspect of the company would adhere to guidelines that would reinforce the brand values and personality. Unless the top management made the commitment to build and reinforce the brand at every opportunity, and shared this vision with everyone in the organization, the company knew it would be impossible for the new brand to reach world-class status. There is now a comprehensive brand management action plan to deliver on the brand promises, which includes:

- "GoKhatak" Smile Shops;
- a "GoKhatak" Customer Relationship Management program; and
- a "GoKhatak" Smile Club, among other initiatives, some still under development.

The management of Phil Corporation has taken brave investment decisions with regard to paradigm shifts of thinking about the new brand that are already bringing in substantial returns on investment.

Chairman Abdullah Fazalbhoy said, "We realized that brand building wasn't only for large companies. At the same time it was difficult to find a successful company that didn't also have a successful brand. In our case we are building our company around the GoKhatak brand and ensuring that everyone in the company signs off on upholding the brand values in all aspects of our working. We are confident that by sweating out the details we can build an outstanding brand and, as a consequence, a world-class company."

For brand managers in the 21st century, there are many complex tasks to undertake, but achieving brand loyalty and lifetime relationships with consumers are the true goals, because only when these are achieved will the brand last and grow in value. Brands are at their most powerful when they determine business direction, and when they bind themselves to consumers through emotional associations.

The power of emotion has been present since life began—it is the great motivator and the prime driver of the human spirit. Make sure your brand develops more emotional attributes, because, although rational attributes may attract, emotional attributes sell.

In the next chapter, I will discuss positioning and many of the strategies available to brand managers. An emotional positioning strategy is one of them, and you will see how this can, and should, be linked with other strategies chosen. When you read the next chapter, don't forget that all great brand positions stem from a well thought-through brand vision, often based on consumer insight.

3

Positioning and Brand Management

HOW DOES POSITIONING FIT INTO BRAND MANAGEMENT?

Positioning is vital to brand management because it takes the basic tangible aspects of the product and actually builds the intangibles in the form of an image in people's minds. It focuses on the chosen target audience(s) and influences their thoughts about the brand in relation to other brands. Through the strategies described in this chapter, positioning seeks the best way of convincing people that this particular product is both different from and better than any other product.

This chapter explains the critical role played by the positioning process in helping to make the strategic leap from being perceived as an ordinary brand to being seen as world-class, with all the rewards this brings. Strong, or even world-class, branding is impossible without powerful positioning.

POSITIONING

If personality is the main part of brand identity, positioning is the other pillar of a brand's strategic platform. It is partly to do with how the core brand values are projected to the outside world. Someone can have a great personality, or a company can create a unique personality for itself or its products, but unless people see it and perceive it as such, it will have little effect. Conversely, positioning can be much more successful if it is personified, because personality is a differentiator in itself.

Avoid the perception gap

All brand managers aspire to build a great image for their brand(s). Brand image, however, may not turn out to be the same as the identity and personality we want the brand to be perceived as having, because image is subject to perception—the way in which people think about something or even imagine it to be. So, if we project the identity wrongly, or not strongly enough, the people to whom we want to acknowledge our identity might view it as something entirely different. They might not see us as honest, or might think our packaging looks cheap. Image can be based on fact or fiction, depending on how people perceive things. The difference between identity and image is what is often called the *perception gap*, which must be avoided at all costs.

To avoid the perception gap between identity and image, we must ensure that what is offered is what is acknowledged—that the target audience sees and relates to our brand personality/identity, and this will depend on their perceptions.

Positioning is also about creating a perception of difference, and brand managers use a variety of strategies to convince and persuade people that they are both different from and better than the brands of the opposition. In positioning a brand, the brand's actual performance can be introduced, as well as its personality. Here are some of the most effective positioning strategies.

Thirteen power positioning strategies

There are 13 strategies that can be used, either on their own or in combination, to establish a powerful position. The fundamentals of these strategies are described below, together with some advantages and disadvantages that need to be given consideration.

1. Features and attributes

This is probably the most obvious strategy and is traditionally the most frequently used in many industries. With this strategy the focus is on those brand attributes that can be used to endorse the perception that here is something that is different, or better, or both.

The motor vehicle industry is a typical user of this strategy, and most car manufacturers have had to do this to stay in the forefront of people's minds. Volvo is one of the best examples, having for many years positioned its vehicles as being the safest on the road. Service companies can also use this strategy, an example being the Ritz-Carlton hotel group which advertises its uncompromisingly high service-quality standards. It gets its staff to think in this way by saying to them, "We are ladies and gentlemen serving ladies and gentlemen."

Advantages

With this strategy there is the potential to own it for a long time, as with Volvo, or it might last only for a short period of time, as in the case of laser jet printers, or 3M with nasal dilatory strips. In either case, it can result in the creation of a rapid market share, particularly if your product is first into the market with a new or distinctive feature or attribute.

Disadvantages

Features and attributes can be copied sooner or later (with increasing speed as technology advances), and this will erode market-share gains. Competitors may produce enhancements that cause your offer to be obsolete, and repositioning might consequently be difficult. Technological change is militating against this strategy by increasing the speed with which products can be copied and by reducing product life cycles.

2. Benefits

This strategy takes features and attributes to the next stage by describing what benefit(s) the customer will receive as a result—for instance, a toothpaste containing fluoride (a feature) helps fight decay (a benefit).

The benefits positioning strategy answers the question consumers have in their minds regarding "What's in it for me?" The safety feature of a car means protection. The introduction of airbags into cars as an additional feature might mean more expense, but in the consumer's mind the benefits of a life-saving attribute outweigh the cost.

Advantages

This strategy helps give a company and its products more appeal by allowing people to see clearly what the brand attributes actually mean. Like features, benefit positioning can establish a short-term competitive advantage, and can lead to market leadership and quick gains. It is a reasonably flexible strategy, and can be extended in a clinical, logical way (aimed at the left brain) or in a more emotional way (aimed at the right brain).

Example:

Feature	*Rational appeal*	*Emotional appeal*
Safety	Protection	For your family

Disadvantages

As with the features strategy, the benefit positioning strategy can be somewhat short-lived, and what is a benefit and competitive advantage today may be part of tomorrow's basic product. It is based around the concept of a USP (unique selling proposition) that is vulnerable these days to easy replication, further enhancements, and technological innovations. I can buy a personal computer with a processing speed of 2,000Mhz, currently state of the art, only to find six months later that there is a new industry standard for that product category.

3. Problem–solution

This is another widely used, and often highly effective, strategy. It is based on the premise that consumers don't necessarily want to buy a product or deal with a company strictly for that purpose. What they really want is a solution to a problem they have that can be provided by the product or company. Here are some examples.

People often regard some banking products as a necessary evil. It is highly unlikely that they will wake up one morning gleefully shouting, "What a great day for an overdraft!" It's more likely that they will lie awake at night worrying about how they are going to solve an immediate financial problem to which an overdraft might be the solution.

Oracle and many other companies use this strategy. (See *Hi-Tech Hi-Touch Branding*, by myself and K.C. Lee, published by John Wiley & Sons, Singapore, 2000, for other examples of technology companies using this positioning strategy.)

Advantages

This strategy is clearly appropriate for certain industries such as financial services, information technology, and communications, but it is also widely applicable. Because problems always have an emotional consequence or impact on the consumer, it is a useful strategy because emotion can be built into this positioning, often being accomplished by suggesting an emotional benefit attached to the solution.

> *Example: Life insurance*
> *Problem:* What happens to my family if something happens to me?
> *Solution:* Life insurance.
> *Emotional benefit:* Peace of mind if a disaster occurs.

Disadvantages

Other competitors can also solve the same problems consumers have, perhaps even improving on the solution. In technology-led industries, this strategy is now becoming so overused that other means of differentiation are essential.

The big crunch can come if you claim to offer the solution approach but don't deliver—for example, with warranties that don't perform. Also, to maintain brand credibility with this strategy (particularly in technology-driven industries), new product development is vital because life-cycle compression means that the rapidity of new product innovations makes today's problems disappear quickly. The pace of change also creates different problems for consumers, requiring you to stay on top of the game at all times.

4. Competition

Every company must always be aware of the competition—what it is doing and what it intends to do. Depending on competitor strategies, it may be necessary to change your position—a reactive strategy. On the other hand, it is possible to be proactive and change your position and thus disadvantage the competition. One of the biggest wars going on at the moment is between Internet software and hardware suppliers. In a full-page advertisement in the *Far Eastern Economic Review* of July 19, 2001, Oracle claimed that it runs SAP four times faster than IBM. Using a large chart to emphasize the point, Oracle also claimed: "That's why SAP customers choose Oracle over IBM 10 to 1. Interesting." You can't get much more direct than that.

Advantages

Competitive strategies tend to be better for positioning companies and more difficult for positioning products. Corporations tend to have more unique characteristics in the form of personality, culture, size, and visual identity that people can more readily associate with, and an image that can help keep a company one step ahead when managed well. However, with products there is often less to work with in terms of differentiators, especially in today's increasingly cluttered markets. Notwithstanding this, if a positioning strategy is based on facts or statistics, it is possible to own a position, as long as consumers believe the figures!

Disadvantages

Competitive positioning can invite retaliation, and in some countries this is prevented by legislation. It can lead to a lot of wasteful expenditure and embarrassing public incidents, as in the case of ambush marketing. The message here is that you had better be sure that your product or company has something to offer to your target audience that others cannot match.

5.   Corporate credentials or identity

Some companies rely on the strength of their corporate name to endorse products, positioning them by the house-brand reputation. This can be very powerful, as demonstrated by companies such as Sony, IBM, and Nestlé. The sheer power and ubiquity of the parent brand name can make life very difficult for would-be competitors trying to establish their own position.

Advantages

The power of the corporate name can help strengthen or make a strong position for even an average product. A well-known name can cross different markets and, in some cases, create global product positions, as in the case of Sony moving into the entertainment industry from consumer electronics.

Disadvantages

If the company goes through through a bad time, so does the product, and the position can lose its credibility. A badly managed corporate image will make life very difficult for products positioned around the strength of the parent's name and reputation. It can also work the other way around, as was the case recently with Firestone, which became a major cause of anguish for parent company Bridgestone and caused huge problems for the end-user, Ford.

6.   Usage occasion, time, and application

This strategy can be an effective differentiator, but it is more appropriate for products and services than for companies and larger institutions. The strategy gains its value from the fact that people not only use products in different ways, but may do so on different occasions and at different times. For instance, some people eat Oreo cookies for a between-meals snack (time usage). A nutritious chocolate drink is used by some people before going to sleep (time usage), and by others as a food supplement at various times of day (application usage). Champagne is usually enjoyed only at celebrations (occasion usage).

Advantages

Products and services can gain a market position that is more easily defendable, and the strategy is as flexible as the capability of the product's possibilities for different usage situations.

Disadvantages

Products with more effective usage may usurp the position, and as consumer behavior changes over time, the time or nature of usage might also change.

7.   Target user

The target user positioning strategy is a very good example of focus in marketing. Companies who know their target audiences well can be effective in positioning a generic product to many customer groups, as is the case with Nike, who basically have the appropriate trainer footwear for each sports group.

Advantages

This strategy is good for getting into, and defending, niche markets, and for building strong customer relationships. It is clearly a winner for developing a product range where a wide range of customer groups exist for a generic product, but where slightly differing needs or applications allow a wide, low-cost product range.

Disadvantages

The strategy relies on accurate segmentation and, therefore, research. Companies that know the market structure and dynamics, but don't understand customers' real needs and wants, may well become unstuck. The strategy can be limiting, and user profiles will change over time. Nike, for instance, found it relatively easy to go from trainers to sports apparel, but less easy to move into leisure apparel for older people.

8.   Aspiration

Aspirational positioning can be applied in many forms, and is very popular with lifestyle brands, but the two most common ones are concerned with:

* status and prestige (related to wealth achievement); and
* self-improvement (related to non-monetary achievement).

In both cases the strategy relies on self-expression, and as most individuals have a need to express themselves one way or another, associating themselves with companies or brands that facilitate this is helpful.

With respect to status and prestige, Rolex and Rolls-Royce are power brands that people use to make a statement about their financial achievements in life, among other things. On the self-improvement side,

Adidas's "Forever Sport" platform taps into the sports lifestyle and sporting achievement.

Advantages

Everyone has aspirations, and they are always emotionally linked. By appealing to these universal feelings, brands can quickly become global players. When combined with other strategies, this one can be immensely powerful.

Disadvantages

Not everyone sees himself or herself as a winner, and thus this strategy can be a turn-off for under-achievers. It is essential, therefore, to know your target audience.

9. Causes

This positioning strategy is also linked to emotion, and focuses on people's beliefs hierarchies and on their need to belong. Avon, Benetton, and other companies target customer groups whom they believe will subscribe to a certain philosophy or will want to relate to a specific group or movement. Shell is focusing on the environment and conservation of the world's resources. This strategy is becoming more widely used and important, as it relates to freedom of thought and speech, democracy, the liberation of women, and other social trends.

Advantages

Companies can own a strong position through this strategy. It can be very powerful when linked to other strategies concerning applications, target users, and emotion.

Disadvantages

Causes can go in and out of fashion, and while being welcomed by some might offend others; thus, proper targeting is vital. Additionally, while a cause is in vogue, the "bandwagon" effect often occurs, as is the case now with literally hundreds of companies giving us steadfast promises that they will do everything they can to protect the environment. If you embark on this strategy with your brand, you are also committed to the long term and to a high marketing budget in order to prove to the cause audience that you really mean what you say.

10. Value

Value is often related to what people pay, but this strategy isn't just to do with price. There are two main elements of value positioning:

- *Price/quality*—that is, value for money, a positioning used by Virgin and Carrefour.
- *Emotional value*—that is, the associations people have when they own, for instance, a Mini car. BMW are trying to bring back these memories and emotions with an enhanced new Mini car, fighting on the nostalgia platform with Volkswagen's Beetle.

Advantages

This is a good strategy when it combines the two elements, and can also be used tactically via promotions. The key is to concentrate on *value*, not *price*.

Disadvantages

It tends to be commodity-oriented when it concentrates on price, and not suitable for those building a power brand and looking for high premiums.

11. Emotion

As a positioning strategy this can exist on its own, but it is often used as an overlay position, adding value and strength to other strategies, as previously mentioned. It is highly important because, as research shows time and time again, emotion sells. Häagen-Dazs ice cream is a case in point, and the brand's success has been phenomenal. It broke into a market dominated by giants such as Nestlé and others, and sold its products at prices up to 40% higher than its competitors. The key to its success was the creation of a unique positioning around the concept of sheer luxury and the enjoyment of the moment. Some of the advertisements portrayed this with romantic and sexual imagery, or by using fantasy.

Advantages

Emotional positioning strategies move people to want things. Emotion creates desire, and can be very powerful indeed. Positioning without emotion tends to be less persuasive and to lack motivation.

Disadvantages

As a strategy on its own, it might not sway the minds of the "cold fish"—the more calculating, careful-planning, thrifty types of people. For those who are very price-sensitive the cost will be the decisive factor, overpowering the emotional feelings.

12. Personality

As mentioned in the previous chapter, brand building based on personality creation can be extremely effective, being frequently used by companies to build world-class brands. But people won't respond to a personality they see as being either not relevant or not likable.

Personality characteristics such as the following have proven to be extremely attractive to most people:

- caring;
- modern;
- innovative;
- warm;
- independent;
- strong;
- honest;
- experienced;
- genuine;
- sophisticated;
- successful;

- inspiring;
- energetic;
- trustworthy;
- reliable;
- approachable; and
- fun-loving.

Advantages

People are very responsive to this strategy, and, when combined with others, it can produce high market share, loyalty, and profitability. It is the only way really to gain and sustain a strategic competitive advantage.

Disadvantages

The strategy relies on a very clear understanding of the target audience, and a great deal of investment, to ensure that the customer experiences a consistent personality on all occasions. Building a corporate personality, for instance, demands that the entire culture of the organization be changed so that all the staff live that personality in their everyday work.

13. Claiming number one

This is an enviable position to have, as it generates perceptions of leadership. In the hi-tech field it can work wonders for the brand and provide a perception of difference, even though product service and quality may be similar between major players. This is essentially what has happened to Amazon.com, which remains the brand leader in its field, even though other companies offer similar products and services. Andersen Consulting, the consulting firm, was the first company to position itself as a technology specialist. All the other consulting firms followed, but the public associated technology consulting with the first mover brand. The firm's change of name to Accenture has, however, eroded its position. The public are now confused about the identity of the brand.

Advantages

Your brand is widely perceived as the market leader, and if you can maintain constant innovation you could own this position.

Disadvantages

The obvious concern here is keeping ahead of the pack when innovation is happening all the time. You will need to invest considerably in research and development.

Gaining power from combining strategies

The power positioning strategies discussed above can be combined in various ways as companies and people wish. A well-known example of this is the sports shoe and apparel manufacturer Nike, one of the world's most admired brands. *Features and attributes* are used, along with *benefits* of improved performance, linked to the *aspiration* of becoming a top athlete, aimed at various *target user* groups, together with *emotion* in advertising materials and athlete endorsements.

Capturing hearts and minds

Whatever strategies are used, the key to positioning is to capture people's hearts and minds by appealing to both the rational and emotional aspects of their psychological make-up. Astute brand managers are those who understand this and know how to combine strategies that satisfy the emotional and rational needs of consumers.

Summary: Choosing a positioning strategy

Whatever strategy, or combination of strategies, you eventually choose, there are certain points you need to remember:

- The position must be salient or important to the target audience you are trying to reach and influence. It is no good communicating messages to them that are of no interest, as they will either ignore them or forget them quickly.

- The position must be based on real strengths. Making claims that cannot be substantiated can cause enormous loss of credibility.

- The position has to reflect some form of competitive advantage. The whole point of positioning is to inform and persuade people that you are different and better than the competition, so whatever that point of difference is, it must be clearly expressed.

- Finally, the position must be capable of being communicated simply, so that everyone gets the real message, and of motivating the audience. The aim of positioning is to provide a call to action to the target audience, and so communications must be created carefully.

REPOSITIONING

As mentioned at the very beginning of this chapter, most positioning is *repositioning*. Unless you have a brand that no one has heard of, you will already have an image in the marketplace, and consequently will need to reposition if you want to change it. In most situations, therefore, it is essential to understand what your image is and whether it actually matches the identity you are trying to portray.

Eight reasons for repositioning

There are eight main reasons why companies attempt to reposition themselves or their products. These are where there is a:

- poor or tarnished (or outdated or inconsistent) image;
- fuzzy, blurred image;
- change in target audience, or in their needs and wants;
- change in strategic direction;
- new or revitalized corporate personality/identity;
- change in competitor positioning or new competitors;
- momentous event; or
- rediscovery of lost values.

1. Poor, tarnished, outdated or inconsistent image

For whatever reason, the image you have may not be all that is desired. The automobile brand Rover had a clear problem here, and even when taken over by BMW, with millions of dollars spent on the brand, it has never regained its former glory. BMW has been forced to sell the brand for a token sum, admitting failure.

2. Fuzzy, blurred image

Sometimes the perception people have of your company or product isn't clear. It's not that it's poor; it may be that people don't think strongly about it one way or the other—they are indifferent, if you like. This is usually caused by unclear positioning and/or lack of brand communications support.

3. Change in target audience, or in their needs and wants

If the marketing focus changes, then repositioning is a must. Theoretically, this might prove difficult to do, depending on how close the new focus is to the previous one. So, for instance, if Coca-Cola decided to target the over-sixties age group, repositioning wouldn't only be necessary, but would be a major challenge, in convincing those people that the product isn't a drink made for the younger set. When considering extending the marketing of your company or product to new market segments, it is imperative that a reality check be carried out through market research to determine whether or not a new position could be a reality, or whether the task would be too large and costly, perhaps even damaging the perceptions held by existing customer groups. For instance, if Coke tried to access the over-sixties segment with the major advertising necessary, what would young people think and do?

In Case Study 5 the generic product is the same, but the focus for the target audience is changing. Interestingly, this has the advantage of growing the whole category.

Case Study 5

LOLLIPOPS

Growing a category by positioning generic products to different market segments

This case may bring back memories for some older readers of the bestselling book by Douglas Adams called *The Restaurant at the End of the Universe*. But the case isn't fantasy or fiction. It's about lollipops. It serves to remind brand managers that there appears to be no limit to branding, or to the criteria for market segmentation and category definitions. Nothing is impossible if you can understand the mind of the consumer.

Everyone knows that lollipops are for children, right? Well, you can stop believing that right now! Adults are the new targets, and lollipops are being positioned to attract new market segments, such as ex-smokers, people on diets, and—wait for it—party goers and drug takers (affectionately known by researchers as Ravers). Lollipops are being multipositioned.

Before you start thinking that I have some kind of strange affliction, or an affiliation to a weird kind of sect, consider the facts and figures. (I should point out that, in the main, the following facts refer to the United States, the home of hedonistic pleasure brands.)

Fact number 1: Annual sales of lollipops have risen from US$138 million in 1997 to US$199 million in 2000. Prudential Securities says that the surge in this category is partly driven by convenience—lollipops are ubiquitous and tend to appear everywhere, in stores as well as in other more unlikely places—but more so by the fact that there is a growing need for foods that can be eaten with one hand! Speculation about what the other hand is doing is not within the scope of this case study.

Fact number 2: Some products have universal appeal, and are capable of being customized to suit many different target audiences. It seems that lollipops are among them. Never slow in coming forward, U.S. confectionery manufacturers such as Tootsie Roll Industries Inc., Mars Inc., Hershey Foods Inc., and Day Spring Enterprises Inc. are all, at this very moment while you are reading this book, held in one hand, capitalizing on this news with extreme alacrity and manufacturing a huge amount of varieties geared to the needs of different market segments, including *you.*

Fact number 3: As a result of segmentation, lollipops are "cool," and "cool" no longer belongs to youth. Lollipops are creating a paradigm shift in consumer thinking. Dieters are being targeted, for example, as lollipops have only an average of 60 calories "per pop." Ex-smokers are a target, as they often take to eating sweet things and are on record, through research, as admitting that they hide lollipops to consume until their children are in bed. Two such consumers (husband and wife) have been recorded as saying, "We limit *their* sucker intake but not our own."

On the line side, producers such as Day Spring have a line of "intense flavors" such as raspberry sorbet. Tootsie Roll Industries has yogurt and hot chocolate flavors. Spangler Candy Co. has fruit punch, orange cream, and buttered popcorn flavors under its Dum Dums brand.

On the brand extension side, Mars and other companies are extending their own brands to on-a-stick varieties such as Fruit Chew lollipops.

And news spreads fast—Chupa Chups SA of Barcelona is already doing well in the 12–34 years demographic market for lollipops in Spain. The company advertises in magazines such as *Cosmopolitan* and *Rolling Stone* with suggestive imagery. Part of this company's marketing mix is placing girls on roller-skates giving out complimentary "pops" at "rave" parties. They have found that the products appeal to consumers of the drug ecstasy, the side effects of which include the compulsion to grind one's teeth and to chew the inside of one's mouth. This is a problem–solution positioning strategy. It is also clearly an ethical issue, but Chupa Chups claim they are promoting their lollipops as drug substitutes, not drug accessories.

All of these excursions into the satisfaction of various customer needs and wants, if successful, will increase the degree of brand loyalty, which in the case of lollipops could be described as—taking a phrase from the Internet branding world—the "stickiness factor."

Fact number 4: Lollipops can be extended in brand terms to include fashion accessories. Day Spring Enterprises Inc. has branded Rainbow Pops, including accessories such as a "popstop"—a stand where you can rest your lollipop if you want to do something with the hand that's holding it, such as make a phone call. Company spokespersons say that this is equivalent to a smoker putting his cigarette in an ashtray for a few moments. Lollipop products are now being sold in very up-market packaging, replacing cellophane wrappers with cardboard boxing, so that they can be sold in appropriate outlets such as Linens 'N' Things.

The brand management message

First of all, it must now be clear that anything can be branded. Secondly, this case illustrates that even the most ordinary or traditional products, and (some might think) those that are incapable of being marketed to many different target audiences, can in fact be successful in growing the category they are in, whether their efforts are perceived as ethically-based or not.

Therein lies the fascination of brand management. There are many, almost limitless, opportunities to grow products into brands, and brands into global experiences.

A variation of this reason for repositioning is where the target audience remains much the same, but the needs and wants of this customer base change. In this situation the company has to try and keep up with these changes (whether in thinking or behavior) if it is going to keep its customers. In the 1950s and 1960s, Brylcreem was a hair preparation that provided a greasy, flattened look for young men. It has since had to reposition the brand to become more modern and up to date and so keep pace with men's fashions. Its existing customer base grew up with fashion-based changed needs, such as a more full-bodied look and then a firm hold (hence, gel preparations). To help in its repositioning effort, the company has used endorsements by some of the top young personalities appropriate to its target audience, such as Manchester United footballer David Beckham. Presumably, the contract had expired when Beckham suddenly appeared with his head shaven, and this probably eclipsed any equity that the Brylcreem brand had gained from the previous endorsement. Repositioning isn't usually accomplished by short campaigns, but by sustained communications.

4. Change in strategic direction

As mentioned, one type of directional change is when there is a need to move from one category to another. This situation usually arises when the category a product is in becomes too crowded, and symptoms of high competitive pressure, such as the erosion of sales and margins, occur. Categories exist in consumers' minds and shouldn't be defined by a company. They depend on how people organize information about the things they see, whether it be by name, usage, attribute, or other descriptors. Successful category repositioning depends on possession of the attributes necessary for acceptance by consumers in the new category, and this should be tested out prior to re-launch as slight product modifications or enhancements and repackaging may prove to be necessary. Care should be taken to ensure correct definition of perceived categories. IBM has significantly repositioned itself away from being perceived as a seller of computer hardware, to being seen as a solutions-based information technology company.

5. New or revitalized corporate personality/identity

This is the corporate equivalent of plastic surgery. Some companies find it worthwhile to change their identity completely—not just with a new logo, but possibly also with a name change, a new structure, and a new personality—in order to overcome problems of the past or to take advantage of new opportunities.

Tag Heuer, the well-known professional sports watch brand, has launched several global advertising campaigns using sports personalities in an effort to move away from its former cold, mechanical, technically efficient image to one which is perceived as warmer and more human. The basic position of mental attitude overcoming adversity and being in control of oneself is still present, but the company says: "Through the association of the brand with these key players in sports, who have succeeded through sheer physical and mental effort, we hope to make a comeback to a more humane face." The brand itself was also given a new personality, and the strategy worked. Tag Heuer's success has been so great it has now been taken over by the LVMH Group (see Case Study 12 in Chapter 4).

6. Change in competitor positioning

Sometimes the competition moves closer in its positioning to yours, and you may feel it is best to move away and reposition. BMW, in the United States, had to do this when Lexus encroached upon its position and started to erode its customer base.

7. Momentous event

Occasionally, a traumatic event might occur which demands repositioning. A momentous event could be a sudden, unexpected crisis. When Coca-Cola had a problem with poisoning at a plant in Belgium, it took the company three days to speak to the public about the incident, and this damaged its image in Europe. Bridgestone and Ford have both had big problems as a result of the Firestone tyre accidents. (Public relations and crisis management will be dealt with more thoroughly in Chapter 6.)

8. Rediscovery of lost values

When a brand has reached the point where consumers are taking it for granted and sales are stagnant or worsening, instead of trying to create an entirely new position, it might be worthwhile looking at successful strategies from the past or evoking nostalgia for past values. Kellogg's once ran a campaign for Corn Flakes with the tagline, "Try Them Again For The First Time." Such a strategy, based on brand heritage, can be very successful, especially when competitors are relatively new and the target audience is open to the emotional value of nostalgia. It can easily answer in their minds the questions of why that company or product is different and better.

REPOSITIONING AND CHANGE—THE NEW PARADIGM

Ten to 20 years ago, repositioning was an event that was fairly unusual, driven mainly by the reasons described above, but in the present day it is becoming more frequent as companies seek to keep up with the pace of change and innovation. As constant innovation becomes mandatory for success, so repositioning follows in an equally mandatory manner. Repositioning of brands is now the norm rather than the exception, taking place on a much more frequent basis, and this means that brand managers have to take a different view of how they sustain and improve their market leadership and/or ambitions.

Factors to consider in repositioning your brand in the world of change include:

- Accept that repositioning is an essential part of brand development.
- Ensure that you don't alter the personality of your product/service/company, as this will place your brand in the "schizophrenic" category.
- Gather market intelligence on what the changing needs of your customers are, and the competitive response.
- Remember that you are dealing in the management of perceptions, and this means that you must budget for it—repositioning means cash outflow in image and product communications to change perceptions and make people *think* you are still, or are now, different and better. The more entrenched the perceptions are, the more you will have to spend.

- Bear in mind that all the products/services you have in the pipeline have to be changed according to your new positioning; if this is difficult, then your repositioning may encounter problems. In the case of motor vehicles, for instance, this can take up to seven years, as products are in the pipeline that will slow down major repositioning.

- Get buy-in from everyone that can make an impact on the brand in your company, or the repositioning effort won't work.

- Remember the basics: in order to reposition, you either have to add more value to the brand proposition, or change the target audience.

SHOULD POSITIONING BE REVOLUTIONARY OR EVOLUTIONARY?

Revolutionary positioning is a term that tends to be applied to a situation where you are starting from square one, say with a new product, company, or personal goal. In such a situation there is no current image, and a position has to be created for the first time. In other words, once you are nowhere, you have to go somewhere. In this case, positioning has to be revolutionary. You have to choose a powerful position amid all the established competitors and make an impact.

Evolutionary positioning, on the other hand, is about developing your image gradually. Here the issue is that once you are somewhere, you have to decide where to go next and not be left behind. This is a repositioning problem and it can be extremely dangerous. The danger lies in suddenly stepping completely away from the position you have been occupying, and to which consumers, particularly existing customers, are accustomed, without alienating them and losing your unique identity.

In most cases, brand managers have the dilemma of balancing the two approaches. For example, Georgio Armani, in an interview with CNN, described his biggest problem as being retaining his classic design styling while at the same time adopting fashionable change. He saw it as a true dichotomy. On the one hand, the existing customer base expects to see his classic style. On the other hand, fashion is moving faster, due to technological advances and media hype. Armani said that the media are now less sensitive to individual style and more attuned to what mass designers are producing. So if the mass-designed latest fashions include the colour red, everyone (Armani included) is expected to deliver something in red. If not, he said, he would be left out of media support for that season. The dilemma for designers like Armani, therefore, is how to remain true to his distinctive style—that is, *positioning*—and yet incorporate the latest trends. His answer is: evolutionary change, not revolutionary change. He has to position his products to satisfy the conflict of identity versus modernity. He must remain constant to his customers and meet their expectations, both of classic style and contemporary fashion.

POSITIONING FOR EQUALITY

Time passes quickly, and people's wants, needs, and aspirations change over time. Sometimes you just have to accept the fact that you are falling (or already have fallen) behind the pack and have to catch up. You have to convince people that you are "with it," not out of touch with the latest trend, are up-to-date, contemporary, and can match what others offer. This means positioning for equality—showing people that you aren't disadvantaged.

Quite often this type of positioning is concerned with the more basic competitive elements of features and benefits, and with keeping up with the needs and wants of the people you are trying to retain or acquire as customers. It is also mostly confined to positioning against the competition in specific categories, such as personal computers. With this category the life cycles have shortened so much that when customers start to use their left brain to analyze and justify which particular brand's features and benefits will both do the job and give value for money, the next range of upgraded models has already made the choice obsolete. Positioning here, then, is aimed at giving your customers the message that you have the necessary elements to be a legitimate competitor in that specific area of interest. So, as a computer manufacturer or retailer, you have to have models with the latest chips, hard disk sizes, memory capabilities, speed, and so on.

POSITIONING FOR SUPERIORITY

Everyone likes to be superior, the best, everyone's choice, but this position is difficult to create and maintain. It goes far beyond equality positioning by seeking to create inequality, a differential advantage, and an image of being a cut above the rest, an undisputed leader. Some companies, including several of the world's leading brands, have already done this. Others have it firmly placed on their boardroom agenda.

Positioning for superiority is only achievable once the target audience acknowledges equality. In other words, you have to demonstrate that you are at least as good as the competition with whatever it is you are offering, and only then can you persuade people that you really have something extra or special to give.

Companies that gain a superior position can be said to have achieved a sustainable competitive advantage (SCA), being the most preferred choice in their field of competition.

THE NEED FOR POSITIONING STATEMENTS

Unless you are in total control of all aspects of creating your image through communications, which is most unlikely, there needs to be a communications brief for people to follow. This is one of the main reasons for having written positioning statements. If positioning statements aren't in writing, there is a real danger that the ideas might be misinterpreted, the strategy warped, and the key messages not be expressed clearly. The result could well be confusion in the minds of the audience. Positioning statements are essential if you are to keep messages clear and develop a consistent image and position.

What are positioning statements?

Positioning statements are internal documents not meant for public consumption. They summarize strategy, and act as a guide for strategic marketing and brand management, and for briefing advertising and other agencies. They state specifically and briefly what you want people to think about you, your product or company, or your country. They not only spell out the desired image you wish to have, but are also a good test for strategy, as they quickly tell you whether the perceptions you wish people to hold are believable, credible, and achievable. Positioning statements aren't easy to write, and often need several attempts. It is best to write them with inputs and agreement from other people. In companies, for instance, a corporate positioning statement would need to be considered by as many senior managers as possible to gain consensus agreement and buy-in, and to ensure execution. Product managers would also need to seek other opinions and endorsements.

Before writing a positioning statement, it is vital that there is a complete understanding of the following areas:

- **Your brand:** This may seem obvious, but you have to be very clear about what you can really offer that will attract the people you are trying to influence. With products, this will mean looking closely at all the features and attributes, and the benefits that people will derive from them. You should constantly be looking for factors that will help differentiate what *you* have to offer from what the competition are offering. The same goes for services. What service standards can you present that will give you the opportunity to suggest a competitive advantage? Companies themselves often have distinguishing characteristics, such as global stature, track record, personality, and other unique features that can be highlighted and used as differentiators.

- **The target audience(s) you want to influence:** Knowing what people need and want is critical, and there is a difference between the two. I might *need* some food to eat, but what I *want* is a curry. More than that, I might want a *vegetarian* curry because that kind of food fits in with my belief structure. It becomes important, therefore, to understand the intangible requirements of people, as well as the more tangible ones. Unless there is precision in customer understanding, the messages we send may be irrelevant and lose us credibility.

- **The competitors you are up against (competitive set):** No strategy is complete without a thorough understanding of the competition, whether you are a football manager, marketing manager, entertainer, managing director, or prime minister. Some of the questions to ask might include:

- ○ Which competitors do customers consider?
- ○ What positioning strategies are the competitors using, and why?
- ○ What key messages are they sending?
- ○ What appears to be their competitive advantage and the key points of difference?
- ○ Why do customers buy from them?
- ○ What image do they currently have?
- ○ What differences do customers see between them and us?
- ○ What competitor would they switch to if they moved from us?

One of the major problems that can arise here is deciding just who the competition is. This issue is particularly relevant for fast-moving consumer goods where the definition of categories becomes extremely important, but it needs to be considered in any positioning situation. Definition of the product category is therefore a critical first stage in competitor analysis, and is vital to the positioning effort.

- **Why you are different from and better than the competition:** Analysis of the above areas will allow you to make some accurate judgments as to what position to choose and which positioning strategy you need to employ in order to influence the perceptions of the target audience(s).
- **The desired perception you would like people to have of you:** Always set a goal in terms of how you want to be seen by people. When you are writing down this goal, try to do it using the language of the customer or persons you are trying to influence. If you put yourself in their shoes, there is a greater likelihood that you will understand how they think and be successful in managing their perceptions, and you will find it easier to track whether or not you have achieved the intended image. When you write your positioning statement, certain things contained in it may be aspirational in nature and some factual. This doesn't matter, as these statements are for internal purposes only. However, the aspirational or desired consumer perceptions must be worked on hard in order to deliver on

the promise. Communicating parts of the positioning may have to be delayed, therefore, until the brand can actually do what it says it can.

Some of the above analysis might entail commissioned research if you don't have the internal resources to carry it out, and this may take some time, but the quality of your communicated position will end up much more focused and accurate. Once you are ready to write the positioning statement, it has to be done in a concise way.

HOW TO WRITE AND USE A POSITIONING STATEMENT

There are many ways of writing positioning statements, but they should all contain certain elements. From past experience I have found the following template to be the most practical.

A POSITIONING STATEMENT TEMPLATE

BRAND X

is better than

COMPETITIVE SET
(The main competitors your brand is competing against in your category, industry, etc.)

for

TARGET MARKET
(The customer group or groups you are aiming for, stated, if possible, in terms of their needs and wants. For a master brand this would be broad, but for each customer segment it would be more clearly defined.)

because it

STRATEGIC COMPETITIVE ADVANTAGE
(The SPECIFIC advantage(s) your brand has, compared to others in meeting those needs.)

with the result that

KEY PROPOSITION
(The real emotional—wherever possible—and rational benefits to be experienced by your target audience, derived mainly from the SCA.)

The brand personality (character)

This is the personality your brand has, as discussed in the earlier chapters. This can be stated separately at the end; or, more usefully, the words that describe the personality can be used in the text of the positioning statement itself.

If you methodically work through this statement, you will achieve answers to the main questions of:

- Why are you better?
- Why are you different?

These two questions are of the utmost importance to consumers, who want to know why they should buy your brand in preference to others on offer. Only if these questions are answered truthfully and adequately will you be able to persuade customers that you should be their preferred choice. Great care must therefore be taken to ensure that the content of positioning statements is credible, believable, deliverable, and relevant to the wants and needs of the audience whose perceptions you are trying to influence.

Example: A positioning statement for an airline

In this particular example, you will see the master brand personality for an Asian airline, which will differentiate it from the other international carriers. You will also see how this can then be transferred down into positioning statements for each target audience. It is important in positioning statements to go into detail for segments, because their needs and wants are different, and so your total proposition will be different. However, the segment positioning statements take direction from the master brand statement to ensure consistency while also ensuring relevance.

This is a real case in which all the major segments of the market are addressed. The main things consumers look for when choosing to travel with airlines are safety, convenience, and a great brand experience via service, whether pre-flight, in-flight, or post-flight. You will find this reflected in the statements. You will also notice that the brand's strategic competitive advantage is carried throughout the different statements.

MASTER BRAND POSITIONING STATEMENT

AIRLINE BRAND X

is better than

Other international carriers

for

All users of airline services

because it

Employs state-of-the-art systems and technology, with global presence, complemented by the naturalness, warmth, and traditions of service of a national personality that represents the very best of *all* of Asia

with the result that

Every customer can have complete confidence in the understanding of their personal needs and wants and the natural, genuine willingness of Airline X people to care.

ECONOMY CLASS
POSITIONING STATEMENT

AIRLINE BRAND X

is better than

Every other international carrier

for

Those seeking a comfortable, safe, convenient journey that offers
new standards in air travel with a fascinating cultural dimension

because it

Employs state-of-the-art systems and technology, complemented by
the naturalness, warmth, and traditions of service of a national
personality that represents the very best of *all* of Asia

with the result that

Their voyage becomes a unique experience and a lasting memory.

SUPER ECONOMY CLASS
POSITIONING STATEMENT

AIRLINE BRAND X

is better than

Every other international carrier

for

Those seeking the space, comfort, and privacy of a new, upgraded standard of air travel, along with the experience of a fascinating cultural dimension

because it

Offers all these benefits at a much lower cost than conventional Business Class travel, with all the naturalness, warmth, and traditions of service of a national personality that represents the very best of *all* of Asia

with the result that

They arrive fresh and less stressed, having experienced the air journey of a lifetime.

BUSINESS CLASS
POSITIONING STATEMENT

AIRLINE BRAND X

is better than

Every other international carrier

for

Business Class travelers seeking a vastly enhanced experience of
pure enjoyment

because it

Offers all the Business Class space, luxury, and special features
expected of a sophisticated global airline, made truly special by
the naturalness, warmth, and service traditions of a national
personality that represents the very best of *all* of Asia

with the result that

They arrive happier, more refreshed, and more relaxed, having
enjoyed a superior form of delivery of all the privileges and
attention they deserve.

FIRST CLASS
POSITIONING STATEMENT

AIRLINE BRAND X

is better than

Every other international carrier

for

Those seeking absolute luxury, convenience,
privacy, and individual recognition

because it

Offers unique First Class privileges and, in the naturalness, warmth,
and service of their attendants, an incomparable experience of Asia

with the result that

Their flight becomes "a journey" in indulgence—given color and
excitement by the fascinating traditions and combined
personalities of the world's most exotic continent.

When you have positioned the company in this way, then these
statements must be applied rigorously to product, service, staff,
communications, and so on. This part of brand management will be
covered in later chapters.

Development of taglines

Taglines are "phrases" that normally appear consistently after the brand
name, supporting its personality and positioning. They are never used in
isolation, always being prefaced by some form of communication. They
cannot (and indeed don't have to) say everything. Rather, they have to
be broad—able to lock down several messages, the thrust of which may

change over time. They should, however, impart a sense of direction and provide the penultimate "full stop"—representing the final impression and, ideally, call to action, conveyed to the viewer, listener, or reader. Once created, they can be very successful in connecting the brand with the minds of target audiences, and in cementing the emotional association. Taglines need to firmly present "difference," claim superiority, effectively cover personality, service, and technical sophistication if necessary, cope with change, and be equally relevant to local and foreign markets. Most of all, they have to convey a sense of promise, excitement, and experience. All in just three or four words!

With respect to the positioning statements for the airline given above, here is one of several taglines suggested: "Your World of Difference."

- This line powerfully highlights the promise of difference, reinforcing the personality-based positioning and related, differentiating product development.
- It attracts interest and a desire to know more.
- It communicates what the airline's developmental process is all about—a quest to be different and better—both to consumers and own staff.
- It implies superiority.
- It is broad, able to encompass and lend power to a host of messages. No specific promise is inherent.
- It becomes a most effective "full stop" for any and all specific messages conveyed in communications, reminding consumers that the benefits featured are not available elsewhere.
- "World" communicates globality, coverage, size (and therefore sophistication), yet in a way which supports the personality position.
- "World" communicates the feeling of a "cocoon," removed from the chaos and inconvenience that can accompany the air travel experience.
- Given context in communications, a "World of Difference" becomes a reference to the country's cultural diversity, representative of the very best of all Asia.

- "Your" puts the emphasis on the customer. It encourages a sense of relationship. It conveys the impression that the airline puts the customer first.
- The line has a "softness" in tune with the brand personality traits.
- It is tight, simple, with ease of recall.
- It is confidently in tune with the strategy of outflanking and enveloping key competitors.
- It is safe. Should a radical change in market circumstances require a shift from the position, the line will still apply to what has become an essential process of differentiation.

The following case concerns the Chinese company Haier. Haier is bravely trying to create a niche position for itself in the United States and to avoid the country-of-origin quality perceptions that might arise. Positioning itself in a mature and sophisticated market will be no easy task for an unknown foreign company.

Case Study 6

HAIER

Positioning an Asian brand in a sophisticated Western market: Those who dare will win?

As a great deal of my time is spent within Asia, I often advise would-be global brand players from Asia to get to the number one position in their home market, then dominate their region, then go global if need be. The rationale behind this is simply that few global brands have ever become global without first being number one in their home market. Secondly, while researching foreign global markets, the common-sense approach suggests that you then go for number one in your region. This second step is tough enough, as Asia represents around half the world's population, but the task is a little easier for Asian companies as opposed to Western ones, as the understanding of cultures isn't a big problem. Finally, when you have size, volume, an established name, and experience, go for the global market if you feel you can support it and can make it into the top two or three.

Fast track

China's top "white goods" manufacturer, Haier, is taking the fast track in contrast to the normal progression suggested above. CEO Zhang Ruimin took a non-driven state enterprise making poor-quality goods, made quality the imperative, and produced a company that is now number one in the China market and had US$5 billion in sales worldwide in 2000. So popular is the Haier brand in China that people pay a premium for it, according to Carrefour, which is located in Qingdao. In fact, its washing machine costs more than a similar U.S. Whirlpool-brand model. But can this brand perception be carried to overseas markets?

Zhang has recently cut straight to his ultimate goal of getting into the top five makers of white goods in the United States by taking Western companies such as GE and Whirlpool head-on, even though his brand is still not a household name in Asia. However, the quality dimension has to be addressed, as no brand can survive without first-class quality, and Asian companies traditionally haven't been associated with this. Zhang has always realized this, and such is his passion that, as a senior manager in the 1980s, he once gathered his staff together and smashed a selection of defective refrigerator products with a sledgehammer to get across his point of view on the vital importance of quality.

Country-of-origin issues

One of the most critical problems facing Asian brands in recent years is the perception of "cheap and poor quality." This perception has persisted for many decades, and has proved difficult to shift. It took 30 years for the Japanese brands to shift a similar perception, but Chinese goods are still in the "poor quality" category, which is why Haier has chosen just this issue on which to fight its battles. And the chief executive really has taken the fight to the commercial "enemy"—the U.S.—where quality begins at home.

The strategy

The strategy for Haier wasn't to build at low cost and export to the U.S. products that would be seen as "made in China." The company realized that while the Nikes of this world could—because of the power of their brand names—market products made in Asia, the Haier brand name would suffer from the home country labeling.

Instead, a strategy was used to reverse the conditions of manufacture so that Haier was made in the U.S. The company bought land enough for several factories in Camden, South Carolina, and spent US$30 million on its first refrigerator plant. This was an important part of "managing perceptions"—what brand management is all about—and establishing a secure base for the future, albeit at an increased cost of production. Staffed mainly by local people, Haier now uses the label "made in the USA."

Haier claims to have helped grow the market in certain categories, citing the increase in growth of the compact refrigerator market of 50% a year after the brand's entry. Haier is also sensitive to the needs of different markets, and is keen to give consumers aesthetic value. The introduction of the wine cooler in the U.S. is a good example of this understanding, with its sophisticated smoked-glass door, curvaceous lines, soft lighting, and chrome racks. It is very much an up-market product, selling for around US$400, and has been featured on the cover of the International Wine Accessories catalogue. This innovation was also brought to market fast, with less than a year from product conception and design to retail availability.

Haier has recognized that the price-commodity trap is waiting, and is trying hard to avoid competing on price and promotions, through a focus on quality, design, innovation, and giving consumers what they really want.

Partnerships and structure

Haier America Trading has been looking for strategic partnerships that will give its brand both recognition and credibility, and has managed to get Wal-Mart, among others, to carry some of its products, mainly small refrigerators and freezers. Haier adds value to its retailers by providing logistical assistance, inventory management, and stress-free customer service.

Speed to market and product innovation are essential items for Zhang, who claims, "In this information age, whoever is the fastest to meet consumer demands wins. I work with whoever can give me the information and technology to meet consumer needs." For this reason, Haier has teamed up with renowned brand names such as Ericsson, with the intention of using Ericsson's Bluetooth wireless technology in its products. Such alliances are giving Haier access to a valuable R&D base that it currently doesn't have. As far as innovation goes, Haier has about 400 new products hitting the market each year. The failure/success rate isn't known, and one wonders if the company can keep up with this rate of change. Zhang's response is, "Wherever we go, the strategy is always to break in with one product, then introduce more and more along the way. The strategy has worked in every market." Zhang says that Haier uses niche marketing and can produce a run of around 30,000 units of one product before moving on to the next. Some of them are clearly *very* niche—for example, a washing machine featuring a virtual fish tank! Currently the company is in 56 categories of products and is practicing mass customization.

Haier has learned from the mistakes of others in managing its brand. Typically, Japanese companies operating in the U.S. have a wholly-owned subsidiary headed by headquarters' executives. Zhang has a different philosophy: he is smart enough to recognize that his staff are still many years behind their counterparts in developed countries, and he actively encourages the joining together of foreign experts and his managers. In the U.S., Haier America Trading is a joint venture between Haier, which has the majority shareholding, and a small group of U.S. investors. The Haier parent company only gets involved in corporate and brand strategy with the U.S. stakeholders, who understand the market and run the operations. They are given a great deal of autonomy, and this enables both speed and flexibility in decision making. According to Michael Jemal, president and CEO of Haier America Trading, it is "the opportunity of a lifetime to launch a brand, to build a brand, to create a market."

Brand culture

While Lexus, the company and brand created by Toyota to break into the luxury car market in the United States, sent their managers well ahead of start-up time to understand the market and U.S. consumer behavior by staying with American families, and placed top Japanese executives to run operations, Haier has again taken a different route. The top managers are American.

The brand culture is important to Haier, and prospective employees must emerge successfully from an initiation program that lasts 40 hours before they are appointed. This program emphasizes teamwork, safety, and the importance of quality. On the factory floor, memorabilia from the Haier heritage are displayed, including a photograph of the Zhang–sledgehammer incident. Employees can earn a trip to China to help them appreciate the values of the company and to experience Chinese culture, which for some is a once-in-a-lifetime experience. Thus, Haier attempts to blend the best of East and West in its employee relations.

The future

Haier has plants in 13 countries and sells its products in over 160 countries. It currently has 30% of the small-refrigerator market in the U.S. The Haier brand is on TV sets, air-conditioners, mobile phones, and PC peripherals, in addition to a restaurant chain and Haier Brothers Cartoons. The financial services category is next on the agenda. Sales in the U.S. are expected to make US$1 billion in 2008, up from US$200 million in 2000. Zhang predicts total 2001 sales of US$7.5 billion, and aims for the company to be among the world's 500 largest by 2006. He also admits that Haier is learning much from the power brands, such as Nike and Dell, and instead of manufacturing most of its output, will seek more outsourcing opportunities.

Haier wants to be a global brand, like the Asian brands Toyota and Sony. In terms of makers of kitchen appliances it is already number six, behind Whirlpool, Electrolux, GE, Bosch-Siemens Hausgerate, and Samsung Electronics. This focus will help Zhang's brand to reach its goal, but the temptation of brand extensions could lead Haier to try and do too much too soon. For instance, an excursion into pharmaceuticals hasn't been successful. There is no doubt, however, that if it can survive in the U.S. and not dilute its brand equity too much by trying to be all things to all people, then a global brand will emerge. The passion is there.

This is just one Chinese company. More entrepreneurs with ambition, passion, and flair like Zhang, controlling huge companies like Haier, will emerge from this tremendous country. And China's entry as a member of the World Trade Organization may mean the end of the domination of global branding by Western companies in some basic goods categories.

I would like to conclude this chapter by emphasizing that good positioning brings about differentiation and brand strength. When a brand occupies a distinctive position in consumer minds, it is difficult for competitors to gain the advantage. The more salient that position is to consumers, then the stronger the brand will be. Good positions are built by really understanding what turns consumers on—the consumer insight I mentioned in the last chapter. When brand managers achieve strong positions, there is always the temptation to try and extend the brand

4

Brand Architecture

Brand architecture is an extremely complex subject, where few rules apply, but no book on brand management would be complete without some discussion of it. This chapter summarizes the basic choices and arguments for different types of brand architecture.

LEVELS OF BRANDING

Several levels of branding can be identified:

- product branding;
- line branding;
- range branding;
- umbrella branding;
- shared branding; and
- endorsed branding.

I will briefly explain below the differences between each of these levels, and describe their main advantages and disadvantages. They represent different degrees of differentiation and origin.

Product branding

This is where a brand name and exclusive position are allocated to one product. Companies adopting this approach give complete autonomy to every brand, and each brand stands or falls on its own merit. There is no apparent connection between the brand and other brands. (For instance, Procter & Gamble use this approach with products such as Ariel and Dash in the household detergent market. And Novotel, Regency Park, and Ibis are product brands of the Accor Group aimed at different target audiences.)

Advantages

- They can occupy precise positions and be aimed at precise target audiences.
- As a result, the multiple brands can occupy the whole category.
- They allow for risk, as failure doesn't damage the parent.
- Retail shelf space may be easier to get, as the brand stands on its own.
- One brand name per product helps customers perceive difference.

Disadvantages

- They are costly, as each requires its own A&P budget.
- There is little room for extension, which is only achieved by product renewal and innovation. (For instance, Tide has had over 70 changes to product, design, and so on.)

Line branding

Line brands offer one basic product under one name, but also offer complementary products, as is the case with Vidal Sassoon shampoos, rinses, hair salons, and so on. Dove not only has soap, but now has facial wipes, body washes, anti-aging cleansers, deodorants, and more.

Advantages

- The brand can be extended to some extent.
- Complementary extensions can reinforce and strengthen the brand image.
- Marketing costs can be shared across products.

Disadvantages

- Lines are limited to the discrete positioning.
- Other extensions are difficult.

Range branding

Range brands have a unique brand positioning but many products under the brand name, such as Bird's Eye frozen foods and Schweppes soft drinks, which have dozens of products under their range names.

Advantages

- Focuses on one brand name.
- Can be a source of heavy brand value.
- Synergy of communications across all products.

Disadvantages

- Excessive extension can dilute brand success, and sub-brands or lines may have to be brought in to liven up the brand (for instance, Lean Cuisine) and develop personality.
- Expenses start to mount up, as various lines under a range need different packaging, and so on.

Umbrella branding

This is where one single brand name, often the company name, covers all products, as with Canon cameras, facsimile machines, and printers. The products don't have names, but tend to have other descriptors, either functional (Canon BJC–2100SP printer) or just alpha-numeric (Mercedes S320).

Advantages

- There are economies of scale across communications platforms.
- Every product contributes to overall brand awareness, equity, and value.
- Entering new markets becomes easier.

- Multiple extensions are possible, but only with good new products.
- Horizontal extensions are easier than vertical ones.

Disadvantages

- A poor umbrella brand image hinders new brand introductions and existing brand success.
- Extensions are easier but are not always accepted by the public.
- Some say the more categories the brand goes into, the weaker the overall image becomes.

Shared branding

This strategy is similar to the umbrella one, except that the products are named (for instance, Calvin Klein's Contradiction For Men, and Microsoft Windows). The product and parent brand share the spotlight.

Advantages

- Parental support.
- Product can ride on parental core values.
- Less expensive to launch than the above brand strategies.
- Products add to parental brand value.

Disadvantages

- Restrained by the core brand of the parent and what it is known for.
- Not as much freedom as the endorsement strategy.
- Failure can damage reputation across the major corporate activity.

Endorsed branding

Here the difference from the above source brand is the fact that the parent brand takes only an endorsement role—for instance, Milo (Nestlé).

Advantages

- More freedom to extend into many categories.

- Parent acts as a guarantee of quality and legitimacy.
- Products add to parental value.
- Failure doesn't transfer across many categories.
- Least expensive way of giving branding support.

Disadvantages

- Bad corporate reputation and performance can affect the product.

The above options represent a continuum from which a company can choose its architecture. However, there is a trend nowadays to the corporate end of the spectrum.

THE COMPANY AS THE BRAND

There is a definite trend toward the company being involved in the branding process, whether through source and endorsement branding, or by other means. Even the master of product branding, Procter & Gamble, now has a worldwide strategy to leverage the corporate brand name by attaching it to some of their product brands as a source reference.

To sum up, there are several reasons for the company brand name appearing in one form or another, including:

- For every product, you get a double message underlining product and company.
- The core values of the company wrap around the product, resulting in consumer confidence.
- There is less confusion for consumers, as they know the source of the product.
- There are more possibilities for brand extensions.
- There are many synergies and cost savings in A&P.
- The financial value of the company brand is enhanced, corporate brands being strategic business assets in their own right.
- And as the late Akio Morita, founder of Sony, said: "I have always

believed that the company name is the life of an enterprise. It carries responsibility and guarantees the quality of the product."

PORTFOLIO MANAGEMENT AND SUB-BRANDS

Having different brands involving different branding strategies, as discussed above, varies by company, and there are no right answers as to what to do. The main reason for holding many brands is that research tells us that no one brand can cover every market, nor even every sector of a market. Some companies take this to the extreme with saturation strategies, like Seiko, with its global range of over 2,000 watches under the Seiko, Lorus, and Pulsar brands. Others like Mars only hold a few "power" brands that are advertised strongly and produced efficiently in volume. Some companies adopt corporate and product brand strategies. For example, Cadbury uses the corporate brand for chocolate bars and product branding for sweets. Toyota, a brand that is well established in most price sectors of the car market, found that the parental image wouldn't transfer successfully to the luxury car segment, and so it had to create a stand-alone brand, Lexus. This was a good move that is in danger of backfiring, so to speak, as the Lexus brand moves down into lower price ranges and opens up the dual possibilities of cannibalization of Toyota brands and a dilution of the Lexus brand.

What must be clearly established, whatever the multi-brand portfolio contains, is that there is no overlap between brand territories. Failure to achieve this will result in consumer confusion and sub-optimization of sales. Finally, it isn't unusual to find a company with many brands neglecting some at the expense of others. It is of extreme importance that annual brand audits are undertaken, and financial valuations of each brand carried out, if possible, to determine which brands are doing well and which not so well, and why. Shell values each of its brands each year and uses this information to allocate market resources to the various brands.

Sub-brands are often confused with product brands, and tend to be used in industries dealing with fashion, trend-related categories, and fast-moving consumer goods where different positions are required for different offerings, and a single brand cannot cover all. Versace presents itself under the main brand for its mature customer base, with Versus for the younger segment. Armani does the same with Emporio Armani. Sub-brands are used to provide variety for different market segments. For example, Gillette manages its portfolio through segmentation, and has Parker pens at the top of its writing instrument range, Waterman for the middle market, and Paper Mate for the lower end.

Sub-brands don't tend to be used when the main corporate brand can cover all products or services, as is the case with heavy machinery, consumer durables, and computers.

Case Study 7 illustrates how a fast-growing brand in a niche market pays attention to building corporate brand value through a consistent naming architecture across its product and sub-brand portfolio.

Case Study 7

RAFFLES INTERNATIONAL
Master branding endorsement

In 1996, there was one hotel in the Raffles Group—the famous Raffles Hotel in Singapore. In 2001 there are 38 hotels under Raffles management. The Raffles International brand started in 1989, built around a famous product associated with top service quality. The word "International" was introduced to add vision to the brand, and now the brand name stands for the promise of product and service excellence. Since then, Raffles has acquired other famous brand names, such as Brown's Hotel in London and Hotel Vier Jahreszeiten in Germany. Many other property acquisitions have followed, including the Swissotel chain. The aim is to have 12,000 rooms by the end of 2003.

But despite this rapid niche area growth, there has been a conscious effort to build a consistent and meaningful brand architecture. The focus of the business of the Raffles brand is lifestyle, not property, and the Raffles International master brand has a two-tier strategy. The Raffles-branded hotels and resorts target affluent leisure and business travelers, while the

Swissotel and Merchant Court hotels aim to give quality and comfort to modern business travelers. The challenge to Raffles management was how to keep the brand equity of all the famous brand names in the portfolio, and yet build up the equity of the Raffles International master brand. The linking is accomplished by keeping the "Raffles International" name in taglines on all hotel corporate identity and communications materials. For example, for the prestigious brand hotel Brown's, the endorsement is "Brown's Hotel, a Raffles International Hotel," while for the Swissotel and Merchant Court hotels each name is signed off with a tagline, "Managed by Raffles International."

It will be interesting to see if consumers actually know the difference, and I am sure that, after considerable education through market communications, some research will take place to reveal what actual consumer perceptions are. There is a slight danger that the prestigious Raffles brand name might suffer some damage to its image when attached to properties of lesser stature.

CO-BRANDING OPPORTUNITIES

This section could just as easily have been included in either of the two following chapters, but I will deal with it here, as it can play an important role in, and potentially do damage to, your attempts to increase the value of the brand name you are managing. Co-branding, sometimes called cross-platform marketing, is increasingly popular as firms look for new approaches to reach their target audiences. Credit cards are good examples of co-branding, linking up with all sorts of businesses. The main reason for co-branding is to reach more of the consumers you want that are currently customers of someone else. Another reason for co-branding is that it shares marketing costs, and this is very important in major campaigns that can cost in excess of US$100 million. An example here is AOL Time Warner joining up with Toyota to promote the 2001 Toyota Camry model in its magazines, cable television channels, and websites in August 2001. Of course, the third major factor in considering co-branding as a business opportunity is to give more benefits to your own customer base and so enhance brand loyalty.

There are many opportunities for co-branding in every industry. French tourism group Accor announced in October 2001 that it would re-brand five hotels in Malaysia and China in partnership with Century International Hotels. A joint venture was formed early in this year by the two companies, and five new Novotel properties in Hong Kong, Kuala Lumpur, and Shenzhen are to be launched under dual brand names. As an example of this, the Watergate Century Hotel Shenzhen will be renamed the Novotel Watergate Shenzhen in China.

Also in 2001, DaimlerChrysler linked its Chrysler brand with Hearst, the company that owns several magazine brands such as *Esquire* and *Harper's Bazaar*. The whole campaign was themed and titled "Designed and Engineered With You in Mind." Also included in this "dream team" was A&E Television Networks to promote the campaign on its channels. (A&E is jointly owned by Hearst, Disney's ABC, and General Electric's NBC.) Finally, the gift retailer Brookstone was included to promote the Chrysler brand via its catalog business and 240 retail outlets. Altogether, it was a massive exercise.

The co-branding effort worked something like this. In Hearst's seven magazines a 12-page section advertised Chrysler designs and Brookstone merchandise. Readers who signed up for test drives received a gift certificate from Brookstone worth US$50. A Chrysler design sweepstakes was featured, and Chrysler brands featured in Brookstone catalogs. Brookstone's Rockefeller Center store held a private event for Chrysler and Brookstone customers. The idea was that everyone could win. Chrysler got much-needed promotion in the right media, and Hearst got revenue in an advertising market that was weakening. Brookstone got access to a wider customer base and a business boost. All contributed to the overall costs. In times of recession, and even in future good times, it is likely that we will see more co-branding partnerships springing up.

One of the latest co-branding exercises is the huge commitment by Coca-Cola to the new Harry Potter movie, *Harry Potter and the Philosopher's Stone* (*Sorcerer's Stone* in the United States). No other company has poured so much money into one movie, namely US$150 million, and Coca-Cola in return receives exclusive global marketing partner status. It allows the beverage company to do what it has wanted to do for a long time, which is reach out to its target young audience without alienating parents. What is more, it gives Coca-Cola better and faster brand communications coverage than traditional advertising. For the movie-maker Warner Brothers, there is a huge funding boost that takes care of its advertising budget worries. The movie was launched in November 2001, and both parties will be hoping for massive sales for a long period of time.

It is important to evaluate the co-branding opportunity before you commit to it, as certain things have to be in place for success to be achieved. One is that unless your customers are going to receive (and see that they will receive) real benefits from the exercise, don't bother. Secondly, ensure that the target audiences of the partners have similar demographic and psychographic profiles. Thirdly, ensure that the partners have brand values similar to those of your brand, otherwise there will be significant strategy problems and working together will be problematic. Finally, make sure that the brand partner you have chosen doesn't eclipse your own brand name. If you get it right, co-branding is a good way of extending the reach of your brand portfolio without product extensions and new product launches.

ORPHAN BRANDS—BRAND TRAFFICKING

Orphan brands are branded products that have been neglected by their parents, and either left to die or sold off to new parents. Usually, they haven't made the grade within major brand company portfolios, and as a result of their mediocre performance aren't given the star treatment.

Global brand holding companies such as Unilever and Procter & Gamble try to sell these orphans in order to regain some of the investment cost, and the brands themselves are often in the ruthless "kill or be killed" categories of fast-moving consumer goods. Other companies with lesser portfolios buy them in the belief that, given more attention and nourishment, they will produce good returns on investment. They also buy these brands because they are already born, have their own identities, have proved to be reasonably acceptable to the public, and don't come with the high costs of market launches. But this strategy hasn't proved to be a successful one for the new "parents."

For example, Aurore Foods Inc. bought brands from Unilever, such as Mrs. Butterworth's syrup for a little over US$114 million, citing a significant growth potential that hadn't been realized due to a lack of corporate support and marketing resources from Unilever in recent years. But Unilever has made a decision to cut its brand portfolio from 1,600 to 400 products in order to reduce costs, and to increase focus on power brands that the company feels are really going to go places. Mrs. Butterworth's is clearly not a power brand in Unilever terminology, and it wasn't surprising that the brand's sales from its purchase in 1996 up to 2000 dropped from US$80 million to US$68 million. Another orphan brand, Duncan Hines (also purchased by Aurore from Unilever), suffered the same fate, with sales reducing from US$228 million to US$220 million during the acquisition time of 1997–2000.

The "buy an orphan" strategy has theoretical promise, but in practice new parents—in this case, Aurore—underestimated the power of the retailers in determining sales through shelf space support, which they often reserve for power brand owners. Also underestimated was the power of the grocery store chains to give preferential shelf space to their own private-label brands.

So, while many retail orphan brands are attractive, unless they receive substantial support they are unlikely to perform. And whether they can ever get to be top performers is questionable if the corporate branding giants have already cast them aside.

HYBRID BRANDING

Hybrid brands are brands born out of the intercourse between two or more companies or brands. The rationale is similar to that of co-branding, but there is one extra ingredient here, and that is that the companies often are similar in what they produce, but come together to combine their experience in the hope of creating a winning brand that they might not be able to create on their own. It is a little bit like a merger, but where a newly formed brand is the focus. An example is

Virgin Atlantic joining up with Singapore Telecom's mobile company, SingTel Mobile, to form Virgin Mobile for the Asian market. SingTel has a good knowledge of Asia but not a really acceptable regional brand name, while Virgin has the brand name but little knowledge of mobile telephony and the Asian markets. Potentially it is an ideal marriage, which in November 2001 was consummated by a grand launch, profiled and reinforced by somewhat fun, cheeky, and very different marketing activities in line with Virgin's brand values.

Another example, set out in more detail in Case Study 8, is that of Sony and Ericsson, where I am less confident of the possibility of success and of the brand management skills of those involved. Case Study 9 then looks at Sundsvall, a brand that didn't make the cut.

Case Study 8

SONY AND ERICSSON
A winning partnership?

Sony Corporation and Telefon AB L.M. Ericsson launched a 50:50-owned new mobile telephone brand and logo in September 2001 called Sony Ericsson Mobile Communications. For Ericsson, one senses an air of desperation, as the brand's market share has dropped consistently over the last few years to under 10%, left, like Motorola, in the wake of the Nokia revolution. Ericsson is literally banking on this new venture to pull it out of the financial problems it currently faces—namely, debt, a lack of profitability, and little consumer confidence in its brand, given a flagging market scenario.

For Sony, whose ambitions reach well beyond consumer electronics into infotainment, the proposition is expected to be a boost to its existing business in a market where it lacks expertise and needs to grow its tiny market share in mobile telecommunications.

The "big idea" is that Ericsson provides the technology capability and Sony the market understanding. The new president of Sony Ericsson, Katsumi Ihara, claims the new hybrid brand makes sense. He says, "We are still complementary. Ericsson is strong in wireless, and we are a little weak in that respect. But we know the consumer."

My opinion of this "wedding" is that there are several obstacles to overcome before both suitors will gel, namely:

- the "logo = brand" mentality;
- spending on product versus spending on brand;
- the volatile market;
- the incumbent giant;
- the fickle consumer; and
- what's the big difference?

Let's have a brief look at each of these.

1. **Logo = brand:** Sony Ericsson has created a new logo that apparently looks like a green throat lozenge, and is to be seen moving on an animated phone screen as well as appearing on ads. On handset screens the logo will react "with emotion," according to company spokesman Mats Georgson. He says it will "behave like it's alive; it can morph and jump around—it's liquid identity or 'another me.' We want it to be something that can constantly evolve and surprise you." To me, this is creative overruling strategy. Logos are only valuable as memory recall devices and are usually consistently applied. This sounds like a gimmick that could backfire. Too much attention and money is given to logo production. Logos don't make brands and aren't prime differentiators.

2. **Spending on product versus spending on brand:** Asian companies are famous for not investing in brands, which is one of the prime reasons why there are few global brands coming from that region. Japanese companies are typical of this and don't manage their brands properly. Hence, we see Sony Ericsson president Katsumi Ihara saying that a big investment in this new brand isn't required because the

name on the logo speaks for itself. He says, "It doesn't make sense to spend a lot of money—people will already know what it is. Instead of spending a lot of money on the brand, it makes more business sense to spend on the product." This is dangerous thinking, as new brands aren't successful without strong promotional support.

3. **The volatile market:** While forecasted sales of mobile phone units were expected to exceed 600 million during 2001, Nokia forecasts only around 400 million. The overall market in many areas of the world has become more saturated, and many consumers are adopting a "wait and see" stance toward 3G, having experienced disappointment with WAP. With the launch of a new brand you only have one chance to get it right, and one wonders if the timing now is right for Sony Ericsson.

4. **The incumbent giant:** Nokia rules the market with a share in excess of 35%. Ericsson's share has slipped enormously, and Sony has never really made an impact on its own. Neither Ericsson nor Sony has created the emotional associations that consumers love, and which breed brand loyalty, and I see nothing to suggest that things are going to be different with the new venture. Indeed, brand spend isn't a high priority as we have seen above, and this is how emotional associations are largely created. Neither Ericsson nor Sony is an expert at branding, unlike their giant rival.

5. **The fickle consumer:** Consumers of mobile phones are already product and brand savvy. Sony Ericsson will have to do a lot of persuading to get consumers to switch from brands they are already familiar—and, to some extent, happy—with. With minimum brand spend this is unlikely to be achieved unless the product itself is spectacularly different. This doesn't look likely to be the case. Moreover, they are more knowledgeable about corporate affairs, and

neither of the two partners has been pushing out great results recently; just the opposite, in fact. Consumers are risk averse.

6. **What's the big difference?:** Mobile phones are commodities, being more or less the same in terms of size, weight, battery life, features, and so on. Nokia is so far ahead of the rest of the market because of its superior branding and design. The question for Sony Ericsson is: Why is its product different and better? Logo differentiation won't be a sufficient reason for success. And we won't know the answer in product terms, as, despite the launch of the company and its logo, the phones themselves won't be available until an undisclosed date in 2002!

Case Study 9

SUNDSVALL
Hybrid branding—one drink too many!

The background

Between 1996 and 2000, the market for liquor shifted in American bars. Seagram Co., the owner of the much-admired and highly successful brand Absolut vodka, saw its power brand downgraded to lower shelves, usurped by newer elite brands from competitors such as Ketel One and Belvedere. In certain bars, Absolut was confined to places under the bar, which formerly was unthinkable. New York's Le Cirque 2000 bar, for example, said: "Being on our shelf is very, very premium."

The knee-jerk reaction from Seagram was to launch a premium vodka, Sundsvall, to be distilled in alliance with Absolut Vodka Co. The new brand's name was actually the name of the town where the liquor would be distilled. This was impressive for the country of origin, but meaningless to the public. The idea was to create a super-Absolut, but three years later the brand was deleted.

The problem

In 1997, research found that Absolut's "early adopter" customers were switching to other brands, such as Grey Goose and Belvedere. These intruder brands were spending heavily on promotion, with literally hundreds of testing opportunities for bartenders, regarded in research lexicon as "indirect advocates." Souvenir glasses with trips to France on Concorde (Grey Goose brand) were offered. The new brands encouraged bartenders and food and beverage writers to look at vodka as a category in its own right, with varieties such as charcoal-filtered, rye-based, coffee-pot distillation, and others. Absolut, despite its great personality, was being left behind.

Consumer pick-up

The perception change among journalists and bartenders inevitably passed on to consumers, who started to select the new brands according to criteria such as prestige and indulgence, matching the status of malt whiskey. So, from being perceived primarily as a mixer, vodka suddenly catapulted into the fashion accessories business. One consumer said that selecting a luxury vodka isn't unlike "choosing what cologne I might wear." Vodka had now come to represent finesse.

Brand architecture, design, and price

Seagram wanted a new brand, but the Absolut management saw it as a trend. Research confirmed that the trend was increasing, but Absolut didn't want its name to endorse the new joint-venture brand. Months of serious discussions focused on packaging, design, and so on. Predictably, Absolut was all for a simple bottle, but Seagram wasn't. Seagram was adamant that the price should be higher than the other premium brands, such as Belvedere, by as much as US$4. Eventually, promotions were arranged, but it was all too late. The vodka was thought by distributors and retailers to be excellent, but the bottle too plain. Sundsvall didn't stand out from the crowd. Media attention was minimal, but the limelight had been stolen by other brands. Limited distribution gave the brand further problems, and it turned out that shelf turn for the one bottle of Sundsvall was three months, compared to three bottles per day for the competition.

The result

In May 1999, Absolut cleared itself of brand responsibility, distancing itself from the Sundsvall brand. By late 1999, production had ceased, while Grey Goose and Belvedere sold 100,000 cases that year. A spokesperson for Sundsvall said, "Sundsvall was so underground it never got above ground."

You only get one chance to launch a new brand, and I am sure both companies have learned from their experience. The lessons are:

- Joint-venture branding can lead to disaster if strategy and execution aren't in line between the partners.
- A win–win situation can only be based on speedy advanced agreement in keeping with market changes.
- Consumer behavior is fickle and can change very quickly.
- Categories can change just as quickly, and brand managers have to stay firmly focused on what is happening.

MERGER AND ACQUISITION ISSUES

Naming and consumer confusion

Mergers and acquisitions (M&As) sometimes give brands problems. For example, if the names of the brands aren't retained, or if the names are joined, as was the case with ExxonMobil and DaimlerChysler, then there is the issue of how to explain this to consumers. In the case of ExxonMobil, the name change was carefully explained to consumers through the press. They ran an advertisement soon after their merger in 1999 that read:

> We're as brand loyal as you are. Loyalty is a two-way street. So along
> the street, road or motorway we aren't about to confuse our customers.
> Yes, we've merged. But our brands Esso, Mobil and Exxon will still be
> there. What will change is the company behind them. ExxonMobil is
> a new name for technology, efficiency and service. Helping our old
> names treat you better than ever.

The ad, which carried the website address, showed the two company
logos, with the sign of ExxonMobil. Here was a company that cared
about its customers and their emotional associations with their brands.
It took the trouble to reassure its customers, and at the same time
promise them a better experience.

By contrast, DaimlerChrysler, which also merged in 1999, have taken
two years to explain their position. In the *Asian Wall Street Journal* of
October 9, 2001, and *Fortune* magazine of October 15, 2001, they
produced what can only be described as an appallingly uncreative
advertisement—and that is being kind—the copy for which showed on
the left page a telephone operator saying: "Good morning. Welcome to
Mercedes-Benz-Jeep®-Dodgesmart-FreightlinerSterlingSetra. How can I
help you?" This was followed by a headline on the right page: "Just call
us DaimlerChrysler." This, in turn, was followed by the copy:

> We don't really need to introduce our brands anymore. They have all
> made history through their own achievements, and their names are
> known the world over. Of course, the fact that they all work under
> one roof means we will always have a wealth of experience and
> innovative ideas to draw on. Something that will help us stay miles
> ahead of the competition in the future. Find out more at
> www.daimlerchrysler.com.

The sign-off was the name "DaimlerChrysler" with a tagline of:
"Answers for Questions to Come."

I am tempted to say, "Words fail me!" Now, I don't know what the
DaimlerChrysler brand personality is, or even whether it has one, but
any company that advertises will create a personality in consumers'
minds, whether by default or not. This ad sends out awful messages

about the DaimlerChrysler personality from the tone and manner of the copy. And I have no clue as to what the tagline means. Have a look at the example of copy analysis for Malaysia Airlines given in Chapter 6 (Case Study 22), and then analyze this example.

When agencies present brand managers with advertising copy, it should be checked against the brand personality to determine whether it is "on strategy" or not.

Brand names and equity

As can be seen from the above efforts, some companies believe there is considerable brand equity in established and famous brand names, and remove them at their peril. Others seem not to care. For example, when Rhone-Poulec and Hoechst merged, they removed both brand names and created a totally new and meaningless name, Aventis. Huge amounts of money have had to be spent to raise brand awareness, but still the brand equity has been lost, and consumers lack clarity about the brand's heritage and what it stands for.

New names, like new logos, have suddenly become a "must have" for some companies, who sometimes pay large sums for nonsensical or irrelevant names. Importantly, the main purpose of branding—differentiation—appears often to be forgotten, as many names are very similar. The end-result is that the consumer is mystified, confused, often irritated, and totally clueless about the message the name is supposed to impart.

In an extraordinary move Acer changed its name in December 2001 to Benq, and intends to spend US$30 million in advertising to promote the name and concept. The name means something to Acer—it is a compression of "Bringing Enjoyment and Quality to Life". Chairman and co-founder of the Acer Group Stan Shih said "We are changing the brand name for the future."

Apparently, market research studies amongst consumers, including focus groups, revealed that people thought it strange but unique, with some pronouncing it Ben-Q and others Beng. President K.Y. Lee said "More importantly, strange name notwithstanding, they said they will remember it."

But memory is one thing and emotional association is another. In my opinion the company may have to spend more than the anticipated figure to re-build awareness and acceptance, and it will take a long time to re-establish the emotional connection between consumers and what was Acer. The case I have written on page 237 shows that it has taken Acer a long time to get to grips with what Acer really stands for internally, and this might now have to be re-thought through also, if "Acerness" is different to "Benqness".

As a final comment, it is most unusual for well-known and accepted brand names to throw away brand equity and value that has been painstakingly built over time, and although I have bought Acer in the past I'm not so sure I would like to buy a Benq!

Dave Barry, in the *International Herald Tribune* of April 7–8, 2001, sums up the situation as follows:

Why do companies keep changing their names? And why do they always change them to names that don't MEAN anything? We consumers like names that reflect what the company does. We know, for example, that International Business Machines makes business machines, and Ford makes Fords, and Sara Lee makes us fat. But we don't know, from the name "Verizon," what Verizon does. As far as I can tell, Verizon consists of some big telephone companies that joined together. So why couldn't they call themselves "An Even Bigger Telephone Company"?

And what in the world is "Accenture"? This is a company that buys a LOT of ads, the overall message of which seems to be: "Accenture—A Company That Buys A Lot Of Ads." I checked the Accenture Internet site, and here's what it says about its name: "Accenture is a coined word that connotes putting an accent or emphasis on the future"... This brings me to my idea for how you can make big money. You start by inventing a new, modern-sounding company name, such as "Paradil" or "Gerbadigm," which are coined words that connote a combination of "paradigm" and "Gerbil." Then you print official-looking invoice forms for this company, and you send out a mass-mailing of bills for, let's say, $20.38 apiece to several million randomly selected people. You enclose an announcement with a perky corporate marketing statement that is clearly a lie, and thus appears to be totally realistic, such as: "We've changed our name to serve you better!"

Barry's article has a terrifying element of truth in it. To summarize, names should be:

- short;
- memorable;
- meaningful;
- relevant; and
- different.

The name "Accenture," which replaced "Andersen Consulting," has not only received poor responses from the media for its budgeted advertising cost of US$175 million (real cost probably more), but has also left the public even more in the dark about what the company really stands for, as the advertising was confusing and failed to send a clear message.

The British Post Office Group was another company to receive a public relations caning when it changed its name to Consignia. Consumers were affronted, offended, and bewildered. One reader of the *Daily Telegraph* wrote: "I hope the new name will be consignia'd to the dustbin."

By the way, are you driving an Acura, Asuna, Altima, Cortina, Integra, Elantra, Sonata, Sentra, or Maxima? Whatever happened to meaningful differentiation?

Here are two case studies. Case Study 10 illustrates how one company, Marriott, absorbed another and found itself with architectural and positioning problems; while Case Study 11 provides an example of how companies have adopted the two extremes of the opposites of brand architecture continuum in their merger/acquisition activities—Carrefour and Ahold.

Case Study 10

MARRIOTT INTERNATIONAL INC.
Acquisitions and the problem of brand fit

In some industries it is difficult to grow the brand and the business via normal means, such as extensions. This is typified by the service industries, such as hospitality, where the process takes too long to accomplish and/or the capital cost of doing so is enormous. Instead, mergers and acquisitions are often the chosen route, providing fast vehicles for business development and returns on investment. Sometimes the brands fit and sometimes they don't. The latter case can prove difficult for brand management, as was the case with the hotel chain Marriott International Inc. when it acquired 114 Renaissance branded hotels for US$947 million in 1997. The Renaissance collection was an eclectic one, comprising large and small hotels; as a result, the brand was somewhat confusing to consumers and franchisees, as well as to Marriott.

Brand schizophrenia

After the takeover, Marriott's operational expertise increased Renaissance's profits significantly, but brand problems still lurked menacingly beneath the surface. Property design was inconsistent and service levels differed tremendously, with the result that guests were never sure what to expect when they made a booking and arrived at their destination Renaissance hotel. In brand terms, the real issue was that Renaissance had no clear and consistent identity—it was a schizophrenic brand. Marriott realized that the long-term future lay in producing a solution to this problem, and that the market confusion caused by this inconsistency didn't augur well for long-term growth, where brand consistency is key to brand power and shareholder value.

Whereas some companies would have been satisfied with short-term gains to the bottom line, Marriott saw the writing on the wall. Other problems also started to appear. For example, Renaissance hotels were found to be cannibalizing Marriott sales, and so repositioning of Renaissance became the focus for brand development. The dilemma was given visibility by Jurgen Giesbert, senior vice president of Marriott responsible for the Renaissance brand, who stated: "When we bought Renaissance, nobody knew what to do with them, whereas Marriott is a clearly defined brand. Everybody knows what it is."

When in doubt, give brand management a shout

Clearly, this wasn't a straightforward strategic brand challenge, but Marriott took several interesting steps. First, it recruited a brand manager from Nike—one of the world's leading power corporate brands; secondly, it brought in a designer from Beverly Hills who specialized in unique, independent hotels. This was a potentially good combination of branding skills, partnering someone who understood and was used to the discipline of focused corporate brand management, with someone who understood the product design elements and markets that Renaissance had grown up in. Then another good decision was made, which was to do some homework. For two years, principally qualitative focus group research was carried out to provide a thorough understanding of the moods and feelings of the desired market segments. In other words, there was a deliberate attempt to gain consumer insight.

Unique boutique?

The end-result of this process was a repositioning of the Renaissance brand into a more focused "boutique" collection of hotels, with an interesting positioning summed up by the phrase, "Give Me A Surprise." Bill Marriott, chairman of Marriott International Inc., revealed that the research clarified that 30% of the total market for hotel accommodation was attracted to the element of surprise in the brand experience.

This significant proportion of the market consisted of people who didn't want the boring certainty and sterility of a predictable "sameness" in whatever hotel they checked into. So, the paradox of branding had become apparent to the company: consistency is key, but there are always sections of the market that want to be different and to experience difference. Marriott had found a niche for Renaissance that would, if managed properly, cater for the needs of a different segment of the market, stop cannibalization between brands, and, at a single stroke, eliminate confusion and create a new and forceful brand identity. But attention now had to switch to the competition.

Product development and competition—out of the frying pan into the fire?

This switch of brand positioning took the Renaissance brand into a new category of competition, where it now has to fight the likes of the Starwood brand and Ian Schrager's designer hotels. Renovation is already under way at numerous key properties, and, if things go well, Renaissance will change its brand identity and image. But there is fierce competition, and it will be interesting to see whether a hotel chain that is renowned and acclaimed for its consistency in product predictability and service quality can develop and succeed by incorporating the repositioning of an acquired brand that is the very antithesis of their traditional way of brand management— namely, the development of a brand that is based around planned *inconsistency*.

The big question for every brand manager is: What would you do if you were given an acquired brand? How do you decide whether your policy is conformity or autonomy?

Case Study 11

CARREFOUR SA (FRANCE) VERSUS
AHOLD NV (HOLLAND)
Mergers and acquisitions—global versus product naming

"To change or not to change? That is the question." (Apologies to William Shakespeare.)

They sound like two football teams, but are in fact the two largest supermarket chains globally after Wal-Mart Stores Inc. Interestingly, they have traveled down different branding routes in terms of naming strategy/architecture in the course of their rapid development over the last few years.

Carrefour is trying to build a global brand by acquiring other chains and changing their names to its own. For instance, it bought Promodes SA in November 1999 for 15 billion Euros in the world's largest retail acquisition. All of Promodes' Pyra and Continent stores in France and Spain were changed to the Carrefour brand name. Even the own-label products of those acquired chains were rebranded. Shoppers weren't pleased, though, and Carrefour's profits and sales since then have slowed, reducing market capitalization by about 30% by September 2001. Consumers claimed they were confused by the new layouts and brands, and loyalty suffered. Bravely, Carrefour says this is a short-term phenomenon, that customers will return, and that the cost savings of consistent branding will pay off in the long term.

Ahold has done the opposite, and operates many names globally—for instance, Superdiplo in Spain, Giant in the U.S., and ICA in Sweden. Ahold spokesperson Jan Hol says, "We know it is more expensive to operate 25 brands around the world instead of one, but we think the benefit of a strong local brand is better." According to Ahold's CEO Cees van der Hoeven, Ahold's brand philosophy is, "Everything the customer sees we localize. Everything they don't see, we globalize."

Carrefour says that it caters to local preferences by tailoring its food products to local tastes in 95% of cases. Carrefour spokesman Christian Honore says, "In China we are Chinese; in Spain we are Spanish." But Ahold's shares are in line with the DJ Stoxx European retail index in 2001, while Carrefour's shares are behind the index to the tune of 7%. Food analysts say that food retailing doesn't behave like other categories, as most shopping for groceries is done close to home. If this is true, they say a trusted single global brand will be difficult to realize. Mmmm—food for thought!

THE BRAND COLLECTORS

The fascination with luxury brands

The ultimate pleasure for any brand manager must be having charge of a luxury brand, with all its concomitant global glamor, prestige, and fame. This isn't to say, however, that competition isn't fierce, but it is surprising that ordinary products such as pens (sorry, writing instruments) can be priced on the same level as rock stars' and football players' salaries. Of course, it's back to basic branding techniques and the management of perceptions, but the returns are huge. One would think that, in times of recession, luxury brands would experience poor results, but this doesn't appear to be the case, as will be illustrated below.

"Watch" this space—opportunities to cross-brand

Typical of a luxury goods category that seems to have an endless range is watches (sorry, timepieces). Everyone appears to be extending their brands into the timepiece category. Calvin Klein has moved into wristwatches that tie in with the overall Calvin Klein clothes look. Emporio Armani has done the same thing, and Versace has a new watch brand called Character. There is an endless stream of others, including DKNY, Adidas, Bally, Benetton, Carven, Chanel, Christian Lacroix, Hugo Boss, Lacoste, Karl Lagerfeld, Lanvin, Nina Ricci, Pierre Cardin, Timberland, Yves Saint-Laurent, and more. The market has exploded, and it is estimated that in the U.S. alone in 2000 over US$6.6 billion-worth of these fashion accessories were sold, and that the market is still growing quickly. Fashion-branded watches come in all shapes, sizes, and prices, but there is little doubt that consumers love them, because they love their brands.

If you aren't into fashion but prefer technology, don't despair. Breitling, Seiko, Nike, Casio, and other manufacturers are producing hi-tech timepieces, in some cases capable of downloading MP3 format files from the Internet or direct from CDs via a home computer. There are watches that monitor heart rates, store electricity, receive emails, measure speed and distance for athletes, and send out distress signals. Many companies are finding that extending their brands via this method keeps the sales tills ringing and brand awareness high.

The dream sellers

But let's move on to real luxury products. The very smart companies are those that have a business strategy of creating and buying luxury brands. These are the brands that cause hearts to flutter, create insatiable desires, and sell more as the price rises. They are the stuff of dreams. They are truly emotional brands and are held by few companies. The two biggest holding companies of these luxury brands are LVMH Group and Richemont. Both of these groups give their brands relative autonomy in brand management, because almost each brand is a power brand in its own right. The corporate branding face is rarely seen, and the brands stand alone. Both of the companies have been referred to as "The House of Brands," as opposed to the branded house.

Richemont (Compagnie Financière Richemont AG) is "a Swiss luxury goods group with a view to the long-term development of successful international brands," according to its website. In addition to its luxury goods business, Richemont also holds investments in tobacco and direct marketing industries. Being Swiss, it is predictably very low key in talking about its own identity. It leaves the talking to its brands, which include Cartier, Van Cleef & Arpels, Piaget, Baume and Mercier, Jaeger-LeCoultre, A. Lange & Sohne, Vacheron Constantin, Dunhill, Montblanc, Montegrappa, Hackett, Old England, Purdey, Chloe, and Shanghai Tang.

In the year to March 31, 2001, Richemont racked up sales of 3.684 billion Euros, but it is well behind its more high-profile competitor, whose profile and ways of managing luxury brands are described in Case Study 12.

Case Study 12
MOËT HENNESSY LOUIS VUITTON GROUP (LVMH)
The house of luxury brands

The net sales of LVMH for the year 2000 reached 11.6 billion Euros. LVMH is a network of over 440 subsidiaries in France and around the world, with 53,000 employees. It describes itself as "a young group, an ongoing expansion." Its brand portfolio boasts around 50% of the world's most powerful brand names across various categories, as shown below. One of these brands, Christian Dior, is itself one of the indirect holders of LVMH.

- **Watches/jewelry:** TAG Heuer, Montres Christian Dior, Ebel, Zenith, Omas, Chaumet, Fred, joint venture with De Beers, the diamond company.
- **Fashion:** Louis Vuitton, Celine, Loewe, Kenzo, Givenchy, Christian Dior, Christian Lacroix, Marc Jacobs, Berluti, Fendi, Thomas Pink, Emilio Pucci, Donna Karan.
- **Wines/spirits:** Moët & Chandon, Dom Perignon, Mercier, Veuve Clicquot Ponsardin, Canard-Duchene, Pommery, Krug, Chandon Estates, Cloudy Bay, Cape Mentelle, Newton, MountAdam, Hennessy, Hine, Chateau d'Yquem.
- **Perfumes/cosmetics:** Parfums Christian Dior, Parfums Givenchy, Kenzo Parfums, Hard Candy, Fresh, Bliss, Urban Decay, Make Up For Ever, BeneFit Cosmetics, Guerlain.
- **Selective retailing:** DFS, Miami Cruiseline, Sephora, Le Bon Marche, Solstice, La Samaritaine.
- **Other businesses:** Phillips, de Pury & Luxembourg, Etude Tajan, D.I. Group, Investir, Radio Classique, La Tribune, Jazzman, Le Monde de la Musique, System TV, Connaissance des Arts, Art & Auction, Sephora.com, eLuxury.

The LVMH vision

But in LVMH's case, at least, we know that this isn't merely random buying of brands. Chairman Bernard Arnault says, "LVMH's vision is to represent around the world the most refined qualities of Western 'Art de Vivre.' LVMH must continue to be synonymous with both elegance and creativity. Our products, and the cultural values they embody, blend tradition and innovation, and kindle dream and fantasy."

The LVMH values

There are five priorities that reflect the fundamental values shared by all group stakeholders, as published by LVMH Group on its website. These are:

Be creative and innovate

Group companies are determined to nurture and grow their creative resources. Their long-term success is rooted in a combination of artistic creativity and technological innovation: they have always been and always will be creators.

Their ability to attract the best creative talents, to empower them to create leading-edge designs is the lifeblood of our Group.

The same goes for technological innovation. The success of the companies' new products—particularly in cosmetics—rests squarely with research & development teams. This dual value—creativity/innovation—is a priority for all companies. It is the foundation of their continued success.

Aim for product excellence

Group companies pay the closest attention to every detail and ensure the utter perfection of their products. They symbolize the nobility and perfection of traditional craftsmanship. Each and every one of the objects their customers buy and use exemplifies our brands' tradition of impeccable quality. Never should Group companies disappoint, but rather continue to surprise their customers with the quality, endurance, and finish of their products. They never compromise when it comes to product quality.

Their search for excellence goes well beyond the simple quality of their products: it encompasses the layout and location of our stores, the display of the items they offer, their ability to make their customers feel welcome as soon as they enter our stores ... All around them, their clients see nothing but quality.

Bolster the image of our brands with passionate determination

Group brands enjoy exceptional reputation. This would not amount to much, and could not be sustained, if was not backed by the creative superiority and extreme quality of their products. However, without this aura, this extra dimension that somewhat defies logic, this force of expression that transcends reality, the sublime that is the stuff of our dreams, Dior would not be Dior, Louis Vuitton would not be Louis Vuitton, Moët would not be Moët ... The power of the companies' brands is part of LVMH's heritage. It took years and even decades to build their image. They are an asset that is both priceless and irreplaceable.

Therefore, Group companies exercise stringent control over every minute detail of their brands' image. In each of the elements of their communications with the public (announcements, speeches, messages, etc.), it is the brand that speaks. Each message must do right by the brand. In this area as well, there is absolutely no room for compromise.

Act as entrepreneurs

The Group's organizational structure is decentralized, which fosters efficiency, productivity, and creativity.

This type of organization is highly motivating and dynamic. It encourages individual initiative and offers real responsibilities—sometimes early on in one's career. It requires highly entrepreneurial executive teams in each company.

This entrepreneurial spirit requires a healthy dose of common sense from managers, as well as hard work, pragmatism, efficiency, and the ability to motivate people in the pursuit of ambitious goals. One needs to share and enjoy this entrepreneurial spirit to—one day—manage a subsidiary or company of the LVMH Group.

Strive to be the best in all we do

Last but not least is our ambition to be the best. In each company, executive teams strive to constantly improve, never be complacent, always try to broaden our skills, improve the quality of our work, and come up with new ideas.

The Group encourages this spirit, this thirst for progress, among all of its associates.

As an expression of what a real brand champion thinks and feels, I think we need look no further than the above statement. But let's have a closer look at how LVMH manages its brands.

In an interview in the *Harvard Business Review* of October 2001, Arnault describes the characteristics of what he calls "star brands":

- timeless;
- modern;
- fast-growing; and
- highly profitable.

And there are fewer than 10 of these star brands in the luxury brand market. The reason for the paucity of numbers is that it is extremely difficult to balance all four of these characteristics at once. For instance, fast growth and high profitability have some tension between them, as do timelessness and modernity.

Timelessness takes years to develop, but Arnault says that the perception of this characteristic can be generated by fanatical, uncompromising quality. Innovation drives modernity, which is harder to achieve as "you must know the past and invent the future at the same time." Much of his design teams' time is spent on this, as star brands have to be current, fashionable, edgy, sexy, and modern—fulfilling a fantasy. Constant brand reinvention is key. Growth is a function of consumer desire, and depends to some extent on advertising to create that desire, but Arnault won't let his marketing people near the advertising; it remains with his design teams, who, in his opinion, can better project the desired image. He stresses:

> The biggest mistake any company can make is to delegate advertising to the marketing department. For example, the advertising for the Dior brand personality (very sexy, modern, very feminine, and energetic) is often created by the Dior design team and John Galliano himself. Profitability for each star brand comes later, of course, after all the innovation, advertising, and other expensive processes have been pumped in.

Product quality and training of staff feature highly at the "front end" of the star brand-building process, according to Arnault. For example, each Louis Vuitton suitcase is "put in a torture machine, where it is opened and closed five times per minute for three weeks. And that is not all—it is thrown, shaken, and crushed." This is how Arnault's company makes an heirloom. "A single purse can have up to 1,000 manufacturing tasks, and nearly every task is done by hand. People who work in the factories are trained for many months before they are even allowed to touch a product." Planning and discipline are paramount in the production process.

As for brand management, Arnault says many brands have the star potential, but are poorly managed. Brand management with luxury goods takes time, because all four elements have to be aligned, and that you cannot hurry. The up-side is that once you get there and manage the brand well, the returns are spectacular.

SUMMARY

Brand architecture is possibly the most difficult area of brand management, in that there are simply no rules, and endless opportunities to try out many variations. Some variations work, while similar ones don't. Corporate branding in one form or another is the trend, but sometimes product branding is necessary. Careful thought must be given to all decisions in this area, and specialist advice may be necessary.

Those companies who continue to believe that spending millions on new logos and names is going to change their brand, its experience and relationship with the consumer, and its profitability are sorely mistaken. Nothing changes unless the customer *experiences* change, so if you are looking for an image change look at changing the brand experience first. If you have to change a logo, do it in an evolutionary way rather than a revolutionary way. If you have to create a new logo, or a new name, choose a local design house or consultancy that will do a good job for a fraction of the price. Don't be taken in by the giant agencies.

Getting brand architecture right isn't easy. The next chapter looks at more tough decisions brand managers have to take regardless of whether their brands are doing well or not so well.

5

Three Great Dilemmas: Brand Stretch, Brand Revitalization, and Brand Deletion

There are three great dilemmas that face brand managers at some stage in their careers, and all are to do with the life of the brand. While brands, if well managed, may live forever, there are situations that occur through both success and neglect that test the skill of a good brand manager. The three great dilemmas are: (1) whether to stretch a brand name into other areas—either inside or outside its existing category—when it is doing well; (2) what to do when a brand has been neglected and needs revitalizing, and whether or not this can be achieved; and (3) whether to kill or delete a brand if the future holds no prospects. None of these decisions is easy, and I will give cases of each type of decision in this chapter.

THE GREAT TEMPTATION: STRETCHING THE BRAND

One critical question that all brand managers have to face at some stage is whether or not they should stretch or extend their brand, to which the answer is: it all depends. At its most basic level, extending or stretching a brand involves producing variants of the same brand in the same category. At another level, there is the issue of stretching a brand so that it breaks into other categories, but still sits in the same industry. Finally, there is the question of whether a brand can be stretched so far that it can move into totally different industries. The temptation is great to stretch a successful brand, and there are no rules to guide the brand

113

manager here, because at the end of the day the consumer will decide, as it is consumers who own the brands. The limiting factor really is the brand promise and personality, and whether or not consumer emotional associations make the connection.

There are, of course, some brand extensions that just wouldn't work, and it is possible to look at various examples and to make some judgments as to when brand extensions are possible. However, first I would like to clarify some of the basic causes of brand extensions, as well as some terminology.

Basic reasons for brand extensions

There appear to be three basic reasons for extending brands.

1. Natural causes

One of the main reasons for brand extensions is what I call "natural causes." This is where a brand may produce a product that is very close to its original offering, but which satisfies the desires of a different, or even the same, audience without significantly cannibalizing existing sales. These extensions are a "natural" development as brand managers uncover and exploit more of the needs and wants of the consumers that exist in their category. Such was the case with the famous After Eight Mints. The Classic Dark Assortment has already been complemented by the White Mint Assortment, and the newest addition to the range is After Eight Truffles, introduced in September 2000. These kinds of brand extensions not only make sense, but are almost mandatory if companies are to grow and keep competitors at bay in their category.

2. Market growth reductions

Companies may try to widen their brand portfolio if their existing market(s) show signs of slower growth. For example, this has happened to Intel—the world's number one semiconductor manufacturer—with a slowdown expected in the growth of its processor unit due to decreasing sales of personal computers. Intel has made a strategic decision to produce other consumer devices such as portable digital music players, ChatPad—an instant messaging and email device, and WebTablet—

which allows people to surf the Net using a hardcover book-sized wireless screen.

Intel is now building devices that connect to, and increase the value of, home computers, especially those that have Intel microprocessors installed. This new directional swing is quite compatible with Intel's existing brand portfolio and will no doubt be readily accepted by the public. The extensions are close enough to existing businesses to avoid consumer doubts, although they will have a tough time competing with products made by Sony, Philips, and Rio.

3. *Confidence in the invincibility of the brand*

While the above reasons are often based on solid market research and a strong degree of common sense, some brands are extended merely on the premise that, because the brand has been successful in one or more categories/markets, it will automatically be a star in others. This line of thinking can be right, but it can also be wrong. The Virgin Group has suffered from over-confidence in a few areas, such as with its Virgin Vodka and Virgin Cosmetics. Thus, while there may be opportunities for stretching a brand, there may also be minefields that can affect the ability of a brand to be stretched. Before we look at more examples, I would like to distinguish between what are often referred to as brand extensions and line extensions.

Brand and line extensions—possibilities and difficulties

Brand extensions involve the use of an existing brand name to move into a new product or service category, while line extensions of a brand use the existing name to offer a new product or service in the same category. Virgin Airlines is an example of the former, and the Mercedes "A" class is an example of the latter.

Examples of where it is possible for one brand, company, or product to line extend include cars, banks, and drinks. Cars can be "flexed" via features such as engine capacity, coupé versions, and so on. Banks can be positioned broadly but be promoted differently to retail, corporate, small and medium-sized enterprises, entrepreneurs, public sector institutions, and so on. Drinks such as Schweppes' soft drinks are flexed via different products such as mixers, mineral waters, fruit and health drinks, with many flavors to appeal to adults and young people, but all of these remain true to the company's basic positioning of quality soft drinks, and all remain basically in the same category. Brand extension can also be achieved in taking the brand into another category or industry. For instance, Ford Motor Company has started a Jaguar Bank, and Virgin has moved into telecommunications. The key to extensions of any kind is that the brand must stay true to its original identity. Only in this way will consumers accept the change.

While a company or product can have only one true, strong position, it can be tweaked, adjusted, and flexed to emphasize particular strengths or values that attract different customer groups, as long as it isn't stretched too far. The amount of stretch available is contingent upon knowledge of various market segments. So, multipositioning can also be seen as line or brand extending, but there are limits to this possibility that mustn't be overstepped.

Harley-Davidson has been successful in marketing its apparel range because it fits well with the needs and desires of the target audience, and with the true personality and positioning of the brand. Associations of freedom, patriotism, heritage, and a macho attitude attract Harley buyers, and the accessories and clothing add value to the consumer experience. They are appropriate to the brand personality and positioning. But even power brands have their limits. The Nike product line extension from footwear to sports apparel was successful, but the step from sports apparel to casual wear was not, because the casual wear segments didn't strongly associate with the true Nike position of athleticism and it appeared that older people didn't feel like *just doing it* anymore. Similarly, Johnson & Johnson's baby shampoo could transfer from babies to children without much problem, but when tried with adults it didn't really make the cut.

On the other hand, Nike seems to have got it right by introducing a line of heart monitors for athletes who want and need to monitor heart rates to achieve optimum performance. The data from these devices download to a wristwatch for training usage. Nike is also set to introduce new watch products that will allow athletes to communicate with their coaches and training companions over the Internet. These new products still fit the brand personality of Nike, in terms of passion, commitment, winning, and getting the best out of oneself. The point, therefore, is that if the brand extension stays true to the brand personality, and therefore matches consumer expectations, it is more likely to be successful.

Another way to analyze the issue of extensions is to look at the nature of the brand in terms of consumer associations, and whether the marketing strategy is to move the brand up or down with respect to associations of price, quality, and, ultimately, value. Essentially, this means looking at whether a brand can be considered as functional or symbolic in nature.

Symbolic and functional extensions—the fit with the consumer mindset

We must remember that brands exist only in the minds of people, and that they can be segregated into two basic types: functional and symbolic brands. This perceptual typology has implications for brand stretch.

For instance, Rolex is a symbolic brand, as it represents more than just a watch to buyers and occupies a position that is associated with high price, quality, status, and prestige. At the other end of the perceptual spectrum, Casio has a position linked to just functionality— it is low in price, with enough quality in terms of reliability and durability to do the job it is supposed to do, but with little association of status or other intangible benefits. (It is at present trying to rectify its rather down-market image with some hi-tech innovations.)

In extending a prestige brand such as Rolex, the only possibility is downwards, but a step-down positioning via a product bearing the same name but with lower quality and price will almost certainly damage the original brand image and alienate its existing customer base, even though it might attract a newer clientele who aspire to own that brand. Rolex considered this matter carefully and created a separate brand for the middle market called Tudor, with no Rolex endorsement. However, the brand communications are cleverly designed to create an air of familiarity.

For brands already positioned at the high end of a market, the distancing mustn't be so great as to eliminate all the positive associations of the strong, core, prestige brand name, and communications strategies must focus on relating the new product to the favorable aspects of the core brand. Too close a positioning, however, may damage both, again through the cannibalization process. The brand manager's task isn't an easy one in the field of brand extensions, and positioning is critical to success.

Thus, although there is a lot of room for positioning new brand extensions with a prestige parent brand, and the rewards can be substantial, great care must be taken to predict whether there will be any dilution or damage to the core brand image. This is the risk, no doubt calculated, that Mercedes has taken with its new "A" class. The further down the quality/price continuum the extension occurs, the greater the damage to image is likely to be, and the "A" class didn't get off to a great start.

Functional brands aren't positioned as high-quality items, and so there is often no room to extend downwards, and any new product introductions will have associations closer to the original brand than might be the case with symbolic brands. The result is that extensions are likely to inflict less damage on the brand image. The downside here is that, because there is less distance between the brands in terms of quality perceptions, cannibalization of sales for both products may occur through customer confusion. Another challenge in trying to extend a functional brand upwards in terms of quality by trying to add status and value to it is that consumer perceptions tend to be locked on to the existing brand image and are likely to be very difficult to shift.

The only way that a functional product can really be branded in the symbolic bracket is by distancing the original brand from the extensions through careful positioning. This may well involve the creation of a new brand name, in the same manner described for symbolic brands considered above. For example, Casio had to create new brand names to break away from an image that wouldn't be acceptable to different market segments; hence the introduction of G-Shock and Baby-G. The Toyota functionally-oriented brand also had to leave its name totally out of the picture in order to position a new product in the status and prestige category (Lexus). This successfully created a luxury brand without the more down-market associations of its other products. The future of Lexus as a luxury car brand is somewhat questionable, however, as the brand appears to be extending downwards into lower engine capacities and smaller cars. Discipline is therefore necessary in brand management.

The bottom line for brand extensions, then, is that you cannot step away from your basic position or proposition as long as the brand name remains the same, because consumers judge perceptually whether or not there is a good "fit" between the brand itself and the extension of the brand. Although the discussion above has concentrated on the most common elements of quality and price, this judgment takes into account other elements of importance, such as usage occasions. It is for this reason that some companies are forced to step away from the main brand name and create a product that stands alone. Coca-Cola has done this with Fruitopia and other beverages. Others play down the brand name of the company to give the product minimum association with the parent. Launching new products in such ways helps to position them with highly individual profiles while retaining subtle usage of brand equity from the parent, as with Levi's Dockers and Toyota's Lexus, neither of which would have been as successful as they have been if positioned as another product line of the same major brand.

Corporate versus product brand elasticity

In general, we can conclude that a brand has more capability to survive being stretched or extended if it is a corporate brand as opposed to a product brand. Let's take the example of a product brand, such as Head and Shoulders Shampoo. It is a very successful brand, and has line extended to provide a range of shampoos under the brand name "Head and Shoulders" for different types of hair and different consumer benefits. However, it wouldn't survive a move into, for example, clothing. I certainly wouldn't be inclined to buy a Head and Shoulders suit or shirt.

Corporate brand names, on the other hand, are more easily stretched because the brand proposition isn't so closely focused and related to a single type of product. They can be successful because they can attach the perceived value of the brand name outside their categories—for instance, Sony has successfully transferred its brand name beyond consumer electronics to entertainment. The perceived value of quality has enabled this to happen in the minds of consumers. Virgin Group has developed many brand extensions, but it hasn't stepped away from its basic brand proposition. Another great example of this is Caterpillar (see Case Study 13), which has successfully entered vastly different categories. Thus, there is more scope for brand management in corporate extensions, and the current trend is away from product branding to corporate and house (endorsed) branding.

Case Study 13
CATERPILLAR INC.
An example of successful brand extension

One of the most unlikely, but seemingly successful, examples of stretching a brand into a vastly different industry is that of Caterpillar Inc. The "construction" company has moved into the fashion business. Seen for over 100 years as a supplier of heavy machinery used in construction activities, it has found a new way of building awareness and recognition (not to mention profits) by penetrating the notoriously difficult fashion industry; in the process, it has been accepted by consumers across multi-segments.

This has, of course, been no accident; rather, it was a carefully planned move by the Caterpillar global brand management group headed by Kimberley S. Neible. The aim has been to boost brand sales among those consumers who also operate Caterpillar machinery products, and to promote the brand to people who normally wouldn't come into contact with Caterpillar.

Caterpillar products are selling well in Europe, competing with the likes of Nike and attracting youth with its edgy attitude. Cat apparel has a worldwide licensee brand in London and a global licensee for Cat footwear based in the U.S., but it has its own stores in mind. With only one store so far—a 5,000-square-foot shop in Illinois, near the company's headquarters—it wants to open several more outlets in cities such as London and New York.

The product range itself is astonishing—everything from casuals to luxury goods. For example, you can buy Cat jeans (with five pockets and a yellow patch on the back). Limited edition jeans, at just under US$300, are on the way, along with sunglasses, sandals, and baby clothes. In many countries there are Cat hats, boots, bags, trainers, baby shoes, watches, and sweatshirts. At the flagship store, up-market products such as a US$500 racing jacket and a US$300 Tiffany & Co. bracelet with a silver Cat chain are available. Cat crosses all boundaries, from the irreverent to the traditional, from the young to the over-sixties (and in some quoted cases, the over-nineties!).

Caterpillar brand personality

The secret to the success of Caterpillar's brand extension appears to be the consistent application of the brand "personality," which could be seen as:

- hardworking;
- tough;
- resilient;
- determined;
- bold;
- rugged;
- independent; and
- a good friend when you get to know it.

This personality has been extended into both the product and the shopping experience. For instance, the boots and shoes look tough. The metal band on the Cat watch (over US$200!) looks like a bulldozer's tread lines. The flagship store's interior is decorated in the bold Caterpillar yellow color and features a replica of a Cat-sponsored racing car. Part of the floor is made of wooden blocks similar to those on the factory floor, and when visitors approach a display, reverse heavy vehicle beeping sounds are activated. It all ties back into the brand personality. Consistency is key, and Caterpillar's brand management has stuck to the rules; by doing so, it has added considerably to the total brand value.

With worldwide merchandise sales for 2000 of US$900 million, Caterpillar has proven that well-planned brand extensions that reinforce and are consistent with the original brand proposition do work, and that when consumers' emotional associations are in tune with the brand personality of proposed brand extensions, the process is made that much easier.

Increasing elasticity via product innovations

There is sometimes the temptation to stretch a brand via an innovation. This can be a problem where perceptions are very entrenched and consumers aren't ready to accept the innovation. For instance, detergent manufacturers trying to market laundry-soap tablets to people who for years have been used to powders and liquids found market acceptance difficult. The problem appeared to be the nature of the innovation—the product attribute/benefit of the tablet itself, with the attribute being the compact size of the tablet and the consumer benefit the fact that consumers no longer have to scoop, measure, or pour. The innovation was aimed at younger working people and small' households that essentially don't like doing laundry and want to minimize the time taken to do it.

Unfortunately, people seemed to want the option to vary the amount of the ingredient to suit the relative dirtiness of the clothes to be washed. The challenge for the brand managers was to convince them of the benefits of convenience and time saving, and has been compared to the problem encountered by the proponents of the teabag in the 1950s. Teabags eventually took off, as we all know, but not without considerable investment in educating the consumer. If perceptions are deeply entrenched, then considerable buying inertia exists, and companies must be prepared for lengthy and costly advertising and promotion campaigns.

In the detergent case, it might be that research had asked only one of the two vital questions necessary to establish consumer acceptance— "Do you like it?"—and hadn't asked the other—"Would you buy it?"

This was the same issue that caused Coca-Cola massive embarrassment when they tried to introduce the new Coke. Taste testing with over 100,000 people reassured the company that they preferred the new drink, but people just didn't buy it, because the old Coke held deeply entrenched perceptions as "the real thing." Anything else was a substitute. When you play around with brands, you are playing around with people's emotions, and brand managers need to understand what these are.

This section concludes with a summary of the advantages and disadvantages of brand extensions.

Advantages

- Extending the brand is less costly than creating a new one.
- The consumer receives a better choice.
- There is less risk for consumers if the brand is trusted.
- There can be some synergy, and therefore savings, in marketing costs.
- They help brand revitalization.
- If successful, they can add power to the main brand image.
- They can keep other competitors from entering the category, and increase coverage.
- They can pave the way for more extensions.

Disadvantages

- If the parent brand has a negative image, it is unlikely that an extension will be successful.
- If not clearly positioned, they can confuse consumers and cannibalize sales of existing brands.
- If not successful, they can damage the master brand image.
- Retailers might not appreciate them.
- All brands have their boundaries, and stepping outside these can dilute brand power.

Whatever the pros and cons, it is possible for a brand to be stretched way beyond its own category as long as it doesn't step outside its basic character and consumers can relate to it. The Caterpillar case study above shows how a major brand can extend into categories most would think impossible. Case Study 14 shows how Wrigley is trying to extend into other categories via product innovation.

Case Study 14
WRIGLEY
Gum does stretch!

Wrigley has been a leader in the chewing gum category since the 1890s and is famous for brands such as Juicy Fruit, Doublemint, and Winterfresh. Extensions have progressed into the sugarless market, where sales have accelerated as consumers are more health-conscious than ever before. It has recently introduced new brands into the U.S. market, such as Extra Polar Ice, Everest (packaged in a tin box), and Eclipse, its first pellet gum.

To fuel corporate growth, overseas markets have been targeted successfully and more than 60% of its sales now come from outside its home country, the U.S. The company is also very strong in Asia, and can be considered a global brand. Its strength is articulated by Deutsche Banc Alex. Brown analyst Eric Katzman, who says: "Not many companies can have 50% of the world market, no debt, very high returns, and that kind of brand awareness."

The company is now looking at new and different brand extensions, the first of these appearing as the brand Surpass, an antacid chewing gum, introduced in February 2001 and marketed as a tastier and chewy alternative to traditional antacid products. Wrigley is also experimenting with a cold-relief gum, and intends to produce a gum that offers dental benefits by forming an alliance with Procter & Gamble, who make Crest toothpaste, among other bands.

But Wrigley has no room for complacency, as other brands have powerful owners such as Pfizer and Hershey. Pfizer Inc. owns the Dentyne, Chiclets, and Trident brands. Hershey

Foods Corporation owns the Carefree and Bubble Yum brands. As at July 15, 2001, Wrigley's had 53.5%, Pfizer 25.5%, and Hershey 13.5% of the global market. (*Source:* Information Resources, Prudential Securities.) And they are fighting back: Pfizer has introduced Trident Advantage Mints and Trident Gum, promising white teeth; and another huge pharmaceutical company, SmithKline Beecham plc, has introduced its Aquafresh Dental Gum.

Wrigley has moved into other categories where the giants roam, based on its singular brand strength of the attractiveness of gum. Whether its health-care and pharmaceutical products will find favor and trust with consumers is another matter. Much will depend on whether Wrigley can manage consumer perceptions well enough to transfer the trust and loyalty it now enjoys into categories where it is not known to have operated before, and where it will be fighting against already trusted brand names. Wrigley seems determined to win, however, and in a new and costly marketing campaign it has signed up tennis icons Venus and Serena Williams to endorse the brand.

THE GREAT GAMBLE: BRAND REVITALIZATION/REPOSITONING

One of the other great dilemmas facing brand managers is when a brand is seen to be going downhill, either through neglect, or because consumers no longer are strongly associated with it, or because competition has eroded the brand position. The decision that needs to be taken is whether or not to revitalize the brand, and if so, how. This is often referred to as brand repositioning, and what is needed is to convince the target audience to change their perceptions about the brand in a more favorable way with regards to the competition.

Sometimes, brands that have lost their shine and market appeal are allowed to continue without substantial repositioning, or even where repositioning has failed (see Case Study 15), while others undergo tremendous changes aimed at making a low-key brand into a global player (see Case Study 16).

Case Study 15

TAB DIET SODA
The customer lifeline

Tab has a shrinking market share of less than 1%, and yet it has been spared the axe by Coca-Cola. The brand, once so successful, now resides at the bottom of the category heap. It was launched in 1963, and immediately became the drink of the "free" generation, the "Beautiful Drink for Beautiful People." But in 1982 Diet Coke was introduced to add more power to the Coke brand, and Tab began to go downhill. Basically, its demise has been determined by a cannibalization of sales by Diet Coke, and a simultaneous competitive attack from Diet Pepsi and other such carbonated drinks. The company made several attempts to revitalize Tab in the 1980s and 1990s, through various product changes (for example, reducing the content of the carcinogen saccharin and increasing the amount of aspartame, adding calcium, and making a clear alternative), and even by repositioning Tab as the drink with "sass." However, all these efforts have failed to revive the brand.

The big question is, why should a company renowned for managing successful brands hang on to one that is certainly underperforming and may even be almost dead? The answer appears to be the fear of adverse customer reaction and publicity. Possibly at the back of Coca-Cola's mind is the terrible mistake they made in attempting to replace Coke with the new Coke in 1985. Customers around the world clamored for the old Coke, which had been positioned so strongly as "the real thing," and the new Coke had to be withdrawn.

In this respect, regular Tab drinkers (although relatively few in number) have been very vocal about their brand, so much so that they have been described as "Taboholics." Those who still drink it are very loyal, and have gone to extreme lengths to prove this. Even though few distributors now stock Tab, some customers have reportedly driven far out of their way to find a store that sells it, and have complained vigorously to the Coca-Cola headquarters about the availability problem.

Herein lies another part of the answer to the question as to why the brand isn't deleted. The Coca-Cola distribution system allows the bottlers some autonomy in production, and if they cannot make a profit from a brand they will tend not to produce it. With many bottlers now not producing the brand, the few that do are meeting the market needs, and Coca-Cola itself isn't out of pocket. It stopped putting marketing resources behind Tab several years ago, but is content to receive a small profit from a select market.

But back to the consumer. What does Coca-Cola say about the Tab situation? Douglas Daft, chairman and chief executive, says it shows the company cares: "We want to make sure that those who want Tab get Tab." Executives are now studying possible ways of selling Tab on the Internet. So, it would appear that some companies, under certain conditions, will continue to support dying brands and not delete them—that is, if the consumers shout loudly enough.

Case Study 16

MAZDA
The revitalization of a brand

This case study should be an inspiration to all brand management practitioners. It isn't only about revitalization of a brand; it's about how leading-edge practitioners take a holistic view of brand strategy, from consumer insight, through personality and product, to internal and external communication.

I have always liked the Mazda brand. I have always thought its motor vehicles had some style and "class"; it's one of those brands that I somehow felt an affinity with. But Mazda, founded in 1920, is also a brand that makes one think, "It has so much potential. Why hasn't it ever become a world-famous brand?" (This question can be asked of many brands that originate from Japan, where brand management isn't a national strength, and therein lies the answer to the question.) Mazda has always kept a fairly low profile, with little advertising or promotion, and despite obvious talent in its design capability the brand had nearly faded into oblivion by the time it was acquired in 1996. (Ford Motor Company's initial investment in Mazda of 25% was made in 1986, with an increased investment to 33% in 1996.)

Since that time, the revitalization of the brand has become a significant focus for business attention, and it appears that Mazda is destined to achieve global brand status in the next few years. However, it is important to point out that the Mazda repositioning and branding is very much Japanese, not Western; the heritage and future would have been blighted by an attempt to impose Western brand values on an Asian brand. It is an example of how Japanese brands are now coming up to speed in brand management, whereas previously they had concentrated primarily on operational efficiency and quality. This case study illustrates how a brand can be totally reconstructed in every way, and how important the role of brand management is in saving a business and then building that business up again. The case also demonstrates clearly the many skills a brand manager must have in order to successfully take on this type of huge responsibility, the importance of including *all* company employees in the brand vision, and how the brand really does drive the business.

The key to business success is the brand

From the very beginning of the business transformation, brand was always at the top of the agenda. Mark Fields, former senior managing director in charge of marketing, sales, and customer service (and now President and CEO), said to Mazda employees in 1999:

> For Mazda to take a giant leap forward in terms of business profitability, we have set the following goals:

- establishing our brand management strategy;
- successful launch of new products, and further strengthening of our existing products;
- maintaining our sales momentum worldwide; and
- bolstering our domestic dealer network.

Fields also commented:

> To promote improvement of our market share and build our brand identity, Mazda must completely understand and satisfy the needs and wants of our target audiences ... And we must continue to offer higher value and deeper satisfaction ... The key to this is brand strategy ... Through our brand strategy, we are aiming at building a brand that differentiates us from our competitors, one that enhances customer satisfaction, improves value—and in the end provides us enduring profitable growth ... As we go forward, all of our activity will be keyed to our brand.

The importance of brand strategy

Fields was clear about the importance of brand strategy and what it means to Mazda.

> First, the brand strategy is about a relationship with the customer. By enhancing our customer insight we can understand their true needs and wants. Based on this, we must establish an emotional connection with them. It is through this and other touchpoints that we present our brand. Customers who come into contact and grow to love our brand become our assets, and their importance is in no way different from other assets such as profitability and our employees.
>
> Secondly, it is a business growth strategy with a consistent management system. Why—because branding requires two aspects—communication and products. Both must work in conjunction, and that makes it a management

system. Since employees, products, sales, service, and the company itself all come in close contact with customers, everything must be coordinated on the basis of brand strategy.

Finally, brand strategy is a means to generate profitability. A brand with a strong emotional connection with customers can employ pull marketing, henceforth creating an efficient and highly profitable business environment. The brand strategy is our focus and core to our business plan.

Fields further commented:

The will and commitment of senior management is, above all, most important. Brand strategy is not a simple matter of image strategy. Therefore the senior management should take full responsibility and not let PR, marketing, advertising, and other communication groups act separately. The management must lead the entire organization to start brand building and create change.

The next most important thing is the cooperation and commitment of management. They must understand and share the management's direction, and promote coordination and cooperation among different functional groups in the organization, to develop products and services that clearly articulate our brand.

Finally, senior management must lead the organization to generate awareness and passion for what the brand stands for.

Push versus pull in brand direction

Mazda has taken steps to ensure that its brand image and company profitability aren't damaged by efforts to buy market share through discounting and rebates—the typical "push" approach that many brand managers become tempted into pursuing as a result of competitor strategies. Instead, it has concentrated very hard on the "pull" approach, which involves giving customers what they really want and engaging them emotionally in the brand–customer relationship. This approach means that the custodians of the brand must understand which particular group of consumers they want to focus on, and then really try to satisfy their needs, wants, desires, add true value and other motivations.

At the heart of every brand is the consumer

It is a fundamental premise of branding that brands only exist in people's minds; that companies don't own brands—consumers do; and that it is consumers, not companies, who build brands. Mazda's philosophy is similar. It is therefore of critical importance that brand managers have a thorough understanding of the consumers they hope to attract and retain, and this means gaining consumer insight through research. For Mazda, this means understanding the deep-seated needs of the target consumer, and not just the generic needs that most people have. For example, Mazda uncovered the following deep-seated needs in the minds of its prototype target audience:

- Aspires to lead a life that is full of new stimulus and excitement, while respecting his personal sense of style.
- Aspires to sustain the sensitivity of a child—moved and excited by the simplest things in life.
- Hates to be constricted by rules and norms, and allows his sensibility and emotions to lead him in pursuing whatever he wants to do.
- Desires to retain his personal uniqueness that invites attention and is respected by others.
- Aspires to enhance his presence as a highly competent person possessing a unique personality and opinions.
- Wants to impress and persuade people around him by expressing his unique values and views.
- By setting high goals for himself, aspires to challenge new possibilities by not adhering to current norms.

The Mazda brand DNA

Mazda takes a life-science approach, which is illustrated by the use of the term "DNA," the very building block of human life. The core of the Mazda brand strategy is the Mazda brand DNA, the essence of the brand, which has two sides: personality and product. The personality side of the Mazda brand can be summarized by the following three characteristics: stylish, insightful, and spirited. This is the driving force behind the Mazda brand's personality and the foundation of the brand DNA; however, in order to understand the Mazda brand DNA, one must understand that key product attributes are included in it as well. These key product attributes are: distinctive design, exceptional functionality, and responsive handling and performance. Hence, a holistic approach encapsulates the entire company, like the human persona, including all the senses and attitudes.

Brand personality

Mazda's brand personality attributes are defined as follows:

- **Stylish:** Every Mazda product should be a self-assured invitation to attention. With this, we acknowledge that Mazda customers are self-confident and truly distinctive individuals.
- **Insightful:** We imply that Mazda has a "street-smart" understanding of its customers' needs and values, and is always taking a creative approach to meeting those needs.
- **Spirited:** We establish that the Mazda brand embodies an enthusiastic and expressive love of life, just like Mazda customers. Together, the Mazda brand personality creates a deep emotional connection with Mazda customers by reflecting how our customers feel about themselves and about life.

It is the brand personality that connects emotion to the customer and enhances loyalty.

Product attributes

Product is an important part of the equation for the Mazda brand, and the elements are defined as:

- **Distinctive design:** The aim for all products is that Mazda products boast distinctive design inside and out; that is to say they are athletic, youthful, solid, and substantial, both on the interior and exterior.
- **Exceptional functionality:** Mazda requires that its products possess exceptional functionality; that means the most intelligent use of space and functional efficiency with a high-quality fit and finish.
- **Responsive handling and performance:** This attribute is a Mazda legacy and creates a sensory driving experience that translates into significant and noticeable driving satisfaction.

It is the product/ownership experience that expresses that brand connection.

While high-level product attributes help toward an understanding of what Mazda would like all its products to represent, they are not specific enough to help planners, designers, and engineers. The company has therefore developed additional tools to help. The first of these is what is called *product philosophy*.

The product philosophy is comprised of quality innovation and design policy. Mark Fields says:

> Our Product Philosophy clearly states our priorities. We wish to be a Leader in these six areas: Design, Craftsmanship, Quality, Stability and Handling, Braking, and Package Innovation. While taking environmental friendliness and safety fully into consideration, our product development aims to take leadership in those six areas.
>
> This hardware exercise is a clear and consistent extension of how the brand DNA is executed within our new products.

The "Design Policy" uses Mazda's design theme of "Contrast in Harmony," a guide to unique and best-in-class design. The new design theme "Contrast in Harmony" aims at creation of Mazda's future products with designs that balance functions and styling harmoniously with each other. "Harmony" refers to the underlying balance and proportion such as details, materials, color combination, configurations, space construction, function, and appearance in our products ... the very foundation of good design.

To further the design direction among products, Mazda has developed the Family Face. The Family Face is a combination of the brand symbol and a five-point grille, and will be applied to all future models to make it a visual expression of Mazda's identity and distinctiveness. For example, some vehicles that are already in showrooms, like the Premacy and the MPV, as well as future concepts, both show Mazda's family face—the distinctive five-point grille with Mazda's winged M brand symbol. The body language shows distinctive "Contrast in Harmony" with a clear contrast of sharp and soft. So the Mazda brand strategy is not merely an image strategy; it is a central business strategy that includes product development. New products that embody all the aspects of the brand strategy will be introduced successively into the market.

The emotional connection

The key element in Mazda's brand strategy is building the "Emotional Connection" with consumers. The key success factors for brand management are "Global Perspective," "Listening to the Voice of the Customer," and "Creating an Emotional Connection." Here are a few examples of the initiatives that have been undertaken to make this happen.

In the area of product marketing, Mazda organized the 1st Shohin Ibento or 1st Product Day in September 1999 with our key domestic and foreign managers, dealers, and distributors from Japan, North America, Europe, Australia, Asia, and the Middle East, providing them with the opportunity to view and drive current and future products. Managers in various markets share success stories and "best practices" regarding new product events and product-focused strategies with the global team. This is a good example of sharing ideas/viewpoints and listening to the customer.

Mazda also ensures global consistency in brand and marketing strategies through quarterly brand summit meetings with key Mazda marketing personnel from Japan, the United States, and Europe. Fields says:

> These meetings drive home a common understanding of the brand and how it is steadily executed in the marketplace. Clear internal communication is vitally important in developing a consistent brand identity worldwide. A simple single brand message is required to support the brand globally. Our major market managers participate in this activity, providing input from a local perspective.
>
> In order to establish a lasting emotional connection with the target customers, we need to deepen our understanding of their values. We need a deep understanding of their latent needs that exist in every human being. Only after we grasp this can we establish a strong emotional connection with our target customers. We call this "Deep-Seated Needs" at Mazda. This is what we use to identify our target customer. And it is with this target customer that we aspire to create an emotional connection and encourage a love and passion for our brand.

Mazda's views on advertising

Mazda has clear views on advertising and on the importance of maintaining a clear and consistent message in the market. However, Fields stresses that advertising is *not* brand.

Advertising is only one aspect of brand. It supports and illustrates our brand identity and makes it clearer to the market. You cannot create a robust brand by advertising alone. Today's customer is far too sophisticated for this type of tactic. What advertising provides is the opportunity to project our brand to consumers in a clear and consistent manner worldwide.

To ensure this, we have developed our "Communication Philosophy." It was developed to manage our overall communications, including advertising. To create tighter advertising consistency with our worldwide brand positioning, we have established a global tagline.

In Japan, our tagline is the same as our brand positioning statement of "Kokoro o Ugokasu shin Hassou," and outside of Japan, it is "Get In. Be Moved." Our global tagline is used in all of our advertisements, and it helps us deliver a consistent message to different markets around the globe. Another innovation to develop a better alignment with our global advertising efforts is our visual identity (VI) ending tag, or what we refer to as advertising VI. I'm referring to the last two or three seconds of our TV advertising and how we illustrate our brand promotional mark at the end of the ad. This VI was developed and researched with customers to ensure that the visual cues are consistent in delivering the Mazda brand DNA. It is our intention to phase this VI into all TV advertising worldwide in the near future.

Again, I would like to emphasize that our advertising portrays a crystal clear picture of the Mazda brand to convey a consistent emotional message. At its most basic level, our corporate message must support our Worldwide Brand Positioning, while providing relevance to our target customers.

To bring our brand to life, we manage and control not only advertising but all of our communications, consistently guided by our Communication Philosophy. For example, our events, PR activities, and all of our press events and conferences are based on the brand strategy, with information, staging, and the format of press releases all consistent with our brand.

Brand management structure and internal communications

Following the development of the brand strategy, other innovative initiatives were implemented at Mazda to create a support process. One of the first was to restructure the organization. The marketing organization was restructured to enhance the focus on branding, and the brand marketing department was established as a part of the marketing division in addition to the product marketing department. Brand marketing is responsible for consistent planning, implementation, and management of product development through the communication process under the brand strategy, and Mazda believes such an organization is indispensable for aggressive promotion of the brand strategy.

The second initiative was to communicate the brand strategy to every one of the employees. Fields says:

A brand cascade event was held for our 1,400 top managers. These managers were educated on basic knowledge about brand and our brand strategy, which in turn they cascaded when they went back to their respective departments and groups. Check-ups ensured that our message was communicated throughout the organization, and by doing this Mazda succeeded in spreading brand knowledge and creating improved awareness to implement the brand strategy to realize the Mazda brand. By maximizing internal communication activity, goals were shared globally.

According to Mazda, everyone is now revising his or her daily tasks in pursuit of these common goals, and in this way the company is moving forward with its self-renovation. This provides assistance internally for everyone at Mazda to be responsible for brand development and execution.

A third innovation was a brand cascade kit, which was specifically developed and distributed for internal education. The brand cascade kit was delivered to all divisions, and brand cards highlighting key words were delivered to every employee. As Fields says, "The brand strategy would never work without a total commitment from every employee. We believe that all of our employees needed to renew their thoughts, and let the Mazda brand direct their everyday job and assignments."

A summary of the Mazda brand philosophy and practice from Mark Fields

First, the brand strategy is about a relationship with the consumers. The brand should establish emotional connection with them, and it is through this and other touchpoints that the brand is presented. Consumers who come into contact and grow to love our brand become our assets, and their importance is in no way different from other assets such as profitability and our employees.

Secondly, it is a business growth strategy with a consistent management system, because branding requires two aspects—communication and products. Both must work in conjunction, and that makes it a management system. Since employees, products, sales, service, and the company itself all come in close contact with customers, every aspect must be carefully coordinated on the basis of brand strategy.

Thirdly, brand strategy is a means to generate profitability. A brand with a strong emotional connection with customers can employ pull marketing, henceforth creating an efficient and highly profitable business environment. More specifically, this means increased conquest sales, enhanced owner loyalty, and improved market share.

The next most important thing is the cooperation and

commitment of management. They must understand and share the top management's direction, and promote coordination and cooperation among different functional groups in the organization, to develop products and services that fully relate to the brand.

Finally, the will and commitment of senior management is, above all, most important. Brand strategy is not a simple matter of image strategy, and so senior management should take full responsibility and not let PR, marketing, advertising, and other communication groups act separately and inconsistently. Management must lead the entire organization to start brand building and promote change. It is senior management that must lead the organization to generate awareness and passion for the brand.

THE TOUGH DECISION: BRAND DELETION

Sometimes, there is no option but to kill (whether it is done quickly or slowly) or sell off a brand. In other words, the brand manager decides to remove the brand from the portfolio. This is usually a consequence of a negative reply to the question, "Can the brand be revitalized?" Killing a brand is often called *brand deletion*, and unwanted brands that are sold off are often referred to as *orphan brands*. A brand may be deleted for one or more of the following reasons:

- There is no foreseeable route to recovery when a brand is heading downhill fast.
- The brand is no longer profitable, and isn't likely to be profitable again.
- The brand has been totally outdated by market innovations.
- The brand doesn't rank highly enough in importance, relative to other brands, to justify a place in the future portfolio.
- The brand's customer base has eroded and is unlikely to return.
- Revitalization of the brand cannot be justified in terms of the return on investment.

- Inadequate brand management has caused the brand to move away from its true proposition and character.

Brands are expensive to manage, keep, and revive. In today's world of intense competition it isn't economically feasible to hang on to a large portfolio. Unilever, for example, is currently reducing its total number of brands from 1,600 to 400, to concentrate on what it calls its power brands. The financial problems intensify with a product branding, as opposed to a corporate branding, approach, because there are no synergies in A&P, and every brand has to make its own way in the marketplace without corporate endorsement. But even when the parent brand is involved in endorsing a brand, markets are so dynamic and consumer tastes so fickle that it is very difficult sometimes to revitalize a brand.

Smart brand managers evolve their brands in line with such changes. Revolutionary changes are often not accepted by consumers and are difficult to sustain, as consumers don't connect with the drastic changes. Oldsmobile is typical of a brand that has become a casualty through a combination of market changes, inadequate brand management, inappropriate product development, and consumer attitudinal shifts (see Case Study 17).

Case Study 17

OLDSMOBILE
The final parking lot

Oldsmobile is a brand in the portfolio of General Motors (GM), and a decision has been taken to phase it out—in other words, to kill the brand. The brand itself is over 100 years old and possesses considerable heritage, but GM feels it isn't going to make any further attempts at revitalization. Previous attempts at breathing life into Oldsmobile have involved massive A&P expenditure during the 1990s and various product improvements. Why is the famous brand now being axed? There are four fundamental issues that GM has had to address in this respect and has failed to conquer.

1. **The name issue:** The word "old" isn't the best one to use in a brand name. One of the obvious problems for the brand is the name itself, which has proven to be a major consumer deterrent for a few decades, so much so that in the 1960s GM commissioned an advertising campaign to change the name to "Youngmobile." However, the problem persisted. In the 1980s, GM even changed the tagline to "It's Not Your Father's Oldsmobile" in an effort to shake off the image that people had of a revered but old-fashioned brand. But despite GM's efforts, the brand still couldn't shake off the age association.

2. **The product issue:** From the 1940s to the 1980s, the Oldsmobile brand heritage and image was one of sportiness and innovation. Its "Rocket" engines and the long, low designs were renowned and admired. But from the 1980s onwards, product developments moved away from this central brand character. Chevrolet engines were substituted and diesel engines given as an option. Even though these product decisions were tied in with the Arab countries' oil embargoes of the 1970s, when big cars were pronounced "gas guzzlers," they nevertheless had the effect of helping to shatter the brand image of Oldsmobile, and triggered off more brand dilution when added to the name problem.

3. **The image repositioning issue:** Attempts at repositioning the name as a luxury brand, accompanied by logo changes and product variations to match European competitors, failed, even though US$4 billion was spent. Major discounting to boost sales worked against these efforts, and consumers were confused. They couldn't accept the widespread transformation of a brand that they perceived was "really not like that," and their associations with the old brand heritage ran deep. Brand sales consequently moved in the direction of fleet purchases and away from individuals.

4. **The consumer issue:** The result of all the above—which amounts to inadequate brand management—is that consumers have fled from the brand in large numbers, seeing no benefits and no differentiation, and no longer feeling an emotional association. GM has at last given up and bitten the dying brand bullet. But like all great characters, according to Hollywood lexicon, the Oldsmobile may not really die: it will just fade away, but still be remembered.

The demise of any brand isn't a joyful time, and one wonders whether or not Oldsmobile could have survived if it had been consistent over time with its initial identity and evolved as a sporty and innovative brand, leveraging on its heritage. The imposed schizophrenia of the brand personality through inconsistent brand communications and product development basically turned people off. Oldsmobile was no longer the trusted and believable personality they knew. The emotional association was destroyed.

The success of any brand depends in part on how well it communicates with its target audiences. Brand managers spend a lot of time on communications, and, as we saw from the Mazda case, these are both internal and external. The next chapter deals with the methods of communications used, but doesn't go into detail on advertising, which has been covered in many other books. It does highlight, however, the growing importance of public relations and integrated communications.

6

Total Communications for Brand Management

There are many options for communicating the key messages you want to be positioned in people's minds, but it is important to note that these are changing very rapidly in their effectiveness, a point that I will address as the chapter progresses. The main channels of communication are:

- advertising;
- direct marketing;
- sales promotion;
- sponsorships and endorsements;
- public relations and crisis management;
- the Internet; and
- integrated brand communications.

Let's look at how each of these channels can be used in brand management.

ADVERTISING

Advertising is a part of what is called paid mass communications, generally meaning space paid for in a publication, or time on radio, television, or at the cinema, although it may also be taken to include posters, billboards, and other outdoor advertising. Its main purpose is to persuade an audience either to take some action or to develop an attitude toward what is being advertised. Advertising is most frequently used for positioning brands.

Advertising achieves image differentiation mainly through repetition of a particular message, which leads to recognition, recall, attitudes, preferences, and action. It is frequently used by companies, but is also becoming more widespread in its application, being a part of national and individual campaigns, where information takes second place in importance to the need for exposure and positive perceptions. A good example of advertising-driven brand building is Absolut vodka, where the personality of the product (intellect, wit, and sophistication) has been consistently marketed and advertised around the world, and positioned so that it appeals to the target audience in terms of exclusivity. The brand has enjoyed a successful campaign relating it to different parts of the world. For instance, one advertisement for the product shows the usual clear bottle, but enormously big and fat, with the caption "Absolut Texas."

Advertising can be executed through the various types of media described above, and all have their advantages and disadvantages, but creative repetition is the key to its success. The nature and cost of commercial advertising space means that only a limited amount of information can be placed in an advertisement, and so the frequency of advertising is also a governing factor in how effective it is. Little perceptual change will be gained by a limited number of exposures, and often companies complain about the lack of advertising effectiveness when the real reason is that the campaign was too short in terms of the message frequency. Advertising agencies have a constant battle with companies over the length and cost of campaigns, because managers in charge of brand communications sometimes don't understand that it takes time, and a great deal of repetition, for key messages to strike home and change human perceptions that evolve relatively slowly. Image advertising, in particular, needs a long-term commitment, but when carried out properly, with good emotional and creative input, it can be a powerful aid to positioning.

The use of emotion in advertising—appealing to the heart as well as the head

There is no doubt that emotion sells, as I have said before. Emotion is still somewhat of a mystery, as far as our understanding of mental processes is concerned, but we do know that it originates in the right brain and manifests itself as a state of arousal. We also know that emotions trigger the brain 3,000 times faster than rational thoughts. Emotion can also be positive (as in a state of happiness) or negative (as in a state of fear). As far as brand image is concerned, it is important to establish an emotional relationship with the people who are to be influenced. If positive feelings and emotions can be associated with what we are positioning, there is a much greater chance of attracting people, and of altering or producing the perceptions we want people to have.

Emotion is increasingly being used by many organizations, especially service companies who are finding it increasingly difficult to differentiate themselves from each other. Financial services companies are typical of many service organizations trying to persuade consumers that they are different and better than their competitors in markets that are becoming increasingly commoditized. They are beginning to realize at last that they have mistaken inertia for loyalty, and people are now switching brands more than ever—brand loyalty is falling with every increase in consumer dissatisfaction. Fidelity Investments, in the United States, launched a series of advertisements in an attempt to present the company as being more human and warm. The advertisements showed their analysts saying why they like to work for the company, and being very helpful to small investors who need advice. In this age of technology, companies such as Fidelity, with large, dispersed customer bases of millions of people most of whom they might never meet, have to show that they are not just cold, impersonal, bureaucratic companies, but have a human side that cares for their customers.

Some of the ways in which advertising can tap into people's emotional feelings include the use of:

- drama;
- shock;

- fear;
- humor;
- warmth;
- aspiration;
- music; and
- sex.

All of these have their advantages and disadvantages, which must be carefully thought through before use, and any agency creative must be examined very thoroughly to ensure that the type of emotion to be used is in line with the company's overall position and desired image. *Appropriate* is the key word in creative selection.

Drama

Drama can be powerful in positioning. One brand of coffee ran a series of advertisements that showed a young couple meeting over a cup of coffee, and followed them as the relationship developed through its ups and downs. It was like a mini soapbox series, and audiences loved it. The coffee was always present, being a part of their everyday lives. Drama was created by means of a story, but demonstrations and narrative can also attract audience attention and brand recall. However, care must be taken not to offend, as was almost certainly the case when the narrator for a 1998 television commercial for a potency drug said: "Attention, impotent men. All 20 million of you!" This example could easily come under the next category of shock tactics.

Shock

Shock tactics can also be powerful influencers, but the dividing line between a positive and negative response can be thin. Some non-profit organizations use pictures of starving children and distressed, abused animals to boost their position, but these tactics can turn off as many people as they turn on. Benetton has created both situations, earning both praise and criticism for its "United Colors Of Benetton" advertisements. For instance, one advertisement featured two horses, one black and one white, attempting sexual intercourse. Pre-testing of advertisements becomes particularly important when using this means of arousing emotion, but with Benetton one suspects that the more people are shocked, the more the company feels it has achieved its brand message—namely, the importance of social and racial equality.

Fear

Closely related to the above is the use of fear. Volvo has used pictures of people who were involved in terrible car accidents, but who lived because of their car's safety features. The "Volvo Saved My Life" club helped the company to establish its position as the safest car, a position it still owns today. Since the terrorist attack on the United States on September 11, 2001, some insurance companies have been excessively promoting the element of fear and peace of mind in their corporate and product marketing communications, which, while reassuring some people, may irritate others.

Humor

Humor can be a double-edged sword. Ethnic and minority jokes can offend, even though many people enjoy them. Care has to be taken to ensure that the surprise element of the humor is followed by pleasure, not pain. Humor, when used well, relaxes audiences, makes them feel comfortable, and reduces their resistance to key messages. The "moustache" advertisements used to promote milk, which feature well-known personalities such as Pete Sampras with a white upper lip, were said to be very effective.

Warmth

Warmth also relaxes audiences and creates positive mental attitudes. Advertisements that project love, patriotism, friendship, caring, and other similar behaviors can be of great assistance to positioning. Johnson & Johnson advertisements for baby and other products have built an amazingly powerful and unassailable positioning of gentleness, caring, and love, which is reflected in the company's global market share. Even sporting events such as the PGA Tour introduce warmth into their advertisements, with golfing celebrity Nick Price describing, with the help of emotion-building shots, how the event has helped many underprivileged people. The commercial ends with the tagline, "Anything's Possible."

Aspiration

Aspirational advertising can be a great motivator. Nike's "Just Do It" campaign is all about self-improvement and success, and advertisements featuring young, successful sportspersons such as Tiger Woods help reinforce their position. Aspiration as a means of bringing out people's emotions is often aimed at in advertisements using children and well-known personalities.

Music

Music is frequently used in advertisements on television and radio, whether as jingles or background. If memorable, it can aid recall of the commercial, but it can also be a source of irritation. Up to 50% of all advertisements use music in some way. It may be used to arouse sentimentality, as done so successfully with the Hovis brand of bread where a northern English brass band plays a very sentimental tune, or to illustrate fun, excitement, seriousness, or other emotions that fit with the desired positioning and perception. Music is liked by every possible segment and can be used to stimulate emotions in all age groups, but it is particularly appropriate for younger audiences. It can, however, be a non-differentiator, as is the case with so many car television commercials playing the same kind of dramatic and opera-type music as the products weave their way through hills, rain, and difficult terrain. A lack of creativity in both scenes and music can cause consumers to take the opportunity to briefly leave the room.

Sex

Caution has to be exercised when using sex. There are no adequate guidelines, but research indicates that sexual images should be linked clearly to the product benefits, and are received better by consumers if linked also to humor and respect, and are used suggestively rather than explicitly. Sometimes, brand management steps over the mark and risks damage to the image of the brand, as Calvin Klein did when featuring children in underwear. Other brands are a little more subtle. A recent example is Martell's campaign for its liquor brand, where a glamorous woman says suggestively, "All great discoveries begin with a question. Like, can you come out and play?" and "If you shouldn't, you should." Similarly, in one advertisement for Chivas Regal's successful, but enigmatic, "When You Know"™ campaign, an exceptionally attractive model, dressed in very little, is shown with the caption, "Yes, God is a man."

At present, the European advertising "watchdog" bureaus are clamping down on what they call "Porno Chic," where sex and nudity in advertising by some brands are considered offensive and indecent. One advertisement that was withdrawn after bureau criticism in France was produced by DDB for the clothing brand La City. A young woman wearing only underwear is shown on her hands and knees beside a sheep. The tagline read, "I'd like a sweater." Subtlety is key to the use of sex in brand communications.

Case Study 18 shows how Jim Beam is repositioning itself around the world through advertising based on consumer insight research which appeals to the feelings of "friendship" that we all have.

Case Study 18

JIM BEAM
Global repositioning and local adaptation expressed through market communications

This case study shows how a global brand seeks to reposition itself consistently around the globe through advertising, following substantial market research.

Brand background

Jim Beam, Bourbon is the number one selling bourbon whiskey in America and across the globe. It is a unique product with a proud heritage spanning over two hundred years. Jim Beam Brands Co. is the largest manufacturer of Kentucky Straight Bourbon Whiskey in the world. Bourbon is not only the largest whisky category in the U.S., where it was born and the only place that Bourbon can be made, but also gaining its popularity on a global basis. "Bourbon follows overseas success with improved efforts in US market." (Source: *Impact* October 2000)

Brand communication

Jim Beam realized the importance of capturing the upcoming trend of bourbon and establishing the brand's own linkage to the new life style. To accomplish this it became critical to portray a consistent image for Jim Beam Bourbon in every market to maintain and strengthen the brand equity.

Global positioning

Global positioning research helped Jim Beam to segment the market, understand its consumers and present an image that was more rooted in sociability and fun. One important fact discovered was that more than 70% of the brand's target consumers enjoy consuming bourbon with their friends.

Jim Beam evolved from its old positioning of "American Cowboy" in global markets to a new positioning of "friendship". The "American Cowboy" image portrayed individualism, rebellion and ruggedness that are hard for today's consumers to associate with. The new "friendship" positioning portrays Jim Beam as a natural part of the friends' bonding process, a part of the group's happy times. The execution of the positioning ensured that potential and actual ads were presented in a relevant and contemporary setting that consumers can identify with, which promotes on-the-spot consumption intention. When you enjoy the company with friends, you enjoy Jim Beam.

Local Adaptation

Adaptation is the key to making global positioning work in local markets. While global image is maintained, the brand equity should be able to leverage on a local level. "Global positioning should allow local adaptation to meet huge cultural differences in different markets, while brand pillars should be maintained on a global basis for the franchise," says Thomas Maas, Vice President of Global Brand Management.

Follow-up regional consumer research studies enabled Jim Beam to adapt its global positioning to different cultural perceptions regarding socializing and friendship. The descriptions of scenario setting, humor and emotional bonding may need to be different, while consumers worldwide consistently endorse the "friendship" appeal.

Example – Asia Adoption and Adaptation

Adoption

Asian consumer research shows a consistent finding that the majority of Asian consumers also drink with their friends. Life is changing. Imported spirits are no longer luxury items intended only for businessmen, government officials and the upper class. Although Asian consumers are still used to picturing imported spirits in luxurious galas and formal drinking scenarios that stemmed from leading premium Scotch and Cognac influences, Jim Beam took this as an opportunity to depict a relaxed friends gathering in a smart casual style. " It's our key to differentiate from competitors and be relevant to today's Asian consumers' changing life style," says Catherine Hu, Jim Beam's international marketing manager (Far East).

Adaptation

The creative process also needs to be sensitive to cultural differences in execution, even though insights are shared across the board. For example, research found that Asian consumers expect to see a deeper and stronger friendship depiction in order to be convinced and stimulated for purchase. As a result, in order to get the buy-in of Asian consumers, the Asian advertisements now reflect these differences by portraying deep values of friendship, such as shared history and longevity. Below are examples of how the look and feel of the brand and its central positioning are flexed to give local relevance.

U.S.   Europe   Far East   Far East

DIRECT MARKETING

Direct marketing is where consumers deal directly with manufacturers or suppliers when buying items, with no intermediary such as a retailer involved. Techniques used here include:

- direct mail;
- telephone selling; and
- press, television, and radio advertising.

To be effective, direct marketing has to be clearly targeted or it can damage a company's image through unwanted solicitation, as with "junk" mail. If done well, it can be highly effective, not just in sales terms, but also in building a strong position. Its specific advantages are:

- It is effective in targeting well-defined segments.
- It can be effective in building relationships over time.

- It contains an interactive quality, thus involving the consumer.

- It is easily measurable in terms of responses.

- It is easily customized to provide specific messages to specific people.

It is absolutely critical for positioning and image building that the personality and identity of the company are visible and consistent, and that the correct values are projected. Dell Computers has built its entire brand identity and position through this means, establishing a first-rate image with low-cost, high-quality products and speed of delivery.

SALES PROMOTION

While advertising tends to occupy a large part of the communications budget for many companies, especially those involved in consumer goods, sales promotion techniques are often used to get new products off the ground and establish positions, to acquire new and lost customers, or to speed up the buying process. Included in sales promotion techniques are:

- free gifts with purchases;

- redemption coupons;

- contests;

- samples;

- price reductions;

- discount coupons;

- self-liquidating premiums;

- "buy one, get one free" offers;

- gift packs; and

- privilege cards.

The danger with sales promotion activities is that consistent promotional activity may weaken brand image. Some experts argue that they shouldn't be used for brand building for these reasons, but companies such as American Express, Citibank, Carlsberg, and others have found them to be useful in increasing their customer base (mainly by getting people to switch brands), increasing individual customer spend, and speeding up the purchase decision. As a general rule, it is better to avoid the price discount type of promotion and go for the added-value type. Adding more value to the brand offering, rather than subtracting from price, gives consumers good perceptions about value without losing quality perceptions. Perceived value for money is rarely a reflection of price alone.

Sales promotion activities are liked by retailers and salespersons for obvious reasons, and can provide a company with a short-term competitive advantage, but there is the tendency for competitors to wade in with their own similar promotion, so the results may be short-lived.

SPONSORSHIPS AND ENDORSEMENTS

Sponsorships and endorsements are now becoming a fact of life for many brand managers, as more and more companies try to boost their brand images by tying up deals with celebrities. The main things to watch out for in this area of brand management are that they are relevant to the audience you are targeting and appropriate to the personality of your brand. The following examples are mainly from the world of sport, but other examples can easily be found.

Brands and sports sponsorships

Sport has universal appeal. It is one category that attracts virtually everyone in the world—a universal audience. It is little wonder, then, that the big brands are equally attracted, and want to be in on the major sporting events and activities that can give them global reach—and that they are willing to pay the substantial prices necessary to get there. An obvious example is the Olympic Games—the ultimate sports event. Olympic revenue now exceeds US$900 million per year, and a great deal of this comes from the power brands. The turning point was the Los Angeles Games in 1984, where the cost of sponsorship and broadcasting rights accelerated tremendously. ABC paid US$225 million for the U.S. rights, and the number of brands allowed to become official sponsors was limited. As a result, a payment of US$4 million got them exclusivity in their category. Coca-Cola paid US$12 million to be the official soft drink of the Games. Nowadays, the premiums are much higher, and the big brands compete savagely for global exposure at the world's greatest sporting event. When six billion people are watching, it's worth it.

Sports personalities

Sports personalities have become very popular with companies seeking global exposure and recognition, boosting the image of the brands (but not in all cases, as shown below) with their endorsements. Here are some well-known examples.

Reebok: Venus Williams

In 2000, Venus Williams became the first African-American to capture the Wimbledon singles title since Althea Gibson in 1958. At the end of 2000, Williams capped a great year with a massive present from Reebok in the form of a US$40 million contract to represent the brand. Reebok had been losing out to Nike in a big way, watching the world leader in sports shoe and apparel products sign up many top athletes and sports personalities, including Michael Johnson, Marion Jones, and Tiger Woods. Although Reebok has been associated with Williams since she was 11 years old, the company regards the five-year contract extension as both a relief and a triumph, with chief marketing officer Angel Martinez saying at the time, "There's no better athlete, no better individual in the world who is better suited to represent our brand. Our goal is not to show Venus as a tennis player but Venus as a lifestyle icon, someone inspiring with the power of her presence." The price tag has lifted the earning power of women athletes to new heights. As Williams says, "For women's sports and women's tennis, it's just so great." Not bad for her bank balance, either.

Nike: Tiger Woods

Other personalities are getting big fees too, and Williams' deal cannot match the US$100 million forked out by Nike for Tiger Woods in 2000. Woods is the sort of sports personality who not only excels at his sport—in his case, being the world number one in golf—but is also regarded as a role model for any aspiring youngster. This alone guarantees him the money, because great sportspeople aren't necessarily perceived as great human beings. Woods himself realizes why he is worth the multi-million-dollar attention of Nike when he says he is a role model who embraces the responsibility of influencing others positively.

Other personalities: The good, the bad, and the ugly

Apart from reminding us that there is big money in sport these days, the following are examples of how the branding of sports products revolves around brand personality, and the personalities who represent the brands. The sports shoe and apparel market has a very young age profile, and the personalities that endorse the brands, such as Venus Williams, have to be relevant to the target audience. Williams is at the height of her popularity, and appeals very much to those young people who identify with being different. Indeed, her new contract was used as a launch pad for the Reebok campaign called "Defy Convention," which began on Super Bowl Sunday in January 2001. Her personality outpaces those of her rivals such as Martina Hingis and Lindsay Davenport, and she doesn't have to resort to physical attributes to sell, unlike Anna "Only the Balls Should Bounce" Kournikova.

Relevance and appropriateness are everything when it comes to personality endorsements. Most of the big brands get involved in this form of promotion, and not just the sports brands. Admittedly, sports watch brand TAG Heuer have Mikka Hakkinen and Boris Becker, but we see this type of endorsement with other brands and non-sports personalities such as Omega (Cindy Crawford) and Rolex (conservationist George Schaller).

With the correct endorsements, the returns are there, but if things go wrong the brand reputation may suffer. Pepsi once had the misfortune to have endorsement deals with Michael Jackson, Mike Tyson, and Madonna when all three entertainers were having their own reputation problems. Hertz Rent-a-Car tied up with O.J. Simpson, who was charged with murder, and by trying to distance themselves from the association brought even more attention to it. Other personalities, such as former footballer Diego Maradona, have also caused extreme embarrassment to associated sponsors.

In February 2001, Coca-Cola was embarrassed when one of China's biggest sports stars wore trousers that were adorned with obscene and sexist English words. Fu Mingxia, who was a triple Olympic diving gold medalist at the time, wore white trousers adorned with the words "bitch," "hysterics," "sex," and "drinking, smoking, and sex," as well as swear words, all of which were displayed in newspaper photographs. The fact that this occurred at a press conference for Coca-Cola's Sprite brand in Guangzhou made things even worse. By the time everyone had worked out what the words actually meant, the damage had been done. The *Beijing Morning Post* quoted a Coca-Cola spokeswoman as saying, "The company is very disappointed. We meticulously planned the event and did not think that, after all, such details would give people cause to laugh." Ms. Fu had evidently not worn the outfit prepared for her, as it was the wrong size, and had borrowed a friend's outfit. The lesson here is *always expect the unexpected*, but the details weren't checked as meticulously as the sponsoring company had said. (*Source: Bangkok Post*, February 25, 2001; reported in Beijing on February 24.)

Of course, you can never tell what will happen when famous personalities are intertwined with a brand, and the public does tend to forgive and forget, but care is essential when choosing the "face" of the brand. It is sometimes easy to grab at opportunities to reach millions of people through personality endorsements without taking the time to look at the possible downside. And even thorough analysis cannot predict how people are likely to behave in the future, so there is always an element of risk in this strategy.

This subject leads us naturally to what is arguably the most stressful part of the job for all top and brand managers: public relations and crisis management.

PUBLIC RELATIONS AND CRISIS MANAGEMENT

I often think of public relations (PR) as the "Cinderella" of brand management, because it works so hard but receives few accolades when brands are successful. While advertising and sales promotion are very visible and tend to get the spotlight, PR is often the unsung hero, capable of achieving a great deal of perception change, yet getting very little recognition for the role it can play.

PR departments are often referred to by a variety of other names, including "corporate affairs," "corporate communications," and "public affairs." The basic work of PR is communicating and developing relationships with various target publics, including:

- the media;
- employees;
- shareholders;
- business partners;
- industry analysts;
- local and foreign investors;
- governments;
- the general public; and
- customers and potential customers.

Advantages of PR

PR is heavily media-related and communicates to these audiences through press releases, press conferences and interviews, advertorials, newspaper/magazine columns, receptions, sponsorships, and other events. Because PR can speak so widely through so many channels, it is critical to the brand-building process, although, surprisingly, many companies don't purposefully use it to do this. I would suggest that more brand managers use PR in a strategic way to build and protect their brands, as opposed to relying on it in a reactive way, as happens with crisis management.

It is strange that PR isn't used more widely in brand building and management, as, although it often uses mass media, unlike advertising it doesn't pay for the space, a fact that might be of great appeal to the thrifty. In many cases it is free, and it can both influence public opinion and build/maintain brand reputation and image at zero cost! It is for this very reason that PR often has more credibility with the public than does advertising. I am not suggesting that PR is a total substitute for A&P

activities, but that it should be in every brand manager's armory, as it can provide valuable support to those activities, just as they can act as a support to PR.

Another advantage of PR, when compared to traditional advertising, is that, unlike advertisements, news tends to be read. The proliferation of advertisements in newspapers and magazines tends to result in readers largely ignoring the messages they contain, merely giving them a cursory glance. Similarly, television commercials are often given short shrift by viewers, sometimes because of poor quality or the company's repetition, but mostly because they have no relevance to them. The tendency of advertising to irritate and alienate people, via whatever medium, is well known. But PR presents messages in a more engaging, newsworthy way that can capture people's attention.

Disadvantages of PR

The work of PR is no easy task; it involves a lot of time invested in meeting and talking with the target audiences, persuading them to listen to a certain point of view and to adopt particular attitudes toward a variety of situations and circumstances. It also involves managing the media; getting people such as journalists to report or say favorable things about the client when many competitors are also seeking comment, especially at times of great importance, such as new product launches. PR is an ongoing process, as opposed to a one-off campaign.

The stories that are generated by PR and sent to the media must be of significance and newsworthy. Nine out of 10 releases/stories that are received by journalists never get printed—they are just not different or exciting enough. PR contributions must therefore be both timely and interesting, and the more expert PR practitioners will generate what in reality are releases that contain ordinary information, but give the material a special twist to make it rise to the top of the editorial in-tray.

Because of the above, the skills of the PR professional must be well honed. In fact, the success of the PR effort depends on the strength of the PR professional's networks and oratorical skills—how they convey their ideas creatively and persuasively.

Points to note

Most large companies have corporate communications departments whose task is, among others, to look after public relations. Some companies and individuals hire agencies to do this for them, whether on a retainer basis or for particular projects, or at times of crisis. Some points to note that have relevance for brand management include:

- Most press releases never see the light of day in the media, and should be used sparingly. Inundating journalists with them isn't going to get results. They look for really newsworthy items, and routine releases are usually filed immediately in the wastepaper bin. Journalists only consider press releases when there is something significant to say that consumers will want to hear about. They are only interested in stories that sell and have a human-interest angle.

- Treat journalists as strategic partners in your business. Relationships are very important, and good relationships are only earned over time. Buying them the odd lunch won't buy you media space. Listening to their views is more important, because they are the ones who are constantly in touch with the public and know what they will want to read, see, or listen to. Also, don't try to be everyone's friend. Choose carefully those few journalists that you believe will, in the long run, be the best choice for your strategy and future situation, and be prepared to invest a lot of time in talking to them.

- Make the best of opportunities that present themselves. An important development in the industry can give you the chance to comment and promote your name. One bank positioned itself as the "Knowledgeable Bank" and managed to get a regular column in an influential newspaper, where it wrote about financial developments affecting people around the world.

- If events are being planned to boost the image of the company or its brand(s), ensure that they are a good "fit" with the company's positioning strategy. The same applies to sponsorships: they have to be appropriate to, and in character with, the brand personality or identity to be projected. When Mattel organized The Barbie Doll

World Summit event for charitable purposes, it brought together children from over 27 countries—an event that was totally in line with the company's personality and positioning strategy. When Rolex sponsor sporting events, they only choose those top tournaments that reinforce the status and prestige of the brand name. And, of course, with both these examples, they were and are sure of getting the right media coverage targeted at the right target audiences.

PR and crisis management: You can expect the unexpected, but can you prepare for it?

Every CEO and brand manager fears a crisis that can influence market and consumer opinion in such a way that it sends the share price rocketing downwards and does serious long-term damage to the brand image of the product or service and the company that owns it. It is also a nightmare for PR specialists, because, when a crisis occurs, everyone else in the organization suddenly seems to distance themselves from the problem and to hand the "hot potato" over to PR. Poor handling of a crisis can spawn more crises and ruin a brand. A good response, on the other hand, can save and even enhance the brand image.

PR specialists are skilled in handling awkward and potentially image-damaging situations, and some are capable of turning a crisis into an opportunity. The problem with a crisis, of course, is that you don't know when it is going to materialize. Nevertheless, many companies are wise enough to develop crisis management manuals and procedures that try to anticipate every disaster situation and prescribe what the response should be. But although crisis scenario planning can, and is, carried out by many leading brands, it is nevertheless simulation, and often doesn't resemble the real event when an actual crisis occurs. However good these preparations are, there is always the chance of something unexpected happening.

Unfortunately, there are no rules for crisis management. But we can look at some unfortunate situations that companies have had to face and glean valuable information about what can go right and wrong, and what can be done and what should be avoided.

The speed factor

In crisis management, the speed and type of response is critical to maintaining brand image. Sometimes, the public initially knows more about a problem or disaster than the company itself does, as news teams tend to be quickly on the scene. In such cases, the company is faced with a lack of information, and yet hard questions are being asked and require answers. As a brand manager, it is imperative that you put out a media statement of some kind, as soon as possible, acknowledging what has happened. You may not have many details, but you must say what you know. Failure to do this can damage your brand image.

In times of crisis, brand managers have to move swiftly, and yet it is surprising that avoidable mistakes are so often made, even by the famous brands. Coca-Cola made a huge PR error when it failed to make any media statement for three days after the poisoning scare in recent years at its canning/bottling plant in Belgium. While people were being poisoned and the media all over Europe were drawing damaging conclusions, head office made no attempt to communicate with the public until it was too late. This wasn't only poor PR and brand management, it was irresponsible. Had the crisis happened to a brand of lesser stature and power, it could have suffered permanent and fatal damage. There is little doubt that this decision, taken at the highest level in the company, was partially responsible for changes in management not long afterwards, and that it caused considerable damage to the reputation of the world's most famous brand.

Other companies have demonstrated a quick response, as in the famous case of Tylenol—Johnson & Johnson's leading analgesic brand. The speed of withdrawal of the product from the market after poison was found in some of the product probably saved the company from catastrophe, and demonstrated how concerned it was about public safety. Its re-entry into the market with tamper-proof packaging reinforced the critical attribute of "We Care."

The "ostrich syndrome": Denial

One critical issue with crisis management is whether or not the crisis should be denied. Many companies opt to deny that there is a crisis until either they work out their response or things get so much worse that they have to admit it. This is the best possible way to destroy a brand image that it has taken time to create. Generally, the best advice is not to deny that there is a crisis situation, even if you think it isn't really significant. What must always be remembered is that you are dealing with human perceptions, and these are very fragile, easily influenced, and difficult to change once entrenched. The message for PR here is that if consumers *think* there is a crisis and that it is important, then there *is* one and it *is* important, especially if those people are from the media. Perceptions can be fact or fiction, but they exist in people's minds; and to those people, their perceptions—which cumulatively form the brand image—are reality.

Maintenance of trust

The world's most powerful brands enjoy the trust of their customers, and this trust creates brand loyalty. In a crisis of any proportion, maintenance of that trust is vital to continued brand loyalty. Reassurance is an essential part of the PR response, and failure to quickly regain trust can mean that the brand image fails just as fast. Soon after President Clinton left office, Morgan Stanley hired him to give his first non-presidential speech at a reputed cost of US$100,000. Customers expressed outrage, with some threatening to take their business elsewhere. Chairman Philip Purcell emailed clients and acknowledged that what he said was an error. "We clearly made a mistake … and we should have been far more sensitive to the strong feelings of our clients over Mr. Clinton's personal behavior as President. We should have thought twice before the speaking invitation was extended. Our failure to do so was particularly unfortunate in light of Mr. Clinton's actions in leaving the White House." Morgan Stanley certainly didn't duck the issue, and probably salvaged some trust as a result of the swift apology of the chairman.

The case of Singapore Airlines (see Case Study 21) demonstrates how a company can avoid many of the pitfalls in crisis management and retain the trust of the public. However, before we look at that case, we will examine two cases that illustrate both quick and slow PR responses aimed at preventing damage to a brand's image.

Case Study 19

HELLO KITTY
Damage limitation—quick response

Hello Kitty, from Sanrio, has enjoyed a great deal of success with many age groups. The little cat with no mouth has managed brand extensions on a massive scale, but the Hello Kitty brand managers are always on the look-out for incongruent exposure. In late 2000, Sanrio learned that two films were to be made in Hong Kong that would tell the story of a woman who was tortured to death. The persons responsible dismembered the corpse, cooked the body parts, and then stuffed them in the head of a Hello Kitty doll. Mr. Soji Nyoi, general manager of the company's distributor Sanrio Hong Kong, said that both films would run against the corporate ethics of the company, and that "Our whole corporate ethic is based on social communications, with love, friendship and happiness." Sanrio was concerned to the extent that it said, "We formally state that we do not support the production of these films, nor do we accept the use of Sanrio's characters." The company was concerned that the tragic event would be used for entertainment and so damage the brand image of Hello Kitty.

Case Study 20

McDONALD'S
Damage limitation—slow response

In Singapore, Hello Kitty unintentionally caused a problem for someone else's brand. In 2000, McDonald's co-branded with Hello Kitty for a sales campaign that blew out of all proportion. The subsidized Hello Kitty figures given away with burgers caused pandemonium on the streets of the island state, with people queuing for blocks to get their favorite little cat. Fights broke out about queue positions, people were arrested for violence, and, to cap it all, customers were entering

McDonald's outlets, purchasing huge numbers of burgers to get huge numbers of Hello Kitty dolls (in one case, 150!), and then throwing the burgers into the waste bins and making off with their feline prizes. A lack of supply of the little animal at some outlets exacerbated the tensions of customers. This adverse publicity damaged McDonald's image, but what the company experienced was a brand management crisis, which wasn't very well handled at the time. In defense of brand management, there was little chance of forecasting the disaster, but the physical customer problems and media response could have been managed more effectively. Luckily for the fast-food giant, the brand image damage proved to be temporary, and in 2001 it has resumed its co-branding activities with Snoopy characters, altogether a safer bet and a better brand fit.

Another implication here is the issue of distribution channels. As an example, McDonald's franchises its brand, and when any company allows this, there is always the danger that the brand won't be represented in the way the brand owner would wish. For those working in brand management and PR, there is the additional problem of helping maintain the consistency of the brand in many markets when those entities representing your brand are not under your total control. This is the reason why many top brands, such as Gucci, are buying back their brand franchises at significant cost, so that they can control the total brand experience.

Case Study 21

SINGAPORE AIRLINES
Thrust into disaster—PR in action

The alpha-numerics "SQ 006" commanded worldwide media attention and created emotional concern when an aircraft from one of the world's most famous airlines and international brands, Singapore Airlines (SIA), crashed in Taiwan on October 31, 2000. This case illustrates well how a brand can be put under the spotlight so strongly by public opinion and the world's media, and how stressful working in PR can be. It also points out to all companies aspiring to be top brands what it takes to deal with an unexpected disaster, and the strength of feelings and emotions that derive from many sources to test brand integrity.

The scene

A foggy, bad-weather environment at Taiwan's Chiang Kai Shek airport. Visibility is low and the winds are high. Aircraft are allowed, under international rules, to take off on the decision of the pilot with airport guidance. The plane moves toward the designated runway that is on the left-hand side. Take-off lights on a runway are seen to the left of the plane in front and the plane moves left. There are no barriers to the runway; nothing to suggest anything unusual to the pilots. Some lights are on and some off, a normal scenario for a bad weather take-off. The pilots request approval from the airport traffic controllers and this is given. The airport controllers cannot actually see the runway because of the poor weather conditions. The plane accelerates, but hits unseen objects on the runway, later classified as construction equipment. The plane has turned off on to the runway before the correct one, which is under repair. The disaster results in the loss of life of 83 people.

No one is prepared. SIA knows nothing of the disaster at this time. But Taiwanese reporters have free access to the airport, and their crews are quickly on the scene to film and report the burning wreckage and casualties. SIA learns of the disaster by default, when the world's media break the story.

The crisis management response from SIA

There is complete and utter shock at an airline that has the trust and confidence of the world. SIA is a major international brand with global aspirations. The company has a crisis management center that immediately swings into action, with its PR staff assigned to work around the clock in two 12-hour shifts. They answer media "hotline" questions without delay. In an immediate response, they announce that they acknowledge what has happened and are searching for more details. They give out what information they have and advise what they don't have.

They *promise* that they will update the media at every opportunity. This wasn't just a promise made by a company about information, but a promise made by the brand itself. What SIA did was to reassure the media that they were acknowledged as being important. When global calls are constantly being received, the PR team has to give out what information it has, and promise to deliver every piece of information as they receive it.

The SIA website was switched immediately from its normal condition to the "crisis site," which replaced all corporate information with crisis information, so that anyone hitting the website would be privy to *sharing* the media releases in real time. And all communications channels started to operate in the same way. This was good crisis management planning. Also planned was that one person only was to address the media, so the airline spoke through and with one voice, leaving no room for error. This person—receiving all reports and constantly interacting with the chief executive officer—gave out not only up-to-date information from the airline's point of view, but also honest reports of what was known, who it was affecting, and what plans there were to deal with these dynamic issues. All media coverage was captured, analyzed, and released to keep the brand promise.

All stakeholders, including employees and investors, were informed and kept up to date, also via the Intranet, as were market analysts. The SIA PR approach was one of total transparency.

Dealing with the public

A brand has only one opportunity to keep the faith and trust of people when a disaster strikes, and SIA made sure that it did the right thing. As soon as the disaster was known, the CEO publicly admitted that the accident had occurred and said that the company took full responsibility for it, as it was its plane. This was a brave and thoughtful decision, made when no one knew the cause of the accident. It gained SIA a lot of respect in the world community, and ensured that it kept the world's trust. SIA also recognized that in situations such as this, those affected need empathy, not sympathy. Examples of how this was done included a 100-day period of mourning for the dead passengers and crew. During this period no advertisements were run by the airline, and the letterhead was altered to omit its famous tagline, "Now More Than Ever, A Great Way to Fly."

All in all, the PR response from SIA was remarkable, and showed how the initials "PR" can, when disaster strikes, become synonymous with the words "public responsibility."

When there are general disasters, there are always PR opportunities at both national and corporate levels. Out of sadness can come hope and resolve; for companies, a massive crisis can offer opportunities to improve their brand strength.

THE INTERNET

The Internet is becoming an extremely important addition to brand management and market communications. (See the detailed discussion of e-brand management in Chapter 7.) Often, however, outside assistance is needed for Web-based and other communications. The trend now is toward integrated communications being offered by single agencies, which can offer companies assistance on a variety of fronts.

INTEGRATED BRAND COMMUNICATIONS

In the past, brand managers have had to rely on different agencies, or parts of agencies, to deliver brand communications via a variety of means, but this inefficient and often inconsistent approach has given way to new ideas on integrated communications that bring consistency to the way in which the brand is presented. Brand managers I have talked to welcome this trend, because consistency builds great brands.

New global marketing and media realities

The marketing and brand communications industry has seen some significant shifts over the last three years or so, driven by the managers of brands and the consumers that actually build the brands. First, there are many more competitors, and many more media opportunities, than in the past—for instance, there are now hundreds of cable channels in the United States. Secondly, more money is now being spent on promotion, as opposed to advertising. Mass media is becoming less impactful, and therefore less fashionable. Brand managers are realizing that in the world of mass customization, mass-media approaches are less successful. Thirdly, consumers are much more discerning and choosy, and are less tolerant of traditional media attempts to influence them.

In response to these global media and marketing realities, the traditional agencies have reacted by producing communications solutions that give brands and consumers more choice and relevance. The latest developments in brand communications are concerned with the bringing together of many communications platforms to create a bigger impact on target audiences, and to add power to the projection of the brand identity. Many agencies are combining their separate units and divisions to create much-improved and more cost-effective "packages" for their clients.

Interactive Advertising

Television and print are still the primary media for most advertising, but the growth of the Internet and digital television promise to give companies more opportunities for targeted and one-to-one advertising. The power brand companies such as Unilever are now developing interactive strategies, using alliances with technology firms such as

Microsoft and AOL to carry ads and banner advertising that links to innovative brand sites.

The interesting benefit of brand web sites is that companies can learn more about consumers. Unilever's Mentadent site saw 125,000 people request samples of toothpaste following an Internet campaign, with over two-thirds of them giving permission to be contacted in the future. Information gathered from this process helped further develop the Mentadent brand to suit consumer needs and aspirations. Unilever has set up three Interactive Brand Centres in New York, Amsterdam and Singapore, to drive the company's market learning and give online consumers more choices.

Analysis of brand communications copy

As we near the end of this chapter, I would like to address one final important element of brand communications: the copy used in brand communications. It isn't always easy for a brand manager to distinguish between creative that is "on brand" and that which is "off brand." I have found that, in far too many instances, the tone of a company's brand communications copy fails to match the personality of the brand. It is critical to speak to the audience in the way the brand as a person would speak to people. Case Study 22 provides an example of how a thorough analysis might be carried out of brand communications copy and appropriate tonal adjustments made to create copy that is "on brand."

Case Study 22

MALAYSIA AIRLINES
Analysis of advertising copy for perceived brand personality

Malaysia Airlines has won several awards for its in-flight service, a fact that it occasionally mentions in its advertising copy. In this case study, I was asked to analyze some advertising copy produced for the airline. (Although the ad itself isn't shown here, use of warmer colors might also have proved beneficial.) The original wording of the materials is given, followed by my analysis and suggestions.

What do you do to the airline that was voted number 1 as Asia's Best Business Airline for three consecutive years? Better it.

Our luxury fleet of B747-400s and the "super ranger" B-777s have two world firsts on board. They are the business center with a laptop computer printer and fax machine and an air to ground retail transaction service.

Receiving the highest honour in the airline industry can only mean one thing: to provide service at a higher level of excellence.

For reservations or information, call your travel agent or Malaysia Airlines.

Analysis and suggestions

General comments

In general, the advertisement has a somewhat dismissive, arrogant, and self-congratulatory tone. It fails to involve the reader in any way, nor does it provide any reason for the customer to be at all interested in this award. There is no warmth or friendliness in this ad. In tonal quality, the airline stands well apart from and above its audience.

Further, it presents a somewhat perplexing line of argument—namely, "We are number one but determined to be better. We have the most modern planes with some special business facilities. Getting the award means a determination to be better. For more, call your travel agent or us."

Fortunately, the headline provides no reason for readers to move on to the body copy, the concluding sentence of which, frankly, is insulting to their intelligence.

Specific comments

- *Headline*: The traits suggested here are: assertive, disinterested, and pseudo-sophisticated.
- *Paragraph 1*: The brand personality traits suggested here are: efficient, manufactured, and systemized. There is no

explanation of what an air-to-ground retail transaction service might mean to the consumer.

- *Paragraph 2*: This assertive statement requires a tortured leap of logic.
- *Paragraph 3*: This just states the obvious.

In summary, the personality traits communicated by this ad are:

- assertive;
- disinterested;
- pseudo-sophisticated;
- efficient;
- manufactured; and
- systemized.

They add up to a personality that is arrogant and dismissive.

Here are my suggested adjustments to the copy to encourage a different perception of brand personality.

Wow!
They say you said we're number 1.

When *Business Travel World* told us Malaysia Airlines had been voted Asia's Best Business Airline for the third year running, we paused for a moment to think about what we might have done to deserve it.

Yes, we have all the Business Class features, facilities, space, and services you'd expect of one of the world's most sophisticated airlines. But three years in succession? When we asked around, we found a very simple, gratifying answer.

It's all about you. It's the way you respond to our people and make them feel. Malaysians are genuine, gentle, and caring at heart, and you have a way of bringing out their natural best. Yes, we train intensively, but an inherent attraction of personalities isn't something that can be "trained for" or "systemized"; it's the way people are.

It's curious, isn't it, that the key difference we're told

makes us Asia's Best Business Airline is not confined to Business Class at all—but there for everyone who flies our airline. To all our friends, a heartfelt "Terimah Kasih."

The key to this suggested copy is that it claims ownership of the award *on behalf of the customers*, in a modest way, while making it relevant to *all* those who fly the airline, not just to Business Class travelers.

Specifically:

- *Headline*: The "Wow!" is disarming, moving far away from any impression of arrogance. "Wow!" is a happy expression, in line with the airline's personality. Reader curiosity is intensified by the impression of Malaysia Airlines' "surprise" at winning the award for the third time. Subliminally, this very powerfully increases the sense of value of the achievement.

- *Subheadline*: "You said" immediately involves the reader. In a single line, the airline claims leadership with no sense of arrogance. It puts the conferring of the award firmly into the hands of a third party—"they." It also creates curiosity, leading the reader into the subsequent elements of the ad. Tonal qualities present a much nicer personality.

The personality traits communicated by the revised ad are:

- *Paragraph 1*: Natural, modest, approachable, interested, and caring.
- *Paragraph 2*: Genuine, natural, modest, approachable, interested, and caring.
- *Paragraph 3*: Helpful, approachable, genuine, natural, modest, interested, and caring.
- *Paragraph 4*: Helpful, approachable, genuine, natural, modest, interested, and caring.

Summary

The tonally revised text still achieves the very important objective of communicating the "win." And in itself, the conferring of the award automatically communicates a modern fleet, sophistication, provision of a very high standard of service, and so on. This leaves us free to sell the far more important, differentiating personality benefit, not only to Business Class passengers but also to the market at large.

From a tonal standpoint, we have:

Original copy	*Suggested copy*
Assertive	Modest
Disinterested	Interested
Pseudo-sophisticated	Approachable
Efficient	Caring
Manufactured	Genuine
Systemized	Natural
Immodest	Happy

The airline is still blowing its own trumpet, but in a way that now endears it to, rather than separates it from, its customers.

I would suggest that any advertising copy that is proposed to be sent out to consumers, via whatever means, be subjected to an analysis similar to that carried out in the above case study.

Brand management exercise

Here is an example of an ad that features in Chapter 8. Have a go at analyzing this one to test your skill.

Double-page advertisement

Left-hand page: Photo of a telephone operator saying, "Welcome to Mercedes-Benz-Jeep®-Dodgesmart-FreightlinerSterlingSetra. How can I help you?"

This was followed by a headline, "Just call us DaimlerChrysler." This was followed by:

> We don't really need to introduce our brands anymore. They have all made history through their own achievements, and their names are known the world over. Of course, the fact that they all work under one roof means we will always have a wealth of experience and innovative ideas to draw on. Something that will help us stay miles ahead of the competition in the future. Find out more at www.daimlerchrysler.com.

The sign-off was the name DaimlerChrysler with a tagline: "Answers For Questions To Come."

Emotional brand communication: Example of a simple, emotion-packed advertisement: Mercedes-Benz

Some of the best advertisements are those that use few words, but are filled with emotion in both pictures and copy. The following is an excellent example.

Source: *Courtesy of Mercedes-Benz. Used with permission.*

The product attributes are clearly shown and referred to, as is the element of human desire. The advertisement is headed:

"The New C-Class Sports Coupe. Let your feelings go."

The copy says:

> How wonderful it is to dream. Of capturing the rush of youth. Of accelerated heartbeats and boundless enthusiasm. Of butterflies in your stomach. Of the pure driving pleasure of a lowered sports suspension that brings every curve and corner to life. Of the commanding power of a supercharged Kompressor engine. Of giving in to temptation.

This advertisement is a perfect example of how a brand makes the emotional connection with consumers and slips in rational areas of competitive advantage. It has a wonderful visual and terrific copy.

7

E-brand Management and Customer Relationship Management

Technology is ubiquitous, and brand management hasn't escaped its intrusion. There are two main ways that technology has impacted on brand management:

- use of the Internet; and
- use of customer relationship management.

We will consider each of these in some detail, as they both can have a significant impact on brand development and management.

INTERNET BRAND MANAGEMENT

We have witnessed the bursting of the "dotcom" bubble, and the reality of having to make profits rather than just generate hype has been a painful lesson for many. The pure online brands have suffered not only from ill-thought-out strategies, but also from the determination of the powerful offline traditional brands to have a piece of the action. The big advantage they have over the new online brands is that consumers already know and trust them, and awareness and trust are vital to brand success. Also, the traditional established brands tend to have deeper pockets.

The future isn't easy to predict, except to say that the Internet is here to stay and will develop substantially in an evolutionary way as more and more people subscribe, driven by their insatiable appetite for knowledge and a desperate need for convenience in a world plagued by time famine. It is my view that the strategy choice for companies isn't one of "bricks versus clicks." Rather, it is how to develop a brand strategy that will use both the physical and the virtual world as a means of acquiring and retaining customers. It is now easy to see that online brands will need to use the physical world to fulfill orders and drive people to their sites, and that offline brands will need a presence on the Internet to promote their brands and carry out e-commerce transactions wherever possible.

The majority of e-commerce still takes place on a business-to-business (B2B) basis, as opposed to a business-to-consumer basis. The rapid rise of B2B e-commerce is due mainly to the fact that the scope of e-commerce is much more restricted for consumer brands. For example, when buying fashion goods, people still want to look around the shop, touch and feel the fabrics, and try on the items. While the Internet can help consumers do this virtually, there is still no substitute for the real brand experience. Hence, some categories of brands will always be bought mainly by traditional retailing. Other categories, such as holidays, financial services, entertainment, and education, will see rapid gains in business. The second reason for the presently limited scope of e-commerce in consumer marketing is that ordinary people are still very wary of giving away personal information via Internet transactions. People have an inherent distrust of technology to start with, and giving away information such as credit card numbers is just one step too far for many Internet visitors.

The issue of trust

Trust is probably the biggest challenge for any online brand. According to research conducted in London for Leo Burnett, reported in the *Asian Wall Street Journal* on June 8, 2000, consumers trust traditional company brand names more than new Internet names. It appears that although many dotcom companies spend substantial amounts of money on advertising to gain a high degree of brand awareness, trust often lags behind. Getting your brand known (brand awareness) is one thing, but if your brand isn't trusted it will never become really successful. Lastminute.com reached a brand awareness level in the U.K. of 84%, but a trust level of only 17% held it back. The problem for Internet brands, therefore, is that traditional brand names will have an easier time gaining the trust of consumers, and online brands are going to have to work very hard, not just to gain awareness but also to gain the trust necessary for success. Powerful brands are trusted brands.

Another main cause of Internet brand failure, still connected to trust, is the failure of some brands to deliver on their promises. Sony had a problem when launching Playstation 2 on the Internet. Over 100,000 visitors in the first minute caused a systems failure and a large number of unhappy customers. Fortunately, Sony had a brand that had high trust levels offline and recovered well, but not until it had learned a valuable lesson.

In the U.S., the regulators have actually punished online brokerage firms. T.D. Waterhouse Investor Services Inc. was fined US$225,000 early in 2001 by the New York Stock Exchange and censured for being unable to process online orders "for various time periods on 33 trade dates" during an 18-month period. Evidently, outraged customers who had tried to place orders by telephone had waits of up to an hour, which is useless when share prices are moving all the time. According to a General Accounting Office Report issued in 2000, 11 online brokers reported 88 outages between January and September 1999. A twelfth had so many outages it failed to keep track of them. Even the big two— Charles Schwab and E*Trade Group—had similar problems. Of course, none of these mishaps were intended, but the best way to damage a brand is to break a promise.

Branding on the Web is different

Branding on the Web is very different from typical consumer branding. With conventional product branding, image tends to be the vital decision-influencing factor. The more you can move your brand away from commodity status, the more influential the brand's image becomes in the consumer's decision to buy. Even with washing powder—to all intents and purposes, a commodity—creating an image requires a lot of marketing effort and investment. When you rise up the scale to prestige items such as fashion watches, then image is everything, and developing brand equity is the name of the game.

When you are branding online, the customer experience becomes more important. This isn't to say that it is unimportant in traditional branding—it is very important—but it isn't the typical experience associated with traditional branding. In traditional branding, the physical aspects of the product or service form a large part of the experience. While the emotional value of buying, say, a prestige watch is very high, the experience of touching and feeling the watch when you consider buying it is very important.

With online branding the experience is different, but nevertheless important. As with traditional branding, consumer interaction with the brand is key, because the very nature of the online process is active involvement. Each online involvement requires the visitor (potential consumer) to actively seek out the brand site on purpose. The motivation of the visit reveals the importance of both traditional as well as online media in advertising and promoting the presence of online brand sites. But regardless of the motivation, the quality of the involvement, which is fundamental to the brand-building effort, has to be positive. It is vital to remember the brand's proposition at this point and to reflect it in the online experience.

The same truth that applies to traditional branding—the customer experience makes the brand—applies also to Internet branding. It doesn't matter whether a brand exists inside or outside of the Internet; all that the visitor is concerned about is getting satisfaction from his or her visit. Navigation buttons transport visitors across varied information and guide them deeper into detailed pages, flash locations of distributors across the world, and bring consumers to feedback mechanisms, real-time forums, and "chatrooms" to share their experiences.

The ability to save time on the Internet and the convenience of downloading information are of major concern; the visitor expects it. Hence, the value of any experience over the Internet is relative to the ease and success of the interaction. In the world of the Web, "what you see is what you get." Needless to say, the better the ability of a website to satisfy its visitors, the higher its value, because it draws the line between being an "effective," attractive website and a "useless" one. This is very much a brand experience.

Website brand impact and design: Some questions to ask

The customer experience remains central to the brand proposition whether you are online or not, and the principles of branding are much the same. However, there are special considerations in Internet site branding which this chapter pays attention to.

Do you need a website at all?

Some companies think they have to be on the Net because it is the thing to do, but once they have a presence they can neglect it or not really use it to great effect. This can be damaging to the brand. Other companies develop a website but don't really need one. The message here is that there must be some real purpose behind your website, and it should have a place in your company's goals or objectives. There is no point in putting up a website just because it is in vogue or because your competitors have got one. So, what is your objective in doing so?

What is your long-term objective?

It is important to get to grips with the real purpose of putting your company, or its products and services, on the Internet, because, depending on what it is, there will be design implications. For example, is your objective:

- To build a virtual business or support your existing offline business?
- To provide customers with specific technical information?
- To increase sales, reduce the salesforce, or increase its effectiveness?
- To offer customers an alternative channel of purchase/distribution?
- To build a customer relationship management program?
- To attract a different segment of customers?
- To gain global reach?
- To raise brand awareness and recognition?

Any one of these, or others, could be a strategic objective, and it is important to gain focus here, as the answer will determine the kind of website you should have.

Having said that, you still need to gain name recognition on the Net. What is occurring at the moment with a lot of Web-based companies is a mad dash to gain brand recognition, because getting established now on the Net is going to facilitate rapid growth as the number of Internet users shoots up over the next few years. So, whether your business is new or old, virtual or physical, you really need to get your brand out there in cyberspace.

Is your website appropriate to your objective?

Think carefully about whether the website you propose to have, or already have, is really appropriate. For example, if you are selling a basic commodity-type product such as household batteries, will being on the Web really increase your sales? It's doubtful. People will continue to buy them from the corner store when they need them. In this case, it would be more appropriate to increase your point-of-sale presence. However, if you are selling industrial-use batteries in bulk to businesses, then e-commerce could generate benefits, by giving potential customers technical information and allowing them to order online at lower cost.

Another consideration may be that an Internet presence can stimulate consumers to buy from traditional channels through promotional features. Even in this case, an e-commerce capability isn't required. But if e-commerce is going to provide customers with massive benefits, you might decide to gear your traditional advertising and promotion to support your website. One of the questions to consider, therefore, is: Which marketing channel is supporting which? Is your website really only to extend your brand awareness through putting up brochure ware, as opposed to giving people other types of information and interactivity?

Who are you talking to?

Your target audience should also be given careful thought. Many companies just put up a site and hope that millions will look at it and keep coming back. There is a lot of naivety about. But getting attention in the first place isn't easy, even if people are looking for it. Getting your site linked to other sites that will attract your particular target audience is essential. So, you must think like a customer. What words would they use to search the Net? Are visuals or text likely to attract them once they are at your site? What exactly are they looking for in a site?

What do you want to tell them?

You cannot be all things to all people on the Internet, just as you cannot in traditional marketing. Selectivity and relevance in presentation is the key. For instance, people looking for fast information don't want to be delayed by aesthetically pleasing but slow-to-download graphics. Animations such as flashes requiring plug-ins may be nice, but are they necessary, and do your target customers have the right plug-ins? Do you need a myriad of colors, or does a relatively simple two-color setting better represent your brand—stylish but simple?

If your audience is looking for up-to-date information, pricing, or bookings, is your site dependable enough in these respects? Are you trying to impart information to a wide audience, or are you trying to engage people in a one-to-one relationship?

How can you get them to listen?

Engaging people's attention is one thing; getting them to stay on your site and listen to you is another. This is what is commonly known as the "stickability" or "stickiness" factor. When people land at your site and are only one click away from going to another site, how can you stop them from doing so? The answer to this question lies in relevance, ease of use, and interactivity.

There are some general-purpose rules to consider:

- *Avoid time-consuming downloads*—fancy graphics may look nice but can be a liability.
- *Ensure quality content*—most people want access to quick, relevant, and accurate information.
- *Concentrate on ease of use and navigation*—give people a good menu with easily navigable routes.
- *Use direct, relevant language*—speak to your audience in the way in which they are used to.
- *Provide an immediate response.*

Remember, one experience is all it takes! Make it a good one, and people will want to come back; make it a bad one, and you may well have lost them forever.

A full discussion of how to develop a great Internet brand is given in my book *Hi-Tech Hi-Touch Branding* (John Wiley & Sons, Singapore, 2000), but here are a few branding tips for building and managing your brand successfully on the Internet.

Branding tips

1. **Be consistent with your real-world branding and personality:** In any brand-building activity, offering differentiation is important. Achieving a unique and differentiated site is a function mainly of design, but the content should be based on the personality and positioning of the brand. Avoid indirect messages in general content as well as in advertisements, as they can mislead visitors.

    If you aren't an entirely virtual company and already have a brand presence in the traditional media, ensure that you are true to the brand identity that people are familiar with. Maintaining brand identity (and, in particular, brand personality) is essential for those brands moving to the Web. The Gap is a good example of consistency, with www.gap.com demonstrating the personality characteristics of direct, straightforward, very easy, and efficient. It is easy to find and purchase products you want. Similarly, there is visual consistency with the blue and white color scheme and the rotating 3D Gap bag. Sony is a bad example. If you log on to the Sony site in different parts of the world, it is difficult to see that it is a Sony site, as colors and fonts are different, and the whole look and feel lacks consistency.

2. **Make things easy:** Consumers who click on your site are task-focused; they are searching for model names, dimensions, prices, distributors, range, opening hours—in short, everything that has to do with your company, product, or service. Insurance intermediary its4me plc (www.its4me.co.uk) allows visitors to do everything themselves, from getting insurance quotes to printing out the final policy. Email and help lines are available, as is a panel of insurance

experts. So every assistance is there, but the carefully thought-out site construction makes it easy and convenient for the prospective buyer.

3. **Boost the brand experience with interactivity:** Internet users, by their very nature, want interactivity. Thus, you can create value by allowing the consumer to interact with the brand in ways that aren't available in the physical world. A good example in relation to this advice is ProphetFinance (www.prophetfinance.com), because it shows a thorough understanding of the needs of its different users. The site allows users to create simple charts, or even more complicated technical analysis charts, when evaluating stocks. Also, the customized facilities can enable users to group charts by industry sector for visual comparison.

4. **Ensure that strategic alliances and networks offer a good brand fit:** Link up with Internet businesses that are likely to have access to the customer base you want to reach. But make sure that their brand doesn't devalue or dilute yours. Online activities should mutually reinforce both brands' positioning, share similar target segments, and have similar brand values.

5. **Make your brand easy to find:** Getting yourself at the top of the pile when people are searching for certain products and services is part of the awareness solution, because it ensures that customers will easily find your brand when they use the search engines. Google is currently one of the best search engines/directories.

6. **Establish trust and deliver on the brand promise:** That powerful brands are built on trust hasn't changed with the advent of the Internet, as I have said earlier in this chapter. Guarantees of privacy and refunds, good-quality products and services, and service recovery are vital to the development of trust and loyalty online. Dell Computers is a good example of this, with a functional experience, neat site architecture, and efficient navigation. You can put together the computer you want with whatever options you need, and delivery to your home is reliable.

7. **Develop brand speed, simplicity, style, and substance:** The challenge of branding effectively on the Internet is also about seamlessly integrating the elements of speed, simplicity, style, and substance into a website for access by visitors 24 hours a day, seven days a week. A well-planned website also provides impressive pre-sale and post-sale brand experience. Yahoo! is a great example of this.

8. **Provide accurate and relevant brand information:** Internet users are basically looking for information that is accurate and relevant. In this regard, be very clear about whom you are targeting, and understand what makes them tick and click. UPS (www.ups.com) seems to know this well. Known for its versatile tracking service through the Internet, the company allows its users to track their UPS bar-coded packages—anytime, anywhere in the world. All the user needs to do is to enter a UPS tracking number on the relevant website. The site also offers the user access to a choice of automated self-help activities such as "Quick Cost," "Transit Times," "Pickup," "Drop-Off," and "Supplies."

9. **Look for a unique brand category positioning:** You have to stand out from the virtual crowd before you can secure consumer perception that differentiates your brand from the others. "Owning" a category position is always a good move, but need not be limiting, as there are always ways to "push" a lifestyle and achievement message. Victoria's Secret "owns" lingerie and related items online after spectacular fashion shows online at www.VictoriasSecret.com. This is also a good example of brand consistency kept between offline stores and online virtual stores.

10. **Balance brand sophistication and simplicity:** Your brand has to look good and different without getting in the way of the consumer experience. It is possible to be sophisticated yet simple, as the Jaguar site (www.jaguar.com) shows. The site is clean and simple, yet stylish and classy, exhibiting understated power, elegance, and prestige. The Jaguar marque is always to the fore, and the

emotional site construction makes the visitor want to click on to see more.

11. **Update your site; refresh your brand:** Immediacy is the value proposition offered by the Web. Therefore, as a rule, weekly information updates are necessary for product sites, and seasonal information updates for retailers, with bi-monthly changes to the upfront look and feel, in keeping with the brand values, of course. Rod Davies, editor of the *Asia Pacific Management Forum* (www.apmforum.com), says: "Be flexible and go crazy with content but be very disciplined that every image, every piece of copy, and even page layouts reflect your single, clean and simple brand message. Brand messages need to be simple and memorable, but experience tells us that the more examples of your brand identity that are provided, the more the message is reinforced and remembered."

12. **Provide brand entertainment:** Entertainment is an integral part of brand building on the Internet, as it enhances a potentially dull experience. Though viewed through a screen, a brand can come to life over the Internet through a myriad of interactive and immersing technologies that include games, animation-cum-sound effects, and other interactive elements. The new official *Harry Potter* website from Warner Brothers (www.harrypotter.warnerbrothers.com) has exciting games; children can try on the Sorting Hat to find out which house they go into, choose their own wand and their own creature, buy memorabilia, play Quidditch, make potions, and send postcards and emails to friends.

13. **Be brand-specific—explore Net niches:** Nike.com has always focused on lifestyle. Thanks to Nike "AIR," everyone knows who Michael Jordan is. (Or should that read the other way around?) Although Nike continues to get the endorsements of big names in sports, the strategy isn't as obvious in the main page of nike.com. The reference to specific sports personalities such as Lance

Armstrong, who in 2001 won the Tour de France for the second time, is typical of multiple links accessible from the page, which reflects the current lifestyle trends in sports—focused and energetic. A direct click from the home page leads visitors to the online store, and to pages where they can customize a sports clip or order a customized shoe. Access to four sub-sites—NikeBiz.com, NikeTown.com, BrasilFutebol, and women.nikejapan.com—enables the brand to cater to specific consumer segments.

14. **Vary content and experience to suit different users:** The key driver in the relationship-building dimension for online branding is an intimate knowledge of each customer. The marketing communications emphasis has shifted from monologue to dialogue, and technology makes it possible to adopt a one-to-one relationship with each customer, enabling companies to:

- identify customers individually and address them personally;
- differentiate them by their value and needs;
- interact with them more cost-efficiently and effectively; and
- customize many aspects of the company's behavior to satisfy customer needs.

For example, in the world of cosmetics, Procter & Gamble has gone online with Reflect.com (www.reflect.com), a brand that fits with P&G's usual stand-alone branding model. What makes this site different is that it isn't just selling already known products—the products don't actually exist until the customer makes them! Reflect.com offers a tailored service that "delights one woman at a time." An example of the outcome of this might be a shampoo where the customer can pick her own fragrance, how much and how creamy the lather should be, shape of the container, and the type of cap. It even gets shipped with a label that says "Made especially for [the customer]," with her name on it. It's hard to resist individualization.

The site also makes it easy and fun for the consumer. When I saw the home page, it provided a "Sneak Preview" and promised

"Products created by YOU. Delivered to you free of charge in under a week. Unconditionally guaranteed." Logging on requires few details, and easy-to-download pages make the site friendly. Touches like having Asian models that come up on-screen for Asian customers demonstrate relevance and understanding, and the whole look and feel is of style and simplicity, with personal attention.

15. **Manage brand loyalty:** How do you manage customer loyalty in a medium that discourages patience while offering more variety than we have ever known? How do we sustain customer interest long enough to make them choose us again? On the Net, loyalty has to be rewarded, or customers will stage a virtual walkout. As one click is all it takes, many companies are using loyalty or rewards programs to keep customers coming back, and thus create long-term relationships with them. The key to this area of activity is to reward people with things that make a difference, not just one-off promotions that cheapen your brand and send consumers looking for a better deal. Remember that the Internet makes it very easy for people to compare competitive offerings, and that universal incentives such as cash and points schemes aren't effective as loyalty builders. The next section of this chapter deals with developing brand loyalty through customer relationship management.

16. **Use the Net for broadening the marketing base:** Some traditional manufacturing companies are embracing the Internet as a marketing tool, while others are still hesitant about doing so. Kraft Foods, which has over US$17 billion in sales, has taken the plunge with www.kraftfoods.com. It also spends a lot of dollars to promote, via this medium, the role Kraft plays in helping families connect over food. Kraft has been promoting this positioning for some time, but the interesting thing is its use of the site. Instead of using the site as a place for consumers merely to gain information about its products, kraftfoods.com functions as a brand itself, with the aim of giving its target audience—mainly mothers—"Real help in real

time," which is the tagline of its recent campaign. Here visitors can find personalized solutions to meal dilemmas, email recipes, online chats with celebrity mothers, and recipes tailored to what they have available in their kitchens. The site then becomes a meal-planning product/service, while the company positions itself as one that understands the needs of today's consumers.

The critical success factor is still the brand experience

All of these tips for online brand building are aimed at giving customers an experience that will be good enough to keep them coming back for more. What isn't unique about Internet branding, as you no doubt will have realized by now, is that whether the brand succeeds or fails depends on the experience enjoyed by the consumer. Providing a great online experience is therefore key. When compared to traditional brand building, online brand building perhaps shows even more clearly that *the experience is the brand*. In some ways, it is easier for companies to control and develop the customer experience because they can control all the customer/brand interactions, while in the offline environment this is difficult, if not impossible, to do.

The development of new and improved software applications will continue to revolutionize 21st-century brand building, especially on the Internet. Any company wishing to develop a great brand must have both an online and an offline strategy, and these should be very consistent in what they offer and how they appear. One of the great assets that companies now have in managing the brand experience in both the physical and virtual worlds is the innovations that have occurred in the activity called customer relationship management.

CUSTOMER RELATIONSHIP MANAGEMENT (CRM)

What is CRM?

One of the most worrying things about CRM is that there are still a great many people who don't really understand what it means and how it can be applied. This section explains briefly what CRM is and how everyone in the organization has a role to play in a CRM program.

Customer relationship management is sometimes called customer relationship marketing, or relationship marketing.

Traditionally, marketing textbooks have suggested that "all customers are equal." But does that old adage really make sense? We all know about, and subscribe to, the Pareto principle (the 80:20 rule). So, if 20% of your customers represent 80% of your revenue, or 10% of your customers represent 90% of your profits, it is clear that not all customers are equal. CRM recognizes that all customers are NOT equal—different customers represent different values to your organization. But CRM takes this knowledge one step further by suggesting that, if this is the case, then *they shouldn't be treated equally.*

The purpose of CRM programs, then, is to recognize the best customers and hold on to them by increasing your understanding of their needs as individuals, meeting the expectations they have of your organization, and making a difference to their lives.

Profitable and nonprofitable customers

CRM is also about looking at customers that may not be big spenders now, but could be if they are encouraged by a really good brand experience. While the economics of focusing on your most profitable customers are compelling, a good CRM program shouldn't ignore all the others. Sure, the level of attention that less-profitable customers may deserve and get may be somewhat lower, but the principles can apply at all levels.

There is no doubt that by turning your organization into one that is centered around the customer, every single customer will ultimately benefit in one way or another. Because once you begin to alter the culture of an organization and your people get used to thinking "customer first," it is virtually impossible to go back to the old way. So, even though a particular customer ultimately may not be among the elite ranks of your "Premier Customer" group, or doesn't hold your "Titanium" card, he or she will surely be enjoying the benefits of all the positive changes that have percolated their way through your company.

Share of wallet versus share of heart

Some people talk about the aim of CRM as being to capture "share of wallet"—in other words, trying to increase the portion of each customer's spend that comes to you. It is a mistake to think in these terms; you might build up short-term sales by this type of thinking, but not enduring relationships. We prefer to think of it as capturing "share of heart"—that is, creating an emotional bond with your customer such that they pledge allegiance to your brand. If you achieve this, "share of wallet" will be a natural by-product. But what is important for your long-term business is that if you appeal to the hearts of these customers, they will themselves become part of your best salesforce—by being your happy and loyal customers and advocates.

Loyalty schemes and CRM programs

In practical application, CRM programs can take many shapes and forms, but it is useful at this point to draw a distinction between a "loyalty scheme" and a CRM program.

Many, if not all, of you will now be familiar with and probably part of a number of loyalty programs, or points schemes as they are sometimes known. Just about every type of retail outlet in every city in every developed and developing country has a loyalty program. It's pretty hard to live life without being part of one. You buy groceries—you earn points; you fill your car with petrol—you earn points; you fly—you earn points; and so it goes on—hotel stays, car hire, even surfing the Internet now earns you i-points or mouse miles. If it's not points or miles, it's in the Starbucks or TGI Fridays mould of collect six stamps and the next coffee or meal is free.

Points programs such as these are designed to keep you coming back for more, and it is true that they might influence brand loyalty to some extent, although the degree of influence is debatable. Do these programs constitute CRM? My view is that they don't, but they can certainly provide a solid foundation upon which to build a CRM program. Normally, these programs have a mechanism—for example, a brief sign-on questionnaire—for collecting a little data about the customer and their purchasing habits, but all too often they fail to take the next quantum leap that makes the difference and turns a loyalty program into a CRM program. That leap is achieved by capturing that data, turning it into knowledge, and using that knowledge in some way to tailor the product or service you offer that customer to make it more relevant, more suited, and more specific to their needs. Without this customization a loyalty program is just a process of "earning and burning" points, and although consumer habits may be affected momentarily, competitors can merely offer more points with the result that the "loyal" customers you thought you had disappear.

Frequent flyer punishment schemes

Let's illustrate this point with an example of a commonly seen marketing initiative that contains elements of both a standard loyalty program and a CRM program. Many of you may belong to a frequent flyer program. These programs typically have an "earn and burn" element, which means customers earn points when they travel and, once they have enough points, they redeem them for free flights. The idea is that customers will pick one airline over another on the basis of the accumulation of more points toward their flights. However, it is all too common that they turn into "disloyalty" programs by punishing passengers who don't redeem points by deducting them. This has happened to me. As a Privileged Passenger of a well-known international airline, and tired of having points deducted for non-redemption, upon trying to redeem my points for a flight two weeks in advance I was told I couldn't do it unless I requested this two months in advance. Of course, I never know exactly where I will be in two months, so the result is that I cannot redeem my points and get further punishment from further deductions. When I asked why I couldn't redeem points for tickets in two weeks, the indignant reply I got from the airline was, "The system doesn't allow such short-term redemptions."

The airlines claim that frequent flyer programs are CRM programs, because the more points people earn the more benefits they get—for instance, using the express check-in, the executive lounge with free food and drink, extra baggage allowance, and a good chance of an upgrade (though I have never managed to get one). Once customers have flown a qualifying mileage, they are invited into the upper tiers of a frequent flyer program. Here they will receive a range of program-specific benefits, designed to make life easier and more comfortable for them. At this level, airline staff are sometimes trained to be able to relate to each customer by their preferred name and to learn to recognize regular travelers by sight. The best programs are multi-tiered with a "Chairman's Club," or similar, at the very top. Here only the most valuable customers get invitations to exclusive events and direct lines of communication to the chairman's office, and never have to stand in line for anything. If it worked like this it would be good, but the "earn and burn" mentality destroys the effect it could have and damages brand image.

Here are a few more questions that people sometimes ask about CRM and how it differs from traditional marketing activities.

Is CRM different from advertising?

Some people ask what the difference is between CRM and advertising. TV commercials, or TVCs to use the advertising trade jargon, are great for creating general corporate and product awareness, and, to some extent, for brand building. They are big broadcast messages, but using them makes it very difficult to target specific groups of customers, not to mention individual customers.

Invariably, TVCs are based on monologue; they are making a statement, but not particularly calling for a response. Of late, TVCs have included free phone telephone response lines where a specific product is being promoted, but this hardly constitutes direct response TV advertising. With the global move toward digital television broadcasting comes an increasing ability to know who is receiving a particular broadcast, for that person to interact with the TV set, and therefore, implicitly, the likelihood that TV advertising will become more interactive within the next few years.

Ultimately, the aim of CRM is to communicate and interact with an audience of one. It is vitally important that marketers, and indeed the agencies which support them, bring CRM into the overall media mix used by their company.

Turning now to some other forms of advertising, there are opportunities to create "interaction" between the audience and the advertiser, but many of these are often missed. How often have you seen a response coupon or phone number in a full-page advertisement in a newspaper or magazine? Many marketing executives don't do this. They run a great advertisement—people like what they are saying or what they are offering—and that's it; the process grinds to a halt. But if they do include a response mechanism, they will achieve several things:

- They will gain some idea of who is interested in the product.
- Their marketing spend (ads) will be made to work harder.
- They will begin to build a database of people who have at least expressed an interest in their company or product (the beginnings of a marketing database).

Fortunately, with the advent of the Internet, most companies now include their website addresses as part of their advertisements. (If you are not doing this already, you ought to include your website address on every piece of advertising or marketing material, including your company letterhead.) This means that for those consumers who have Web access, at least there is an opportunity to respond or find out more.

Is CRM different from direct marketing?

Direct marketing at its worst can involve "cold mailings" to a list of names, sourced from a bureau, about whom the marketer knows very little, other than that they apparently conform to the specification he or she supplied to the bureau. The brand manager has no idea whether or not these people are interested in buying the product they have to sell.

A good direct marketer will segment the list into control groups and try different creative styles and different incentives in an effort to find the magic formula that generates the highest response rate. But even the best direct marketing campaigns run in this manner may deliver only a 1–2% response. Not surprisingly, the consumer normally regards this type of marketing negatively, because the chances of it being something they need, and of it being delivered at a relevant time, are pretty remote. This type of mail-out has rightly earned the label of "junk" mail—because, for most recipients, that's precisely what it is.

Having said this, those direct marketing campaigns that are run by a company trying to sell more to an existing customer can enjoy significantly higher responses to a well-thought-out campaign. Campaigns have seen percentage responses ranging from the mid-20s to the low 30s, by sending offers to those who have already bought from a company and are happy with the product and service, and who know that the company has taken the trouble to offer them other products that are relevant to them. Again, think about human relationships—if someone you had never heard of asked you out on a date, what is the likelihood that you would go? Compare that with a situation where this is someone you've known for a while, you know that they can be trusted, and you have some idea of their personality—isn't it far more likely that, in those circumstances, you would accept the date?

Is CRM *different from customer service?*

The simple answer to this question is that the two are very closely related, because CRM is all about building brands by giving customers wonderful experiences. In fact, product and service quality are at the center of all the great brands. Traditionally, customer service has always been an important part of brand building for every company, and especially for service companies. It has offered great opportunities to companies to get close to their customers, and to build up long-lasting relationships with them.

Unfortunately, many companies have failed to take advantage of these opportunities and have damaged their brand images as a result. Instead of leveraging the brand experience by giving excellent customer service, they have, in some cases, treated customers like irritants. Sometimes they haven't listened to them, or have been unable to help because someone else dealt with the customer last time, or they haven't been able to answer queries that aren't in their area, or they may have been under so much pressure that they have made customers feel unwelcome. We all come across poor customer service stories on almost a daily basis. But each time customer service fails to delight the customer, it is another nail in the coffin of the brand; poor customer service kills brand value fast. Even the millions spent by some companies on training their staff in customer service techniques still only manage to inculcate generic interpersonal skills at the end of the day. So, how does CRM work to better advantage than the activities mentioned above?

How does CRM work?

CRM works by:

- **Creating a continuous communication loop between your brand and your customer:** This can be phone-based, face-to-face, by mail, the Internet, or any combination of these. But the critical thing is to open the communication channels and make it easy for the customer to interact with you.

- **Getting to know the customer:** Use this new-found communication channel to get to know your customer—not just their name and address, but also:
  - Who they are.
  - Who is in their family unit.
  - What they do for a living.
  - What their ambitions are.
  - Their likes and dislikes.

  You can only get this information by asking them directly.

- **Using existing customer data:** You need to look at the information you ought to have already about the customer. Included here would be information such as:
  - How often do they buy from you?
  - How much do they spend when they do?
  - When was the last time they bought from you?

- **Asking the customer what they want from you:** For instance:
  - What might they buy from you if only you supplied it?
  - What do they like about your brand?
  - What do they dislike about your brand?

- **Establishing the unlocked potential:** This involves finding out:
  - What brands they buy that are competitors of yours.
  - Why they don't buy everything they need from you, if you offer it.
  - What you would have to do to persuade them to buy more from you.

- **Creating the knowledge:** Marry all the foregoing data together to create the most powerful database in your entire organization. This database will now drive every piece of targeted sales and marketing activity to your customer base.
- **Reusing the knowledge time after time:** Each and every time a customer interacts with your brand, make sure that the person the customer interacts with has the knowledge in front of them and can thus talk to them like a friend they have known all their life. It is this concept of intimacy that really helps in the brand-building process.

The concept of lifetime value

Since the 1960s, supermarkets have only been interested in transactional data—how many units of product have been sold today. Banks are just the same. Only now are they beginning to realize that, by understanding more about the actual person buying the product, they can make more profit. The case study of Hang Seng Bank (Case Study 23) at the end of this chapter is a good example of a bank getting closer to customers and offering them more channels by which they can do business. Lifetime value of customers is a reflection of how often a customer buys from you, how much they spend when they do buy, when they last bought from you, and what they are likely to buy from you during their lifetime.

The concept of brand intimacy

Knowledge is power, and if you can get knowledge about your customers, then you can really become close to them and deal with them on a one-to-one basis. It is the ability to create this degree of intimacy between your brand and the customer that will lock out the competition and maximize the profit for your company. It means concentrating on, and streamlining, all your marketing efforts so that the customer and your brand become one.

In Asia, relationships are a fundamental part of social and business life. Some companies realize this. Jakob Meier, president of Giorgio Armani Asia Pacific, says: "In Asia, the personal relationship with the customer is more important. We work much harder with the database in

Asia. We try to capture more about the customer, how he reacts to different products. The relationship becomes quite close."

Getting closer to or becoming more intimate with your customer means you are going to be in the best possible position to sell them something at the time they need it. You will be their best friend, the person they turn to when they need help, guidance, and, ultimately, someone to buy from. This isn't pressure selling, but quite the reverse. It is sound brand strategy. And by using your customer knowledge base, you will be putting offers to your customers only at a time when you already *know* they will need you. Your advances will therefore always be welcomed. You are adding value to your brand proposition constantly, and not being a nuisance. Consumers like intimacy, but not intrusion, and good relationship management can determine whether your brand is perceived as a really close friend or as an unwelcome visitor.

Good brand management needs consumer focus

For brands to be successful, there needs to be a total shift toward consumer-centricity. In other words, the consumer should be the sole focus for all brand initiatives. So, whether it is the website, product development, advertising, the CRM program, or anything else that will influence the brand image, all activities have to reflect the brand consistently and appropriately. In many cases, this means that companies have to change their structure to make it easier to be close to the customer, and with CRM this is usually inevitable. The results will be worth it. You can build an outstanding brand very quickly. The companies that have developed the most powerful brands have done so by always thinking from the outside in, starting with a thorough understanding of what consumers need, want, and feel.

The challenge for brand management: Becoming the customer manager

Some of the most powerful brands in the world have major organizations based around product, with brand and product managers being the most important people in that structure. But they are changing, and so can your company.

Brand managers must be prepared, at the very least, to become more immersed in the brand–customer relationship, and at best to assume a role at a higher level, whereby they are responsible for the way in which the whole company deals with customer relationships.

It is essential, then, that brand managers are given responsibility, not for a product or range of products, but for all aspects of delivery to a selected group of customers. Look at the way management responsibilities have changed in companies like Tesco, the supermarket chain based in the U.K. For years, the store manager's key responsibilities were the day-to-day store operations—making sure the shelves were stocked, that the delivery orders were placed, and so on. Now, this is all delegated activity. The store manager's prime focus now is getting to know each of the store's highest-value customers by name. Each store manager makes phone calls on a regular basis to ensure that their highest-value customers are happy with Tesco: Is there anything they have done to upset them this month? What could Tesco be doing more of? Why? How? Tesco has realized that these top customers represent 80% of its profits, and that if any of them are unhappy and take their business elsewhere, Tesco's profits are walking out of the door at the same time, decreasing the value of the brand name in the process.

Brand management must be both macro and micro

The end-result of the new innovations that are sweeping across brand–consumer relationships, enabled by the sheer power of technology, is that those responsible for managing brands have to be prepared to manage them from a macro point of view—looking at markets and groups of consumers, as well as from a micro aspect—building individual relationships between a brand and each individual customer. This is no easy task, and requires that brand management be prepared to work more closely with all functions of the organization.

The branding opportunity

CRM represents a great opportunity for brand management, because the CRM technology that is now available allows a company to gather more and more detail about each individual customer, such as their preferences, dislikes, and so on. Importantly, it gives every brand manager the capability of interacting with each customer individually, and of treating each customer differently with customized offerings. Unfortunately, this one-to-one approach has rarely fulfilled that potential, because companies have rushed into buying technology without thinking through what information they want to collect and what they want to do with it. In other words, they have failed to develop a CRM strategy.

The toolkit in the appendix at the end of this book contains a complete list of questions for companies to consider when embarking on a CRM program. Those of you who are interested in the details of implementation are advised to read *Romancing the Customer: Maximizing Brand Value through Powerful Relationship Management*, by myself and Martin Trott (John Wiley & Sons, Singapore, 2001).

To round off this chapter, Case Study 23 is of interest because it shows how a bank (and banks are not noted for their attention to customer relationships) introduced e-banking, but did so by involving all staff, using all communications channels, and really giving its targeted consumer group what it wanted. It is a good example of a company creating an online/offline brand strategy with a CRM base.

Case Study 23

HANG SENG BANK
Forging an e-image

Hang Seng Bank is the largest Asian bank, excluding Japan, in terms of market capitalization (*Source*: *Finance Asia*, August 2001), serving more than one-third of the population of Hong Kong. In the Internet age, "e" has become more than a delivery channel for Hang Seng Bank. The bank's communications program has focused on shaping an e-image around its distinctive brand that isn't only consistent with its core brand values, but also tells how it is evolving to meet changing customer needs as a modern bank. Or, as its new corporate tagline puts it, "Hang Seng Bank. Exceed. Excel."

"In the crowded marketplace, the brand and its image

remain the only thing that distinguishes a company or product from the competition. They differentiate us from the competition and can pre-sell the product to consumers," Walter Cheung, the bank's assistant general manager and head of corporate communications, said. "Given changing consumer preferences, we must maintain the relevance of their messages. Consumers are casting their clicks with brands that are evolving with their needs."

The need to change

The bank's brand has tried, from its earliest days, to project progressiveness, trustworthiness, premium service, and customer caring. However, despite the bank's pioneering role in offering solutions, such as Hong Kong's first seven-year mortgage loans in 1967 and its first virtual credit card in January 2000, its image was still perceived as relatively conservative.

To help signify change, the bank launched its e-image campaign in July 2000, including the introduction of the Hang Seng e-Banking brand name and the "Hang Seng Bank. Exceed. Excel" tagline. The campaign highlighted the bank's strong customer focus and how it is constantly reinventing itself to meet new consumer aspirations. Backed by a comprehensive external and internal communications program, the e-image campaign has helped build a modern and progressive image for the bank, as well as its standing as a major e-player.

"In a business environment of 'innovate or evaporate,' we believe the forward-looking message of our image positioning will help ensure customer loyalty and protect our market leadership," Cheung said.

The success of Hang Seng's e-image campaign won the bank an award for excellence in the Gold Quill Awards of 2001. It was the only Asian winner in any of the eight categories of the awards, organized by the U.S.-headquartered International Association of Business Communicators.

The growth of Hang Seng's Internet banking services, launched at www.hangseng.com/e-Banking in August 2000, has been rapid. As of September 2001, more than 160,000 customers have registered, and Internet transactions now make up in excess of 8.5% of the bank's total transactions.

The perception of Hang Seng as a progressive bank increased from 36% in November 1999 to 51% in December 2000 after the launch of its e-image campaign, according to an AC Nielsen Image Perception Report. In particular, the bank was highly successful in reaching its primary target of consumers aged 18 to 39. This age group accounted for 73% of total enrollments at the end of June 2001. According to analysis from Nielsen/NetRatings, hangseng.com had the third-largest group of Web-surfing women aged between 21 and 34 in Hong Kong in March 2001, at 33%.

"Our new image has promoted mass awareness of our commitment to reliably offer consumers what they want today and will need tomorrow, and to give them a great experience. A great experience creates loyal customers who are often willing to pay a premium for something they enjoy," Cheung said.

The new marketplace

Given the growing popularity of the Internet, today's increasingly sophisticated customers are spoiled for choice and only a mouse-click away from a competitor's website. Business models have been changing dramatically as a result. "In order to enhance our market competitiveness, we had to roll out Internet banking or risk losing market share," Cheung said.

Besides offering customers a convenient and value-added channel for financial transactions, the bank's e-Banking services tied in well with its drive to encourage customers to switch to lower-cost automated channels.

A major challenge was that the bank wasn't among the first to launch, although its website had provided comprehensive banking information since 1996. Some banks had launched

Internet banking services more than a year earlier. "We found that being a first-mover is not particularly important in the online world. What counts is getting it right with the security, reliability, and scope of services offered," Cheung said.

Hang Seng realized that alongside its e-Banking services, it needed a more powerful image that would allow it to get closer to customers, attract new customers, and increase cross-selling ratios. Cheung said, "Developing an e-image seemed appropriate to demonstrate to consumers that our use of leading-edge technology and innovation is helping to improve their lifestyle. The e-image is also targeted at value-seeking investors and at attracting, retaining, and motivating the best employees."

The bank was ranked third in Hong Kong for being "innovative in responding to customer needs" in the "REVIEW 200: Asia's Leading Companies" survey by the *Far Eastern Economic Review* in 2000. It was the only financial institution on the list.

e-Banking has become an important part of the bank's integrated, multi-channel delivery network. In a clicks-and-mortar approach, its branches have been converted into financial sales and advisory centers and cater to customers who prefer face-to-face contact in their banking.

E-image build-up using all communication channels

Hang Seng's e-image built on its 1996 corporate identity redesign, which improved its image as a modern, customer-caring, and user-friendly bank. The new tagline, "Hang Seng Bank. Exceed. Excel," is derived from the bank's "Because We Care" spirit, and highlights the bank's pursuit of service excellence and its commitment to exceeding customer expectations in the e-age.

The elaborate campaign was kicked off in July 2000 as a prelude to the launch of e-Banking services the following month. Two e-image TV commercials and corporate print ads highlighted how the bank is making life easier for customers.

Due to the development of the new corporate tagline and a specially created e-Banking icon, the bank's stationery and marketing communications materials were revised in order to drive a consistent e-image.

PR activities had an e-focus wherever possible, such as backdrops, the 2000 annual report theme, and interviews. Major speeches of senior executives highlighted things "e" at every opportunity. Outdoor advertising in the form of a giant bulkhead light box at the bank's headquarters and a larger than 1,000-square-foot poster on the exterior wall of the Hang Seng Building attracted wide attention. Eye-catching buntings, posters, and banners were also hung at the bank's premises and selected branches.

August 1, 2000, the official launch date of the bank's e-Banking services, was designated e-Day at the bank, and specially designed T-shirts were worn by staff.

Since August 2000, the bank's results announcement press conferences have been Webcast live and made available online as part of its efforts to promote its e-image. The bank received the second-largest number of applications—about 24,000—when Hong Kong for the first time introduced e-IPO services for the MTR Corporation Limited in September 2000.

The bank's campaign reached out to the whole of Hong Kong through a series of e-related community programs. The Hang Seng Olympic e-Wish Campaign in September 2000 encouraged the public to pledge their support to Hong Kong's athletes by sending them messages of encouragement through the Internet.

The human touch was strengthened through features such as Lunar New Year e-cards of the God of Wealth and the Hang Seng coin box charity e-auction in 2001. Over 20,000 e-cards were sent out by customers and non-customers in two weeks and about HK$330,000 was raised for the Community Chest through the e-auction of 39 collectable coin boxes issued by the bank in the 1970s and 1980s.

Developing the brand culture

The e-image campaign was extended internally to all 7,400 bank staff from the very beginning, as it was essential to create an e-culture within the bank before Hang Seng could successfully deliver its messages to the public. "Customers want to be reassured not only about services but about the people behind the services too. We wanted our e-culture to excite staff and encourage their contribution to success. We wanted them to walk the talk and deliver the brand promise," Cheung said.

Various e-education programs—including large-scale seminars, circulars, and regular morning broadcasts to staff at headquarters and all branches—on Internet-related developments cultivated the e-mindset of staff. E-corners were set up at different locations in the bank, including the canteen. Newly designed uniforms in a silvery gray color projected a hi-tech appearance.

A culture of innovation was reinforced among staff. The bank's managing director and general manager was appointed as Innovation Champion to lead the bank-wide drive to exceed, excel, both in the bank's business and personal development. Staff whose ideas for business improvement were adopted were recognized and rewarded. Staff were also invited to try out the Internet banking services before the formal launch. This also served as a trial to ensure that the system was ready for use by a large customer base.

Business strategy tie-in and results

From the start, the bank's e-Banking strategies have been incorporated into its overall business plan to deepen customer relationships by gaining a larger share of their financial spending. "Our e-Banking services have become a major means to deliver wealth management services, including securities trading, to customers. This is part of our efforts to counter narrowing interest margins by increasing fee income and higher margin businesses," Cheung said.

Initially, e-Banking was available only to the bank's integrated account customers. It has since been extended to its credit card holders, employees enrolled in Hang Seng MPF Schemes, and sole proprietors. e-Banking has proved a success in product cross-selling. The monthly average of integrated accounts opened between August 2000 and June 2001 increased by 36% compared with July 2000, and the monthly average of securities accounts opened increased by 248% over the same period. Currently, over 50% of the bank's securities transactions by count have been migrated to the Internet.

The monthly average of new investment fund accounts grew by 276% from December 2000 to June 2001, compared with November 2000. A customer satisfaction survey in January 2001 recorded high overall satisfaction of 96% with e-Banking services.

The bank continues to expand its e-Banking services as part of its efforts to become more customer-focused. Plans are afoot for the redesign of its website and the launch of business Internet banking. "No matter how our business develops, we will ensure that the Hang Seng brand will always stand for extraordinary service that satisfies changing consumer needs," Cheung said.

The Internet and CRM are fast becoming ways by which brand managers can acquire and retain customers, but they have to give those customers rich experiences if they are to be successful. What is more, they have to be backed up by a strong organizational culture that supports all brand initiatives. The next chapter looks at how to build a strong brand culture that will motivate employees and delight customers.

8

"Long Live the Brand!": Creating a Brand Culture

MOMENTS OF TRUTH

Moments of truth determine success or failure, weakness or strength, loyalty or desertion, resolve or retreat. Moments of truth aren't defined by companies or brands, but by everyday people who experience things that make an impact on their lives. Some worldwide defining moments are chronicled in history, such as the attack on the United States on September 11, 2001, when the World Trade Center and Pentagon buildings were the targets of terrorists. Others go relatively unnoticed. The world of politics and its fundamental pursuit of perception management is little different in theory or practice from the world of branding—both seek to influence public opinion, reputation, and loyalty. And both worlds subscribe to the Darwinian dogma of survival of the fittest.

The really smart companies in the world of branding accept the fact that powerful brands are the only route to survival and differentiation. They occasionally have massive worldwide defining moments of truth in the form of a major crisis, such as those described in Chapter 6, but they also recognize that they face moments of truth every day in terms of the brand–consumer relationship. As brands exist only in the consumer's mind, then every contact with consumers can potentially be a moment of truth. This philosophy is similar to that described by the former chief executive officer of Scandinavian Airline System (SAS), Jan Carlsson, who simply and effectively told his entire workforce that with 12 million customers a year and an average contact rate per customer of five SAS people on a single journey, this translated into 60 million moments of truth—60 million moments to get the brand experience right or wrong. His message was that all touchpoints with all consumers count, and that companies have to look meticulously at how they can manage these. That's brand management thinking.

"If only it was that easy!"

Many people with responsibility for company and brand image might respond, "If only it was that easy!" If we study Carlsson's strategy, we can see that it wasn't just rhetoric—he changed structure, systems, and technology, along with many other things, and, importantly, he empowered front-line staff to take decisions that impacted immediately on the consumer's brand experience. He succeeded in bringing the SAS brand to life by motivating and empowering employees so that they recognized their contribution to the value of the brand and the business. In short, he created a massive organizational change project based around the brand–customer relationship, involving every function in the company—no easy task.

The big challenge for CEOs such as Carlsson, and brand managers in charge of major corporate and/or product brands, is to bring the brand(s) to life through strategy and change, and to motivate people to deliver on the brand promise. This is particularly important for those people involved in any business that uses a corporate- or house-endorsed branding approach. This chapter examines how this can be achieved through careful management of the brand management wheel, shown in Figure 8.1.

The wheel is important, as it shows how every aspect of the consumer experience, every touchpoint, must be carefully managed. Few companies do this well. For most, the reason for lax brand management here is the absence of a brand strategy to drive out from the center to the spokes of the wheel. If a company has a clear brand strategy, then it is much easier to manage the outer areas. The inner part of the wheel, labeled "Brand strategy" in the figure, gives everyone in the organization a guide as to how the execution of the brand should be carried out in each area of responsibility.

Figure 8.1: The brand management wheel

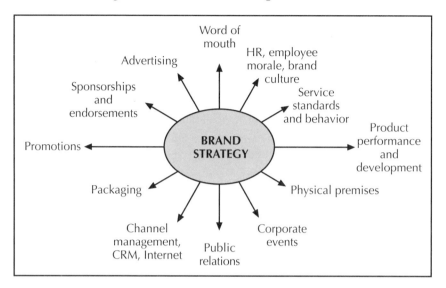

Without a clear brand personality and positioning, there is little hope for brand consistency, as there is no guide for practitioners who manage these different areas, and the tendency is to use the spokes in an ad hoc way. The result of this is usually a confused, mixed, and relatively poor brand image, and those responsible for brand image come under fire because they are receiving ratings that are perceived as detrimental.

The absence of a clearly defined brand strategy also means that agencies commissioned by the company have little idea of what the brand stands for, what the brand platform is, and what the key messages should be to address the different target audiences. In the case of one of my clients, I was called in to find out why the advertising agency wasn't portraying the brand messages in a way that met the client's expectations. When I asked the client if the agency had been given a proper brand brief, the answer was "yes." But when I asked to see the brief, the client said it had been verbal, not written. The client hadn't clearly defined its brand positioning or personality for the agency, and so interpretations of the brief by the advertising creative team were far removed from the client's expectations. This accounted for the history of continuous misunderstanding with respect to what was required of the agency and what the client actually got.

Here are some brief descriptions of what the "spokes" of the wheel mean for brand managers.

Advertising

It is difficult not to use advertising in some form, but companies often get lured into tactical advertising as opposed to image advertising. What is needed is a combination of both—tactical to deal with changing competitor moves and brand features, attributes, and innovations, and image to build the consistent brand message.

Sponsorships and endorsements

It is very important that all sponsored activities related to the brand, every co-branding opportunity, and every endorsement made by external parties and individuals are appropriate to the character of the brand. For instance, Marlboro has a brand character based around strength and independence; it therefore wouldn't sponsor synchronized swimming, but it does sponsor Formula 1 racing.

Promotions

Use promotions sparingly so as not to dilute the image of your brand. Continuous "special offers" and other promotions can make the brand appear cheap. If they are co-branded promotions, again ensure that they are relevant to your customer base and appropriate in terms of brand fit.

Channel management, CRM, and the Internet

I have said a lot about CRM and the Internet in Chapter 7, but with regards to channels of distribution, beware when putting your brand in the hands of other parties. Ensure that they represent your brand properly, and focus on fighting other brands in the market as opposed to fighting other distributors on price who are also offering your brand. Poor representation by channels has led companies such as Gucci to buy back all their franchises.

Public relations

This has been thoroughly discussed in Chapter 6, but public relations is a good source of brand building. Use the various means at the disposal of PR to take every opportunity to get your brand name out in the market, and be quick to respond if crises occur.

Corporate events

Any corporate events held by your company or outsourced for execution by event management companies are high in profile. Meticulous management of these, so as to maintain the right image, is imperative.

Physical premises

Even your buildings and offices represent your brand, so ensure that they are also appropriate and kept in line with your desired consumer perceptions.

Product performance and development

You cannot build a strong brand without top-class quality. These days, innovation is a basic requirement, not a luxury. Make sure that you achieve both.

Service standards and behavior

Service quality is one of the most difficult elements of brand management to get right, but also one of the most essential. If it is poor, it can damage the brand forever. Continuous attention to all aspects of customer service is essential—regard it as a never-ending process and not just a one-off training course.

HR, employee morale, and brand culture

As discussed in this chapter, the whole brand has to be brought to life. The culture and morale of the organization have to be good if people are to go the extra mile to support your brand initiatives. All aspects of human resource development and management must become involved.

Word of mouth

One of the most powerful ways of building brands is through word of mouth from happy customers. Yahoo! built its brand this way, not advertising at all in the early years. Customer advocacy can only come from a consistently great brand experience, and so we come full circle. Do all the other things right, and word of mouth will become your biggest brand-building weapon.

Great brands are built on consistency, and this necessitates consistent and appropriate behavior in all areas of operation. But consistency depends on a clearly defined brand strategy. This is where the skills and influence of brand managers need to be at their peak. My suggestion is that you take a really hard, analytical look at the "spokes" of the brand management wheel, and ask yourself and your colleagues:

- Is our brand vision and platform clearly articulated in written statements?
- What is currently happening in each area to manage the brand consistently?
- What needs to be done to improve on management of the brand in each area?

Every "spoke" of the wheel is vitally important, although some of them might be more relevant to your brand than others. An action plan should be developed incorporating the improvements, and this should be reviewed frequently at meetings of those people responsible for managing and guarding the brand.

What all of the above really boils down to is the need for companies to build a strong brand culture. Here are some practical ideas as to how that might be achieved.

LIVING THE BRAND: DEVELOPING A STRONG CORPORATE BRAND BEHAVIOR AND CULTURE

Companies are judged by their behavior. Everything they say and do affects their image and reputation. In order to build a powerful corporate brand with a corresponding image, the behavior of the company has to be controlled and shaped in such a fashion that people's perceptions of it are always favorable. This also makes for good customer relationships;

corporate behavior perceived in a negative way will give rise to poor relationships. One of the roles of brand guardianship is to manage corporate behavior, and this role is both vital and wide-ranging.

The ideas presented in the brand wheel must be applied to products, services, and companies. However, to develop a powerful corporate brand image, where the company is the center of attention and customers interact frequently with the company's representatives, a whole brand culture has to be built around the brand personality/values.

Corporate image, branding, and culture

Corporate culture is a much-discussed topic these days, as companies try to accommodate modern work practices and change management styles. Many sophisticated training and organization development initiatives are implemented by internal and external specialists to suit current corporate cultures, and to help promote efficiency and effectiveness for the future. Corporate culture, in its crudest form, is described as "the way we do things around here." Essentially, it is the sum of a complex blend of employee attitudes, beliefs, values, rituals, and behaviors that permeate a company and give it a unique style and feel.

Corporate culture can have a profound effect on both staff and customers. For staff, it can provide an invigorating, stimulating, and exciting place to work, or it can make going to work a dismal daily experience. It can empower people or enslave them. Because culture is ubiquitous, it inevitably has an impact not just inside, but also outside the organization. Customers who come into contact with staff can feel it through the morale, attitudes, and expressions of the staff, and see it in the staff's comments and service standards. Corporate culture impacts considerably on corporate image, and thus has to be controlled.

When a company tries to develop and maintain a good brand image, it has to create a suitable culture. If the company is creating and maintaining a corporate brand, a service brand, or whatever, then the culture has to be appropriate to the essence of the brand. Branding is a very positive and well-received way of changing the culture of an organization, for reasons that will soon be discussed.

Companies wanting to build a new corporate culture or change the existing one often do so by establishing some corporate values as a behavioral guide for people to follow. The most attractive (and often most successful) way to build a brand is to create a personality for the brand—a personality that summarizes what the brand really stands for. If a brand platform is built through developing certain personality characteristics or traits, then it is easier for consumers to connect with it, and become attracted to it. And once the personality characteristics have been chosen as the building blocks of the brand, then the culture of the company can, and must, follow that same identity.

Corporate versus brand values

Most companies that decide to commit to building a brand already have some corporate values defined in the organization, although staff may or may not be well versed in them. A word of caution here: too many values may cause confusion among staff. There is a consequent need to explain the difference between corporate and brand values to every employee, and this is usually accomplished through a combination of brand literature and training.

One way to explain the difference is to use the analogy of a building. In the construction of any building, a strong foundation is critical. Without a strong foundation any building is likely to collapse. In a corporate sense, the corporate values are the foundation of the building; they define the ways in which the organization members will work together. They are typified by values and beliefs such as teamwork, commitment to quality, integrity, and customer-orientation. But once the foundation based on such values is built, then the focus switches to the style and appearance of the building. In corporate terms, this is how the company wants to be seen by the outside world. It is the brand values—usually worded by way of personality characteristics—that represent this external face, or style, of the building, and hopefully will influence profoundly the perceptions of people outside the company.

If the company already has a set of corporate values at the time it embarks on a branding exercise, then decisions will have to be made as to whether to keep the existing corporate values, replace them with the new brand personality, or to use both. If the corporate values are somewhat similar to the brand values, then the corporate values can be maintained, and the personality used to reinforce and add more strength to the practice of these values. For example, if the company has reliability as a corporate value, then the personality characteristic of dependability would translate into roughly the same message. On the other hand, if the corporate values are far removed from the brand personality, there is a choice of discarding some or all of the old values and starting to inculcate a completely new culture based on the new core values of the brand. The company may want to retain some of the old values that are still regarded as important to its future (for instance, quality), and there is no harm in doing so as long as the value doesn't conflict with any brand personality characteristics. Indeed, some companies have a mixture of conventional values and personality characteristics. What does matter, though, is that the people in the company are not confused if two sets of values exist.

As every brand change agent knows, with the dissemination of corporate values, brand values must also be defined and explained at every level of the organization. This involves helping business units to apply the brand values strategically to everything they do by integrating the brand into business planning. It also involves integration of the brand into all the jobs of employees. These activities are now discussed in more detail.

Develop brand strategy plans for all business units

I have found it useful for business units, divisions, and departments within companies to produce plans for the short and medium term with respect to how they are going to deliver on the brand values. It is critical to include support services in this activity, as unless they also change the way in which they do things, those departments impacting directly on consumers will find it difficult to implement their plans. For example, in a telecommunications company it is difficult for a marketing or sales business unit to improve performance on the value of "friendliness" if customers receive separate bills for fixed line, mobile, Internet services, and so on. Customer-friendly billing would give them just one bill covering all transactions. So, it is often necessary to change systems and procedures in order to provide a total impact on, and change in, consumer perceptions.

With this in mind, all divisions or departments—such as information technology, finance, research and development, human resources, production, credit control, logistics, marketing, corporate communications, and others—have to develop strategic and tactical plans to demonstrate to top management how they intend to implement each brand value. These plans shouldn't contain vague statements of intent, but be concrete action plans detailing timing and accomplishment criteria.

Brand strategy workshops are the best way of helping departments articulate these plans. Once managers get used to developing such plans, the establishment of the brand is easier to achieve and control, and departments will find it easier to define people's jobs more clearly in terms of the brand.

As an example of brand strategy execution, let's take "innovation" as a key brand value or personality characteristic. Many firms have this as a brand value, but execute it in different ways to ensure that products and services are truly innovative. Gillette does so via its policy of insisting that over 40% of annual sales come from products introduced in the last five years; 3M has a ratio of 25% to help implement the same value. Kao, the Japanese personal-care-product company, concentrates heavily on innovation, and approximately 2,000 of its 7,000 employees are dedicated to research and development—around three times that of the giant Procter & Gamble. Kao's aim is to become a global player, but states it can only achieve this through producing a constant stream of new products to aggressively seize international opportunities.

Disney Corporation created a section called "Imagineering" devoted to developing innovations for its six divisions—a think-tank employing over 2,000 people. Within this section are highly paid scientists with expertise in fields such as flight simulation, artificial intelligence, cognitive psychology, neuro-anatomy, mathematics, neural networks, and other disciplines. Their task is to create the future where, for example, there will be virtual theme parks, or where children's wishes for a toy can be conjured up on the company's website. This is an example of a company living its mission of making people happy.

The message, then, is that every brand value or corporate personality characteristic has to be very carefully defined, not just at the corporate level but also at departmental and job-specific levels. The brand has to live in every strategic way possible. Beyond this, the brand also has to be brought to life by every employee in the organization. Case Study 24, on the Virgin Group, illustrates how one of the brand values is brought to life in one of its businesses.

Case Study 24

THE VIRGIN GROUP
Let's have some fun!

Inspired by the freedom of the 1960s, Sir Richard Branson has developed his brand consistently over the last 30 years. This is a prime example of how the founder of a company can create a brand in his own image, and whose charismatic style has influenced his various businesses and encouraged their people to "live the brand!"

The extent of the Branson empire is an interesting example of brand stretch from a corporate brand viewpoint, which I mentioned in Chapter 5 as being easier to extend than product brands. From the not-so-humble beginnings of Virgin Records, the Virgin brand has now extended into many different enterprises and industries, such as cola, bridal-wear, cosmetics, rail travel, financial services, mobile telecommunications, Internet-related businesses, wines, and air travel.

Although not highly successful in all its business initiatives, the Virgin brand has largely been able to accomplish this amount of brand extension through single-minded commitment to its values, which are:

- the best quality;
- innovative;
- good value for money;
- a challenge to existing alternatives; and
- a sense of fun and cheekiness.

To get a sense of what this means commercially, consider that although Virgin management is inundated with requests for joint ventures and 90% of the projects it considers are profitable, none get the green light until they satisfy at least four out of these five values. The Virgin values don't in themselves constitute what I would call a "brand personality," but Branson himself adds that dimension, so that personality is his, particularly with the "sense of fun and cheekiness" and the "challenge to existing alternatives"—the underdog role he plays so well. Quality, value for money, and innovation are now regarded as "must haves" and no longer as differentiators. Companies such as Virgin do incorporate these values, however, to remind themselves of what the brand stands for and what they believe in.

We can see the values applied meticulously to all consumer touchpoints, as in the case of the value "sense of fun and cheekiness," examples of which are given below in regards to Virgin Atlantic and other brands in the stable.

Brand value: Sense of fun and cheekiness

Product: The airline has been the first to introduce product innovations such as personal massage, live rock bands, and casino opportunities for fliers. Even the top-price seats are cheekily called "Upper Class."

Service: In-flight staff are friendly, happy and fun-loving, enjoy jokes with customers, give out hats to wear, and so on; all done to create a fun atmosphere. They also go the "extra mile." Once while traveling with the airline I tore my trousers getting up from my seat. There was a great deal of hilarity from other travelers and cabin crew, but one flight attendant sat me "trouser-less" in the galley while she personally sewed up the embarrassment!

Website: When I accessed the Virgin Atlantic website, a plane in Virgin colors appeared and went across the screen, and a little hand waved at me through a window. Another element of fun was the reference to the "Cyber Espionage Centre" which invites visitors to "report back" on their findings.

Public relations: Every opportunity is seized by Branson to put across this brand value of fun. When he was about to climb into his hot air balloon in the attempt to break a world record that nearly got him killed, one astute reporter evidently noticed a British Airways (BA) seat in the balloon, and asked why a Virgin Atlantic seat hadn't been used instead. Apparently, Branson quipped that there was less chance of him falling asleep in a BA seat.

Events: At the announcement of the signing of the deal between Virgin and Singapore Telecom—a joint venture to form Virgin Mobile—the journalists and other media representatives were treated to a lion dance, the traditional way of celebrating in Chinese culture. After a few minutes the dance stopped, the lion removed its head, and there was Branson. He had taken the trouble to learn lion dancing, and to provide the unexpected and a sense of fun. At the press conference later, a more serious Branson told the audience that Virgin and Singapore Telecom were not forming a company, but were creating a brand together. Dressing in drag as a bride was another experience created by Branson when launching the Virgin bridal-wear brand, and running naked out of the sea was another. When finalizing the deal with Singapore Airlines (SIA), the final figures were discussed, and Branson eventually passed across a note to the CEO of SIA, which read something like: "I agree to the figures, but who's paying for lunch?" This is an example of the "fun" value extending into the most serious of discussions. By the way, SIA apparently paid for the lunch.

Brands that live their values attract not just customers, but partners too.

What will happen when Branson goes?

This is the big issue with brands based around their founders. Of course, we hope he stays around. But retirement comes to everyone, and it will be interesting to see if, as with Walt Disney, the legacy and the brand values will continue to be brought to life, so enhancing the consumers' brand experience and carrying the company to further successes.

Define brand values for every employee

It isn't good enough simply to select brand personality characteristics and inform everyone that they now exist. These personality characteristics must be closely defined at two distinct levels.

First, they have to be defined generically at a corporate-wide level, so that employees can see how they fit into the goals of the organization, and understand each characteristic or value. If we continue with the "innovative" brand value example, this could be broken down into the three key behaviors of "creative," "resourceful," and "proactive." It is important that all employees are informed of the brand values and the reasons for bringing the brand to life, and why the behaviors included in the definitions are so important to the branding process. This step alone calls for a substantial awareness and briefing effort on behalf of the company, and may take the form of many short training programs or a significant brand launch event.

Secondly, and importantly, the personality characteristics must be defined at a job-specific level. For a company to brand itself properly, everything it does must reflect the brand personality characteristics— this is the way forward to meeting the moments of truth successfully. This means that every employee, from the CEO downward, must attempt to live that personality in the job that he or she does. The reason for this is simple: an employee may understand the new brand personality and the general descriptions attached to it, but what they really want to know is what it means for their particular job. If they don't know how to apply the brand values, then they are likely to treat the whole exercise in a superficial way, and if this happens the customer is unlikely to feel much impact. This means that brand management has to ensure that staff are not only aware of the corporate personality characteristics and know what each characteristic means, but also that they know how to apply these values to their particular jobs. Brand managers have no choice but to work closely with the human resource function to make this happen, as the biggest obstacle to realizing brand potential is a lack of clarity about the brand, what it stands for, and what it means to the individual.

There are no short cuts

In the case of a characteristic such as "caring," the company would need to explain through training what this brand value means to a customer-service assistant, a receptionist, an IT manager, a production supervisor, and so on. There is no short cut to brand building, and the more time and effort that is taken, the more successful the brand will be. If one of the brand characteristics is "innovation," the company has to be prepared to tell a van driver, a salesperson, an accounts clerk, a human resource executive, and every other individual in the company, what that characteristic means for them in carrying out their jobs. Only then will they know what specific behaviors, attitudes, and relationships they should adopt in order to make that personality come alive. Some companies such as DuPont put all employees through training to help the brand values come to life. This company has a value of innovation, for example, and has put 26,000 people through innovation training programs, in the belief that everyone can come up with good ideas. Disney has four brand values and has trained 32,000 people in them, from cleaners to the CEO. Every Disney employee gets a two-day values training program on entering the company. Each value is then defined and taught for every job, so that every person knows how to apply the values to their jobs.

The training of staff in the job-specific implications of the brand is no easy task and has huge implications for human resource management, development, and training. But it isn't optional. It is vital to a company's performance and the achievement of brand consistency that everyone gets involved. There must be no short cuts. For companies that pursue this course of action, the rewards can be spectacular. Don't worry about acceptance of personality-based values by staff. In my experience, staff take to them very easily, and can understand why these values will differentiate their company from all the rest. Every employee can see a sense of purpose with a brand personality that they may not see with other training and project initiatives. This is because they are used to dealing with personalities, and have a tendency to judge companies they come into contact with (brands) in personality terms.

Develop extensive training for brand values

Training is an integral part of achieving good performance on brand values. Briefing staff on the company's brand strategy, and identifying how staff can apply the values to their jobs, is, of course, important. But, however well defined the brand values are, staff may need to learn new skills in order to perform well. It is important to look at each value and decide what these skills are. A fruitful way to do this is by analyzing the behavior of employees who have been identified to be performing to a very high standard on one value. Look at critical incidents that have happened to the staff member when they had to bring that value into action; find out what they did and how they did it. Also, interview people who knew about the incident. This research can be very revealing, not just in identifying the skills associated with particular values, but also in terms of what the organizational implications are for helping staff bring that value to life. As an example, the following are the results of a series of interviews with the employees of an Asian bank on the value of "caring."

Personal skills required	*Organizational implications*
Showing empathy	Encourage openness, honesty
Emotional resilience	Improve coaching, counseling
Suspending judgment	Train more in interpersonal skills
Listening	Develop teamwork
Giving positive and negative feedback	
Self-discipline	
Openness and honesty	
Combining formality and informality	

In this example, it was found that it wasn't easy to really care about others (including staff, subordinates, customers, suppliers, and others). It is an attitudinal-related skill, which goes much deeper than just being friendly, and can be extremely stressful. An intensive coaching and training effort is required if all employees are going to live the value of "caring" and bring the brand personality to life. Yet, it is absolutely critical to the corporate vision, mission, brand strategy, and credibility. There are no short cuts to building a strong brand. Some companies go to extreme lengths to ensure that their employees understand and apply the brand values. Intel is one such example (see Case Study 25).

Case Study 25

INTEL CORPORATION
Training for maximum brand performance

In the 1990s Intel made serious inroads into the definition and inculcation of its values for employees. For each of Intel's six brand values, the company defined clearly the behaviors associated with it, how performance on that value could be judged, and then complete training was given. One of Intel's values was "risk taking." The following summarizes what happened in the process of Intel's helping its people to apply that value.

Apart from linking all values by internal communications to the mission, objectives, and strategy of the company, everyone, level by level, was exposed to a one-week training program, where senior managers gave talks linking the values to Intel's success. They also stressed the importance of people becoming role models on the values.

"Risk taking" was found to be a difficult value for people to understand and apply. Employees found themselves being punished for taking risks that failed, despite the good intentions of their managers. Problems also occurred in the practical application of some other values. As a result, an Intel Values Task Force was formed, which identified five key behaviors for each value. For "risk taking," these were:

- embrace change;
- challenge the status quo;
- listen to all ideas and viewpoints;
- encourage and reward informed risk taking; and
- learn from our successes and mistakes.

Intel found that people still needed more questions answered, such as "How can I take a risk when it might be detrimental to quality?" Intel went further than most companies do by providing people with the necessary tools to help them through the process. For example, there was a self-assessment survey that evolved into a 360-degree core management survey used around the world. Under each key behavior for each value, employees had to rate themselves and have others rate them. For instance, for the key risk-taking behavior of "encourage and reward informed risk taking," ratings had to be given on how often each person acted in the following way:

- Fail to clearly define expectations and limits.
- Reward only successful activities.
- Communicate that failure isn't tolerated.
- Provide insufficient time for implementation.
- Criticize employees for pre-approved risks that fail.
- Insist on clear ownership and accountability.

The use of role models and training kits

Intel searched for role models—people who demonstrated success in the values. Their behaviors and skills were analyzed in a similar fashion to that done in the bank above. Risk taking was the top priority for Intel and was the first value to have its own training kit featuring 10 items that included team and individual exercises, written and video interviews with the role models, advice on specific issues of concern, and a list of further resources to use.

Values "owners"

Intel appointed an "owner" of the role-model strategy, and "owners" of a value or value process had to prove they could implement it and recruit others who wanted to be co-owners. Laurie Price was the owner—or values champion—and she produced courses for employees that were based around the following two questions:

- Do you know what the values mean?
- How does your behavior match them?

Pre- and post-testing of results was used, and results showed not just greater awareness of the values, but significant improvements in performance. Eventually the whole program was offered to all employees via Intel University.

The Role Model Advocate Award

All nominations for this annual award are accepted, but the selection process is rigorous, with only three or four awards a year being given out. Winners not only have to demonstrate that they are role models for all values, but also must be outspoken advocates of them.

Intel itself is a role model. It serves to remind us that there are no short cuts in getting people to "live the brand"—it requires well-planned hard work. Every company must make every effort to help its employees create a brand culture by whatever means. It must also be prepared to assess what constitutes good and bad performance on the brand values. The diagnosis of what makes a good or bad performer on brand values isn't easy, but it can be done.

Reward and recognize "brand performers"

Whenever a company introduces a new process, it must remember that, however loyal and enthusiastic its employees are, they want to know what is in it for them. The universal truth is that employees always perform better if they gain some kind of recognition and reward for changing their work practices. The acceptance of personality characteristics into corporate culture is usually supportive, but to increase the speed of the process it is a good idea to think of ways by which employees can gain recognition and rewards.

Rewards

It is not unusual now for companies to allocate a certain percentage of the employees' remuneration packages for values performance. General Electric, for example, links 50% of its annual review to this. Performance on values for Toro accounts for 25% of incentive compensation, with Levi Strauss tying in one-third. With Levi's, poor performance on brand values is a career killer, involving the loss of promotions and increments. The actual financial amount varies with these companies, but it is never treated lightly. To do so would dilute the importance of values recognition. Putting brand values into performance management and appraisal schemes ensures that the values are translated into corporate behavior, so that the consumer sees and experiences consistency. This influences perceptions and has a major impact on the brand image of the company. Further, it increases profitability. Harvard Business School research reveals that companies implementing "performance-enhancing cultures" achieve profit growth of several hundred percent more than those that don't.

Recognition

It is not only financial rewards that can motivate employees to perform well on brand values. Here is a list of ideas that have been tried in client companies I have been involved with, and that have worked well:

- *Role models*—seek out people who perform outstandingly well on all values, and those who perform outstandingly on one or more but not all values.
- CEO *awards*.
- *Competition awards*—for teams, departments, business units, and so on.

- *Newsletter and magazine recognition*—give people exposure to everyone in your company and companies you deal with.
- *Customer recognition awards*—highlight people in your company that have helped give customers outstanding brand experiences, and have made customer delight happen.
- *Peer group awards*—poll peers at different hierarchy levels to nominate and choose best of class related to brand values.
- *Outstanding team awards*—for innovative contributions to the development and practice of brand values.
- *Brand ambassadors*—select people who are really committed to the brand and enjoy the respect of others in the organization; allow them opportunities to talk about the brand, their thoughts on best practice, and success stories. Wherever possible, choose senior managers in every market the company operates in, and let them make recommendations to top management for improving brand execution.

The company has an obligation to help people understand the brand and bring it to life. In addition to the strategy facilitation and training described so far, corporate literature can help in the creation of a brand culture.

Brand manuals and corporate identity manuals

Some companies have manuals to establish clearly what can and cannot be done with the company's brands. These are usually written with reference to the visual aspects of the brand, and are usually referred to as corporate identity manuals. The more difficult decisions are those that cannot be prescribed in advance, such as whether a television commercial reflects the brand personality and positioning properly. Often, the danger here lies in delegating this task to a level that is too junior. With high visibility, such decisions must be taken at the top. However, for day-to-day brand management, and as a reference for advertising, promotion, and other agencies, corporate identity manuals are essential.

Brand manuals are for all employees

Brand manuals are for all employees, and their purpose is to explain what the brand means to everyone. They are often distributed either at a brand launch initiative, or at brand-related training events, where employees are given the opportunity to ask the questions, "What does the brand mean to my job?" and "How can I incorporate the brand values into my everyday work?"

Brand manuals typically include:

- a message from the CEO about the central importance of brand to the business future;
- a section on what a brand is;
- examples of powerful brands and the benefits they bring to companies and employees;
- an explanation of the brand values chosen by their company;
- examples of how they can bring the brand to life in their work; and
- questions for people to answer as to what actions they are going to take to "live the brand."

I have found that brand manuals that invite employee interaction, by including quizzes and other activities, are more effective than purely descriptive text. If brightly colored and creatively designed, they also tend to be referred to more often by everyone, and to stay in sight and in mind. I have also found that training at departmental/section levels, to ensure that every employee knows what each brand value means to their job, best supports brand manuals, as there are many questions people have about how they can implement the company's values in their everyday work.

A SPECIAL NOTE ON CUSTOMER SERVICE

The role of customer service in brand delivery is absolutely critical, whatever business you are working in. Customer service is all about staff attitude and values performance, as opposed to public behavior and "customer first" scripts. Customer service training should therefore not rely on generic interpersonal skills courses, but on dedicated values performance courses. The brand values should be layered on top of the generic behavioral skills. Companies such as Singapore Telecommunications, for example, are training their service staff not just in how to deal with customers, but in how to enhance the perception of trust through the use of special words, phrases, and body language.

Also essential for outstanding customer service is the empowerment of employees to deal with problems. It is no good training people to understand and graciously appreciate customer problems, when they then have to refer the problems upwards to various levels. Many companies are now allowing front-line service people to take direct action to solve problems on the spot, and in some cases, are defining amounts of money a member of staff can spend to get problems fixed.

Nor is customer service confined to front-line interpersonal action. Many other things that form part of the "value" package in consumers' minds are a part of the service issue, including:

- warranties;
- speed of breakdown visits;
- staff dress and personal presentation;
- tone of voice and verbal style;
- written response times and style in letters and emails;
- product and service knowledge;
- retail layout and window presentation;
- telephone response (without pressing several buttons and ending up precisely nowhere); and
- call center practices.

All factors affecting the brand–customer service experience should be benchmarked against best practice.

The Technical Assistance Research Programs Institute in Washington D.C. has published some alarming statistics that show just how significant customer service problems are:

- Complaints about service have increased 400% since 1983.

- Ninety-six percent of customers with problems will never tell you they have a problem. They simply take their business elsewhere.

- For every customer with a problem a company knows about, there are 26 others that it doesn't know about.

- The average customer with a problem talks to nine or 10 other people about it.

- Thirteen percent of customers with problems will tell as many as 20 other people.

- For every customer with a problem, there are 250 people who have directly or indirectly heard negative comments about the supplier.

- One of the primary reasons customers switch loyalties is due to perceived neglect or indifference—68%, in fact!

Conversely, according to the Strategic Planning Institute in Cambridge, Massachusetts, companies noted for outstanding quality and service:

- charge, on average, 9% higher prices;
- grow twice as fast as the average company;
- experience yearly market share increases of 6%, while the average company loses 2% per year; and
- receive an average annual return of 12% (the average during the research period was 1–2%).

These statistics are no more than typical, so you need to both communicate and live out the brand values in words and actions! This is why AT&T Universal Card:

- collects and analyzes *daily* more than 100 measurements for customer delight;
- uses these to form the basis for company-wide and departmental indices;
- gives everyone a bonus for the day when global numbers exceed the target;

- gives the bonus on total company indices so that departments cooperate with each other; and

- carries out 5,000 customer calls per month for follow-up interviews.

Why do companies go to such great lengths to build cultures based on values and to ensure that customers are happy? Look at the results below and you will see.

REWARDS FOR CREATING A VALUES-BASED CULTURE

Research by Kotter and Heskett in their book *Corporate Culture and Performance* showed that "performance-enhancing cultures" such as those based on the principles I have illustrated above bring enormous bottom-line benefits to companies. Covering 200 companies in 20 countries over four years, the research revealed that companies with a strong culture based on shared values outperformed others by huge margins, as the following shows:

Average % growth with a performance-enhancing culture		*Average % growth without a performance-enhancing culture*
Revenue	682	166
Stock price	901	74
Profit	756	1

The message is simple: define your brand values carefully and reinforce them with consistency, repetition, and rewards.

Who is responsible for brand management?

The role of the CEO

Although CEOs cannot be solely responsible for brand management, they most certainly have to drive branding from the top and help create the conditions necessary for strong brand management to take place. Without forceful leadership at this level, brand managers find life very difficult, as they often don't have the power to influence the other functions upon which their success often rests, such as human resources. One of the best ways to ensure that the brand culture is built properly is for the CEO to be involved in the brand process by way of boards of management and other control committees. The Philips case study (Case Study 26) shows how a forward-looking CEO understands the need for a good brand guardianship and management structure, and its implementation.

Case Study 26

PHILIPS
Brand philosophy—making brand guardianship happen

Gerard Kleisterlee, president and CEO of Philips, has clearly stated his commitment to value creation through a strong Philips brand. He doesn't believe that building business value and brand value are different processes. He has also stated that the way to create value is to understand consumers better than the competition can, and that this skill is at the heart of the marketing function.

A big part of the current effort in building brand value at Philips has been in strengthening overall marketing competence right through the company. This is done structurally, as well as individually. Philips believes that the brand is important because it can deliver a potent promise with the power to make people choose its products, its jobs, and its stock in preference to those of other players on the market. In other words, the bottom line is that Philips believes that the brand, and what it stands for, has a profound impact on its consumers, its employees, and its shareholders.

The Philips brand values are summarized by the promise of "Let's make things better." This represents the company's ability to enhance people's quality of life with its wide range of products, as well as by the jobs it creates and the way it tries to become part of the societies in which it operates. In this way, Philips feels it clearly differentiates itself from other brands in the market.

Brand structure

The Brand Equity Board (BEB) has been set up as the highest marketing body within the company. This board has the task of clearly setting out the fundamental values of the company, and then creating the means for them to be applied consistently right across the company. The BEB's "agreed" definition of brand equity is "positive associations that drive the net present worth of a brand's sustainable or potential contribution to profits and market valuation."

Philips is now charting a course to fully leverage the power of the Philips brand and improve its equity. This started with the founding of the BEB and Global Brand Management (GBM) and has been invigorated with the recent announcement of management by brand as a corporate core process.

The key driver of this process is the president and CEO himself, who announced: "The Philips brand is a significant company asset and its proper care and development is critical for the company to achieve it goal. Its addition as a corporate core process represents the clear intent of the board of management to re-emphasize the brand and its values in the company's approach to the market and to its stakeholders."

The Brand Equity Board was founded in mid-1999 when Philips determined there was a need for a cross-divisional entity to help enhance Philips' brand equity and share best practice. Currently, there are 11 members, representing each consumer product division, regional organizations, and corporate staff functions. The president and CEO is the chairman of the BEB.

The purpose of the BEB is to ensure that brand management strategy and policies are developed in concert with the organization and, consequently, have the full support of, and full deployment into, the organization and the businesses of the company.

The mission of the BEB is "to build premium brand equity for Philips." This will be accomplished by:

- developing the ways and means to create a balanced, cohesive, and relevant face to the market, and a deeper and more significant relationship with the stakeholders;
- creating networks, forging specific processes, and fostering discipline and synergies to leverage the power of the brand across Philips; and
- building and strengthening the Philips company culture through a stronger customer and market orientation.

GBM supports the board of management in developing brand strategy and managing issues around the Philips Group's portfolio of brands. It develops and monitors global brand standards and guidelines, and challenges the businesses and the regions to set appropriate brand goals, contributing to raising the standard of marketing competence in the company.

GBM's mission is to: "Increase the value of the Philips brand by ensuring its development and protection, and encourage a stronger consumer/customer focus within the company."

GBM's objectives are:

1. **Brand strategy:** Through the creation of a brand platform, to set standards and goals for the development of the brand through corporate and product division initiatives.

2. **Setting global standards and targets:** GBM consults with the product divisions* and regions on developing appropriate marketing efforts to achieve brand objectives, advises the board of management when discrepancies exist, and develops plans to counteract them, if necessary.

3. **Competence building:** To build the company's overall marketing communications competence through training, sharing best practice, advising on key relevant personnel hires, and agency relationship management.

4. **Brand health reporting:** To hold quarterly brand health "barrel" reviews with the board of management. These are scheduled meetings between the brand and Philips business groups/core corporate functions, with the purpose of reviewing progress on core strategic competencies.

* There are six product divisions—three business-to-consumer and three business-to-business divisions, namely:
   • *Consumer:* Consumer electronics, domestic appliances and personal care, and lighting; and
   • *Business:* Semiconductors, components, and medical equipment.

Finally, many people ask me: "Who is responsible for brand management?" The answer is "Everyone," because everyone can make an impact on it. Every department and every employee can, and should, help manage and guard the brand. Acer, a company that is still in the process of establishing what its brand culture should be and how it should be delivered, is discussed in Case Study 27.

Case Study 27

ACER
Model of brand anatomy and management

Acer has developed what it calls a total brand management (TBM) system. The reason that this mechanism was introduced, said Acer's founder and chairman Stan Shih, was that "we had not effectively and consistently conveyed our image to the general public" and that "if you're not clear on the brand image you want to create, anything you do may conflict with that image and all effort is wasted."

Acer's brand anatomy

The first step in this was to develop the anatomy of the Acer brand, as shown in Figure 8.2.

Figure 8.2: Acer's brand anatomy

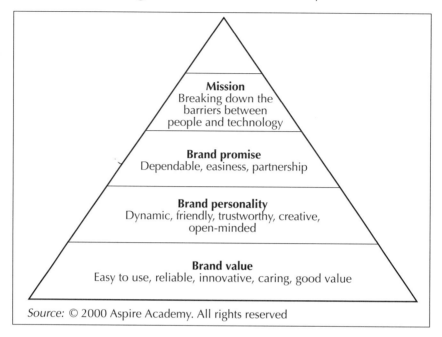

Mission
Breaking down the
barriers between
people and technology

Brand promise
Dependable, easiness, partnership

Brand personality
Dynamic, friendly, trustworthy, creative,
open-minded

Brand value
Easy to use, reliable, innovative, caring, good value

The mission for the Acer brand was defined as "breaking the barriers between people and technology." Acer has referred to this philosophy many times in the past in various ways (slogans, speeches, and so on), but it now became clearly defined. Following from this statement, Acer developed three brand promises relevant to the mission, but intended for the brand's three major segments or customer groups. For the OEM group, they promised to be a reliable partner; for corporations, the promise was to be a company that they could depend on; and for individual consumers, the brand promised "easiness" in terms of convenience and simplicity.

A brand personality was chosen carefully to focus on five characteristics that would support the brand mission and promises, namely:

- dynamic;
- friendly;
- trustworthy;

- extremely creative; and
- very open.

Finally, Acer asked the question, "What is the value of the Acer brand?" This meant: "What value are we adding to the lives of partners, consumers, and customers through our brand?" The answers were:

- ease of use;
- dependability;
- innovation;
- concern for users; and
- good value for money.

You can see clearly how each step supports the previous stage. After applying and managing the brand in this way, the results were mixed and, in the U.S. especially, brand awareness wasn't prominent, which led to the question, "What exactly does Acer stand for?" Acer had a slogan, "We hear you," but there was a feeling that the message wasn't clearly understood and universally consistent. The company set out to build a brand culture by answering the question that would bring the brand to life across all employees, channels, and customer groups. This is summarized in Figure 8.3.

Figure 8.3: What is "Acer-ness"?

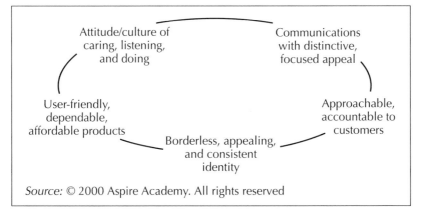

Attitude/culture of caring, listening, and doing

Communications with distinctive, focused appeal

User-friendly, dependable, affordable products

Approachable, accountable to customers

Borderless, appealing, and consistent identity

The full story of the Acer brand creation, development, and management is told in the book from which these diagrams and quotations are taken: Stan Shih, *Growing Global: A Corporate Vision Masterclass* (John Wiley & Sons, Singapore, 2002).

Stan Shih says that TBM was introduced and put on an equal footing with TQM (total quality management). "We stressed that just like product quality, brand management was everyone's responsibility. Beginning with me, every person in the company has to get involved in TBM." He goes on to say, "Without effective brand management, it is very difficult to establish brand value." His words are a fitting summary of the message contained in this book.

Until this point, the book has covered many topics concerned with generating and maintaining brand strength. The next chapter focuses on how brand managers might assess brand performance and strength.

9

Measuring Brand Success: Market Research and Brand Valuation

Continuously tracking the effectiveness of your brand against the competition is vital, especially at times when the stimuli that consumers are exposed to are constantly changing. I won't regurgitate here many of the well-known ways in which brand effectiveness can be measured, as most readers will be well aware of these. Instead, I will examine a few concepts that have more potential for use in effectively measuring brand success and for helping brand management to track brands differently and make better decisions about the future.

CONTINUOUS TRACKING OF BRAND PERFORMANCE

There are many items that can be tracked to help brand managers assess how their brands are doing in the marketplace, and what effect certain market interventions are having on brand equity. For instance, purchasing, consumption, brand, and advertising awareness can be tracked against advertising spend, pricing policy, product launches, and in-store promotions. Also, tracking by demographic segments can enable brand managers to assess whether marketing campaigns are influencing the target consumer groups. Some companies also track their brand values and personality characteristics against the competition, to see whether they are gaining or losing ground. There are many available research methodologies that cover such areas of interest, such as BrandVision™, which can measure important variables such as "share of mind," "share of heart," and "share of sales."

Brand managers normally use all of these things as an ongoing part of their work, but I would like to focus this discussion on how to track brand strength, which is of the utmost importance.

BRAND STRENGTH

The real purpose of measuring brand strength is to know whether our customers are likely to remain with us. For many companies, measuring and increasing brand strength is a key goal of marketing efforts worldwide. However most measures of brand strength only tell you how people acted in the past, and not which brands they are likely to choose in the future. Research that measures past or current behavior alone can only tell us where we are, but to be truly actionable, we need to know where we are going.

The Conversion Model™ is the world's leading measure of brand strength. It is a psychological analysis of commitment to brands, incorporating measures of how to increase commitment and exploit weaknesses in the competition. Its diagnostic analysis allows brand managers to focus communication strategies on the most relevant consumers. Developed in South Africa in the late 1980s, the Conversion Model™ is now licensed worldwide. It was originally developed to understand religious conversion, and was expanded into politics and then business with enormous success in a wide variety of brand types.

There are two sides to the model—the strength of commitment and the balance of disposition—and through these measurements the model provides a complete overview of a brand's position in the market.

Predictive psychological segmentation

The heart of the research is an immensely powerful psychological segmentation that can be used to assist many marketing decisions. Behavioral and/or attitudinal segmentation currently used by many marketers isn't enough, as these methods only tell you where you are. The Conversion Model™ is predictive: it tells you where your brand and your market are going. By providing a full understanding of brand equity, it can also predict swings in customer loyalty. Numerous validation studies have proved the power of this prediction. The model has:

- frequently identified shifts in the market before they actually took place;
- been rigorously validated through longitudinal studies in a variety of product categories and markets; and,
- in numerous studies, has correctly identified which products or brands stood to lose or gain market share.

Complete market segmentation

The research provides data that fall into the following segments:

- *The Entrenched*—highly committed to use our brand, and won't switch in the foreseeable future.
- *The Average*—committed to our brand, but not as strongly as the Entrenched.
- *The Shallow*—not content, but waiting for a better alternative.
- *The Convertible*—discontented and actively seeking alternative brands.
- *The Available*—actively considering conversion, and may switch immediately.
- *The Ambivalent*—attracted to our brand, but need motivation to switch to us.
- *The Unavailable*—not interested in switching in the foreseeable future.

In other words, the Conversion Model™ successfully segments your market, giving you the ultimate edge, because you know:

- who to target to increase sales; and
- which brands pose the greatest threat.

AMI's PinPoint™ within the Conversion Model™

Asia Market Intelligence (AMI) was founded in 1991, and now has over 900 full-time staff. In March 2000, AMI joined media communications specialist Aegis plc, making it part of a global research and marketing consultancy network. A unique AMI proprietary approach to the interpretation of the brand image data described above has been developed which provides actionable information on brand positioning and strategy:

- By understanding brand image relative to the competition and brand-differentiating consumer preferences:
  - Yours and competitor brand images.
  - What images drive brand preferences.
  - How consumer wants and needs are changing.

The analysis

AMI PinPoint™ analysis begins by grouping image attributes in terms of their relationship to the consumer. It then goes further to rank these image attributes in order of relative importance in driving consumer preference. The more important attributes can better discriminate the preferred brands from the non-preferred ones. It then standardizes the image data to identify the true strengths and weaknesses of each brand relative to its competitors. This removes the "familiarity bias" associated with both brands and image attributes. Standardized scores are calculated using prescribed formulas.

The second step in the research analyzes the true reasons for brand preference. Attribute importance measurement scores are calculated on a respondent-by-respondent basis, showing not only what is important to consumers but also the relative importance of these attributes.

The strategic output

There is a very clear visual output with this research model based on strategic matrices. For example, the matrix shown in Figure 9.1 is typical of one that a brand manager might get. The two axes of the matrix are the relative importance of the brand to the consumer and its relative performance compared to competitive brands. The output also provides several strategic recommendations based on what is important and where each brand's strengths lie. These may include enhancing a brand's performance or leveraging its strengths.

Figure 9.1: Strategic matrix interpretation

		RELATIVE PERFORMANCE		
		WEAK	AVERAGE	STRONG
RELATIVE IMPORTANCE	HIGH	THREATS (Remedy)	COMPETITIVE (Enhance)	CORE STRENGTHS (Maintain)
	MEDIUM	WEAKNESSES (Enhance)	LOWER PRIORITY	OPPORTUNITIES (Increase salience)
	LOW	LOWER PRIORITY	LOW PRIORITY	POTENTIAL OPPORTUNITIES (Increase salience)

Areas with no clear image position

Areas/ priorities for image correction

Reasons for current franchise and must be maintained

Increased salience of such existing strengths can significantly enhance positioning

Source: Asia Market Intelligence.

Four key areas for consideration

The output of the matrix can be condensed into four key areas for brand strategy:

1. **Competitive action (enhancement) strategy:** This is where the brand is only performing averagely on attributes falling in this area. The brand manager might consider strengthening perceptions in order to solidify what currently is a weak image.

2. **Removing threats (remedial) strategy:** Here is an area where attributes are considered by consumers to be important and where the brand isn't performing well. Remedial action must be taken immediately, since this is a serious brand image weakness.

3. **Core strengths (maintenance) strategy:** Attributes in this area of the matrix are important to consumers, and if the brand is currently

performing well on these, then the recommendation is to take action to maintain these strengths, because they are the real reasons why consumers prefer your brand.

4. **Opportunities (increase salience) strategy:** This section is where the brand is performing strongly on the attributes shown that fall into this quadrant, but relatively they are not important to consumers. The brand manager might be able to manage the perceptions of these attributes so that consumers see them as more important, and so increase brand strength through an improved positioning.

Brand management exercise

Figure 9.2 illustrates the use of the research in the beverage market. Have a look at the figure and decide what you would do with a brand that has this profile, taking into account the four key strategy areas indicated above.

Figure 9.2: AMI Pinpoint™ analysis—an example from the beverage market

		PERFORMANCE		
		Weak	**Average**	**Strong**
IMPORTANCE	**High**	*Growing*	*Attractive packaging* *brand* *Easy in pubs*	*Always fresh* *Buy best* *High quality* *Good tasting*
	Medium	*Promoted in bars* *Trendy*	*Modern* *Easy to drink* *Good advertising*	*International standards*
	Low	*Locally made* *Younger*	*Easy shop* *Good value* *Expensive* *Hear a lot about brand*	*Special occasions* *Strong*

Source: Asia Market Intelligence.

Case Study 28 shows how research data derived from the above model was used to leverage customer profitability and satisfaction.

Case Study 28

LLOYDS TSB
Tagging customers for increased profitability and satisfaction

Background

This case study is about the use of the above research methodologies to look at "committed" and "uncommitted" and "low value" and "high value" customers in the bank, and to resolve strategies for better customer relationship management, brand loyalty, and increased profitability. The bank was concerned about the leakage of business to competitor brands and decided to research this in order to discover the degree of "brand commitment" among its customer base.

The research

The bank had a monthly magazine that was sent out to high-value customers on a monthly basis. To ascertain the degree of "commitment" of these customers, a questionnaire was included that achieved a response rate of 10% from a base of 350,000 customers. What essentially was revealed through the data was that there were both "committed" and "uncommitted" customers. Of the "committed" customer group, the research showed that 20% were likely to take up new product offerings that would result in an increase of profitability of 9% over a six-month period. The research also revealed that there was a large "uncommitted" group of customers, and that although defections were expected to be limited, they would result in a decrease in profitability of 14% over the same time period.

Both sets of customer groups were analyzed using the Conversion Model™, and the database "tagged" with their level of commitment. A typical customer report would look like the one shown in Figure 9.3.

Figure 9.3: An example of what the report could look like

1. Customer name	1. John Doe Enterprises
2. Customer ID no. and branch code	2. 10001/123456
3. Length of time a customer	3. 6 years or more
4. Main business account is with	4. Retail bank but has secondary a/c at Bank B
5. Overall satisfaction score out of 10	5. 7
6. Does Bank B perform better than us?	6. Yes, 9 out of 10
Etc, etc.	
13. In what areas are we giving poor service (score out of 7)?	13. (3) Business manager doesn't stay in place for reasonable length of time
	(1) Business manager doesn't know and understand my business
	(1) A bank that doesn't make me feel valued as a customer
14. Overall level of commitment (1–4)	14. 4
15. Bank importance rating (1–10)	15. 10
16. Contact priority (1–40)	16. 40

Source: Asia Market Intelligence.

The action taken

For the "committed" group a program was launched in January 1998 called "The Personal Choice Program," with the aim of maintaining customer commitment and cross-selling product. The key features of this program were:

- Each customer was assigned a personal choice manager.
- Customized financial statements were provided.
- Customized money-management magazines were given.
- Tailored products and services were offered.

The results were increased customer profitability from:

- lower levels of attrition;
- higher sales levels; and
- improved balances.

For the "uncommitted" group a program was launched in September 1998 with the aim of eliminating service problems and responding better to individual needs, unofficially called "Attempted Seduction." Profitable "uncommitted" customers were identified, and a letter was sent to them that said, first, "We know that you're unhappy ..." and then assessed their:

- channel preference;
- interest in products and offers;
- life events tailored to financial needs; and
- open-ended opportunities to state their service problems.

The results were:

- a willingness to consider new products that rose from 24% to 66%; and
- a 5% increase in product holdings within six months.
(Source: Asia Market Intelligence).

Comment

As you have seen, using the right kind of research methodologies for the problems you face as a brand manager can result in a rapid and significant impact on the bottom line and lifetime value of customers. In this type of case, the matrix output from the research process adds value to brand management by suggesting strategic courses of action for different situations.

PERFORMANCE TRACKING USING BRAND VALUATION

Brand valuations are increasingly being used as a management tool. The strategic use of brand valuation techniques is becoming more prevalent in many blue-chip organizations, allowing senior management to compare the success of different brand strategies and the relative performance of particular marketing teams.

Background

In the late 1980s, many investment analysts and fund managers were still basing investment decisions on traditional measures of financial health, principally earnings per share, dividend yield, and balance sheet asset values. Such measures can fundamentally misstate corporate value.

The main impetus for an acknowledgment of the value of brands, and other intangible assets, came from the corporate raiders and asset strippers of the 1980s who targeted brand-rich companies and paid significantly more than their net asset value. This resulted in huge "goodwill" values that had to be accounted for. Alarm bells rang in the boardrooms of many underperforming branded goods companies as directors realized there was a clear need for a method of accounting for brands that would recognize their true value in the balance sheet and avoid arbitrary write-offs that damaged investor perceptions.

A realization that the full value of brand-owning companies was neither explicitly shown in the accounts nor always reflected in stock market values led to a reappraisal of the importance of intangible assets in general, and of brands in particular. This in turn raised the question of how such assets should be valued and disclosed. Although the accounting profession has only partially adapted to a world in which intangible assets are the main drivers of value, business leaders and investors have been quicker off the mark.

There is currently a global merger and acquisition boom in progress. Brands have played a significant role in this activity. In 2000, French Telecom paid around US$30 billion for a mobile phone brand that has only been in existence for six years. Within its home market, Orange boasts higher customer acquisition, retention, and usage rates than its rivals—all key factors of a successful brand. Orange has achieved that magic ingredient which positions it as a lifestyle brand. It has already been licensed into new geographies and is tipped to move into other product categories.

Instances such as this bring the value of specific brands into the public domain, but the bulk of intangible asset value remains "off balance sheet." A recent research study carried out by Brand Finance indicates that brands and other intangible assets now contribute the bulk of shareholder value in many sectors. This U.K.-based study reviewed the annual reports of 344 of the FTSE 350 companies with year-ends up to and including December 31, 1998.

It seems bizarre that 72% of the value of the companies surveyed wasn't reflected in published balance sheets. This percentage varies considerably by sector, highlighting the varied importance of intangible assets between sectors. Brands form a significant part of this "unexplained value." Other intangibles such as patents, customer lists, licenses, know how, and major contracts also play a role. Patents, for instance, are a major component of value in the pharmaceuticals sector.

Brands will be major drivers of corporate value in the 21st century. Investors and business leaders have recognized this. Marketers are increasingly using brand valuation models to facilitate marketing planning. They should go one step further. Investors need and want greater disclosure of brand values and marketing performance. Marketers should play a leading role in ensuring that such information is adequately communicated to investors, rather than waiting for statutory disclosure requirements to catch up with reality.

Recent developments

During the last five years, brand valuation has become a mainstream business tool used for the following purposes:

- merger and acquisition planning;
- tax planning;
- securitized borrowing;
- licensing and franchising;
- investor relations;
- brand portfolio reviews;
- marketing budget determination;
- resource allocation;
- strategic marketing planning; and
- internal communications.

A particular trend has been the increasing use of brand valuations as a tool to aid marketing management. The focus here is to increase the effectiveness of the marketing effort and aid brand management. A prime benefit in this regard is the fact that a brand valuation model is linked to the company's business model and provides a financial measure that is understood throughout the organization and by investors.

A well-constructed brand valuation pulls together market research, competitive data, and forecasts of future performance. This increases the understanding of the brand's value and its contribution to demand in each segment and identifies opportunities for leveraging the brand. A dynamic brand valuation model can be used for scenario planning purposes.

The ability to place a financial value on a brand within each key market segment isn't the only output of a valuation study:

- Research into the drivers of demand yields information that aids a range of decisions, including portfolio planning and product positioning. It can help define the focus of the advertising message.
- An identification of causal relationships within the business model facilitates an increase in advertising effectiveness.
- The competitive benchmarking study that forms part of an assessment of the risk attached to future earnings provides a gauge of the brand's strength, in relation to competitors, from segment to segment.

Some examples of internally focused brand valuations that Brand Finance has carried out during the last four years are discussed below.

The first example illustrates the use of a brand valuation to help resolve a specific issue. The impetus for the project had been the acquisition by a global financial services company of a number of new brands. This had resulted in a cluttered portfolio that required rationalization. The brand valuation was segmented by product and customer for all of the group's brands in the U.K., Europe, Australia, Hong Kong, and the U.S. The project formed the framework to inform brand rationalization and brand architecture decisions.

In the case of a retail bank, a brand evaluation project was carried out in order to assess the contribution of the brand in the corporate, as opposed to the consumer, market segment. The study was also segmented by major product groups. Consumer research was commissioned to quantify the drivers of demand. The study impacted on the allocation of marketing resources between market segments and was applied to measure the effectiveness of marketing investment.

A global insurance company provides an example of a valuation initially carried out for a specific purpose, but which has now been repeated. In this instance, brand valuation and competitor benchmarking techniques were combined to determine the optimal global advertising investment behind the client's corporate brand. The results were used by senior management to set corporate advertising levels. Periodic repetition of the exercise has been used by management to understand and monitor the effect of brand investment decisions on corporate brand value.

In the case of a listed food manufacturer, brand valuation was conducted in order to communicate the value of the company's main brand to analysts and investors. Management commissioned the study, as they believed the shares were undervalued and that the company was vulnerable to takeover.

A major tobacco company illustrates the use of a brand valuation model on an ongoing basis. The corporate marketing finance team commissioned the construction of a brand evaluation model to monitor the performance of key client and competitor brands in local markets and at a global level. The brand valuation has been placed on the company's intranet and is supported by a manual that clarifies what information is required to be inputted into the model and how the results can be used. The model is kept up to date by operating companies in 60 countries. The data produced by the model informs local decision making as well as group planning.

Brand economics

How do brands add value? In economic terms, the answer is simple: they impact on both the demand and supply curves.

On the demand side, brands enable a product to achieve a higher price at a given sales volume. Strong brands can also increase sales volumes and decrease churn rates. Price and volume impacts are, in some instances, achieved at the same time. An example, taken from *The Economist*, is of the GM Prizm and Toyoto Corolla in the U.S. These vehicles are virtually identical, coming off the same production line and having similar levels of distribution and service levels. However, the Corolla trades at an 8% premium and sells at over double the volume.

Brands also establish more stable demand, through their relationship with consumers, and this helps establish barriers to entry. The relationship with consumers is due to both functional and emotional attributes. On the functional side, brands ensure recognition and further aid the purchase decision through a guarantee of quality. From an emotional perspective, they satisfy aspirational and self-expression requirements. This is most evident in the luxury goods and fashion sectors.

A further benefit of branding that has increased in importance in recent years is the ability to transfer the equity or values associated with a brand into new product categories. In order for brand stretching to be effective, it is necessary that the core values of the brand are image-, rather than product-, based.

While there are numerous examples of successful brands that have achieved significant price premiums or higher volumes, the impact of branding on the supply curve is often ignored. Brands tend to shift the supply curve downward, for the following reasons:

- Greater trade and consumer recognition and loyalty, which results in lower sales conversion costs and more favorable supplier terms.
- Lower staff acquisition and retention costs.
- Lower cost of capital.
- Economics of scale achieved through higher volumes.

There is an increasing body of research supporting the fact that successful brands add corporate value. There are, of course, examples of successful brands that have fallen from grace and of branding initiatives that have failed. The challenge is to identify how your brand, or your client's brand, impacts on the business model, and to monitor whether strategies are successful in adding value to the brand.

Best practice in brand valuation

A number of methods can be used to value brands. Cost-based brand valuations are rarely used, as the cost of creating a brand tends to have little similarity to its current value. Market-based comparisons, on the other hand, are unsatisfactory as a primary method of valuing a brand, because of the scarcity of comparative data and the uniqueness of brands. However, where available, market comparisons are useful for testing primary valuations.

A more commonly used approach is the royalty relief method. This method is based on the assumption that if a brand has to be licensed from a third-party brand owner, a royalty rate on turnover will be charged for the privilege of using the brand. By owning the brand, such royalties are avoided. The royalty relief method involves estimating likely future sales and then applying an appropriate royalty rate to arrive at the income attributable to brand royalties in future years. The stream of notional brand royalty is discounted back to a net present value—the brand value.

Although the royalty relief method is technically sound, it provides little understanding of how and where the brand is creating value. It might therefore be an appropriate method of valuing a brand for balance sheet or tax purposes, but will be of limited use to a marketing director wishing to leverage the value of a brand.

The economic-use method integrates consumer research and competitive analysis with the brand's forecast earnings. As such, it provides a foundation for brand management in addition to determining the value of the brand by market segment. As this method is of most interest to marketers, and is the most widely used method of brand valuation, it is discussed here in more detail.

The Brand Finance methodology has been used by leading brand owners across the world and will be used to illustrate a marketing orientation valuation. A snapshot of this valuation framework is provided in Figure 9.4.

Figure 9.4: Brand Finance methodology

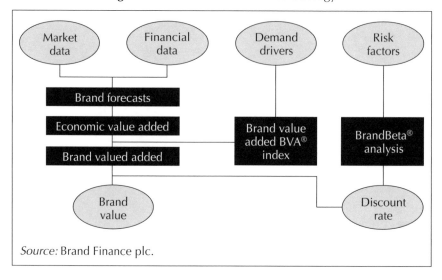

Source: Brand Finance plc.

The focus is on the return earned as a result of owning the brand—the brand's contribution to the business, both now and in the future. This framework is based on a discounted cash-flow (DCF) analysis of forecast financial performance, segmented into relevant components of value. The DCF approach is consistent with the approach to valuation used by financial analysts to value equities and by accountants to test for impairment of fixed assets (both tangible and intangible) as required by new international accounting standards.

For some purposes, market-based valuation or the royalty relief method of valuation may be possible. However, DCF valuation is the most widely accepted approach to brand valuation and provides a greater depth of understanding of the dynamics of the brand.

While brand valuations can be based on a multiple of historical earnings, it is clear that past performance is no guarantee of future performance and that investors base value judgments on expected future returns rather than actual historical returns. However, historical results are crucial for an accurate valuation, mainly because they provide information and data relationships that help to forecast the future more accurately.

Valuations based on projected earnings are therefore the preferred approach by Brand Finance, with the caveat that forecasts must be credible. Where forecasts are credible, the valuation results are both robust and actionable.

A brand valuation study typically consists of four work streams:

- financial forecasts;
- Brand Value Added (BVA®)—analysis of the brand's contribution to demand;
- BrandBeta® analysis—determination of the risk attached to future earnings; and
- valuation and sensitivity analysis.

The BVA® section of the analysis can be extended to incorporate a study of causal relationships within the business model. This facilitates the development of a dynamic brand valuation model, as discussed later.

Prior to commencing these studies, however, it is necessary to decide on the most appropriate level of segmentation.

Segmentation

In applying the valuation framework, one of the first and most critical tasks is to determine the nature of the segmentation for valuation purposes. It is then important to identify how internal financial and marketing data, and external market and competitor data, can be obtained in a way that fits with the chosen segmentation. The principles behind effective segmentation for brand valuation purposes are as follows:

- Homogeneous geographic, product, and customer groupings to ensure that the valuations are relevant to defined target markets.
- Clearly definable sets of discrete competitors in each segment to ensure that we are comparing apples with apples.
- Availability of market research data to match the chosen segmentation.
- Availability of volumetric and value data for competitor brands to match the chosen segmentation.

There is little point in choosing a valuation segmentation based on an aggregation of product or customer groupings that obscures important underlying differences. Equally, there is little point in choosing a particular detailed segmentation against which it is impossible to obtain volumetric or value data to the appropriate level of detail. Without these it may be difficult, if not impossible, to estimate relative market shares and to compare performance and forecasts against competitors.

Much of the success of a brand valuation lies in the selection and planning of the relevant segmentation and the sourcing of suitable data.

A dilemma in relation to customer segmentation is that below the broad categories lie many more specifically defined demographic, socioeconomic, or psychographic sub-segments. The marketing and market research teams may well want to "drill" down to a more detailed level for new product development or communications planning purposes, while the valuation may need for practical reasons to be cut at a higher, more aggregated level. It is often impossible to sub-segment the financial valuation to the same level of granularity that may be desirable for a market-mapping segmentation. The brand valuation team therefore needs to ensure that the segmentation for the valuation cascades up from a more detailed underlying segmentation if one is used.

Another difficulty in relation to product segmentation is that volumetric or value measures for each product group may be difficult or impossible to obtain, particularly in less well-developed or well-defined product and service areas or countries. It is also common to find that, in some client segments, it is difficult to obtain reliable data for total market size, as competitor data may be unavailable. A pragmatic approach and a medium-term strategy to populate data gaps may be required, allowing subsequent years' valuations to have an increasing level of detailed comparative analysis.

The difficulties of selecting and populating the chosen segmentation with data have been noted to highlight the need for care and experience in planning and constructing the brand valuation.

Financial forecasts

Typically, explicit forecasts for a period of three to five years are used for such valuations and should be identical to internal management planning forecasts. An important part of the brand valuation process involves ensuring that forecasts are credible.

Forecast revenues

Macroeconomic review

It is necessary to conduct extensive due diligence on each of the markets in which the brand operates to ensure the valuation takes into account all the macroeconomic factors likely to affect the level of demand for the brand. These could be technological, structural, legislative, cultural, or competitive. The brand valuation exercise needs to consider the likely trends for both volume and value for the market as a whole and for the brand being valued. This often involves detailed discussion between the brand valuation team and the internal competitor analysis, corporate strategy, market research, and marketing departments.

Microeconomic review

It is necessary to consider the factors that have historically affected the performance of the brand in each of its markets. This can involve econometric modeling or some other form of statistical analysis of past performance to show how certain causal variables have affected revenues.

One of the key issues in terms of branding is to understand the causal relationship between total marketing spend, pricing, and sales results. It is equally important to understand the relative effect of different media on the overall level of sales. The task of the brand valuation team is therefore to ensure that brand and marketing factors are being accounted for properly in the modeling and analysis taking place, and that results are used to obtain the most appropriate forecast sales values.

In the same way that it may be desirable to use econometric analysis of past influences on sales, it may also be appropriate to use projective price elasticity research to predict the effect of price on sales. Price elasticity modeling of this type is typically based on large sample quantitative research and is used to improve the accuracy of future sales forecasts. To the extent that this isn't already being done, we recommend that this should be considered as an input to the brand valuation process to help refine forecast earnings.

Forecast costs

It is also necessary to understand fully the basis on which forecast costs have been determined. The brand valuation team will need to confirm that the basis of cost allocation is sensible between each of the geographic, product, or customer segments on a current and forecast basis. The same principle applies to the allocation of capital to different segments and the resulting charges for capital made against the segmented brand earnings streams to arrive at forecast economic value added. Economic value added is the starting point for the brand valuation. A proportion of the identified economic value added is ultimately attributed to the brand in the brand valuation calculation.

Calculating brand value added (BVA®)

This is the heart of any valuation, as it determines the proportion of total economic value added to be included in the brand valuation. Having selected an appropriate segmentation and populated it with comparative volumetric, value, and market research data, we next need to identify, for each of the competitor brands under review, the extent to which the brand contributes to demand. This is done with trade-off analysis based on quantitative market research.

It is usual first to identify the key drivers of demand by reference to existing qualitative and quantitative research, or by means of management discussions. It is possible to reasonably estimate the relative importance of different factors in determining demand by means of detailed management workshops. However, it is preferable to eliminate the inherent subjectivity of this approach by using large-sample, customer-based research. It is ultimately more robust for justifying a financial valuation and more useful as a barometer of the relative importance of the different factors that drive sales demand. It is therefore more usable as a line management decision-making tool, rather than simply as a valuation technique.

Drivers of demand

Trade-off analysis can be conducted at a number of levels to identify the importance of the brand to the purchase decision from:

- one brand to another;
- one time period to another;
- one target audience sub-segment to another; and
- one product class to another.

It is an invaluable, statistically robust means of attributing income to the brand in a brand valuation. In addition, it can be used for tracking the changing importance of different drivers in given markets, for planning resource allocation behind different drivers of demand, and for tracking the effect such resource allocations may have on the profile of factors affecting demand for the brand. It can also be used to assist in anticipating future demand.

Assessing brand risk

The final step in the brand valuation is to determine the appropriate discount rate to use in the DCF analysis. Brand Finance has developed an approach to discount rate determination that is a transparent adaptation of the capital asset pricing model. The appropriate discount rate is built up from first principles, as follows:

- Discount rate = [BrandBeta® adjusted cost of equity × (proportion of equity funding)] + [cost of debt × (proportion of debt funding)]
- BrandBeta® adjusted cost of equity = risk-free rate + (equity risk premium × sector beta × BrandBeta®)

The 10 years' risk-free borrowing rate in the geographic market under review is the starting point. The equity risk premium is the medium-term excess return of the equity market over the risk-free rate. This can be obtained from investment data providers and a number of risk evaluation services. So, too, can the sector beta, which is used to determine an average implied discount rate for all brands in the sector under review.

This sector-specific discount rate is finessed to take account of the relative strength of different brands in the given market. We call this BrandBeta® analysis and base it on 10 key criteria for which data are

usually available and which in our view represent the best indicators of
risk. The generic list of BrandBeta® attributes used by Brand Finance is
shown in Figure 9.5. It must be stressed that these are evaluated in each
instance to ensure that the most appropriate grouping of risk measures
for a specific sector is identified.

Figure 9.5: A standard BrandBeta® scoring template

Attribute	Score
Time in the market	0–10
Distribution	0–10
Market share	0–10
Market position	0–10
Sales growth rate	0–10
Price premium	0–10
Price elasticity	0–10
Marketing spend	0–10
Advertising awareness	0–10
Brand awareness	0–10
Total	**0–100**

Careful planning will be required to define which competitors need to
be monitored and evaluated, and in which sectors. There may also be a
need to change the competitor set over time if the focus of the business
shifts into new areas.

A score of 50 implies that the brand offers average investment risk
in the sector under review and therefore attracts a BrandBeta® of 1.
This means that the discount rate used in the valuation will be the
average composite rate for the sector. A score of 100 implies a
theoretically risk-free brand which would be discounted at the risk-free
rate. A score of zero implies a particularly weak brand that doubles the
equity risk premium.

The review of data for the BrandBeta® analysis provides invaluable
insights into the competitive position of the brand in its market and acts
as a useful focus for a balanced scorecard for the brand. Where available,
perceived quality of brands is a strong alternative to simple "brand

awareness" in the BrandBeta® scorecard. The scorecard is data-driven, transparent, and produces supportable discount rates.

Point-in-time valuation

The result of the foregoing analysis is a branded business value for each segment identified. The branded business value expresses the full net present value of the intangible earnings in each segment. In addition, the valuation team produces a detailed competitive review with risk scoring and a robust estimate of the contribution the brand makes in each segment. This is used to drive a value for the brand alone within the total value of the branded business. Also produced is a sensitivity analysis indicating the impact on value of altering certain key assumptions.

An important philosophy behind a brand valuation exercise is that the model should become a simple and comprehensible rallying point for the whole brand team, not a sophisticated model for the initiated only.

Dynamic brand evaluation

A point-in-time valuation methodology discussed thus far provides a robust point-in-time brand valuation model drawing directly on financial, analytical, and marketing research activities that either are, or should be, in place already. In a sense, it merely brings together existing measures and processes in a coherent way. It is therefore a suitable way of producing valuations on a periodic basis by and for internal management. In our experience, it is often preferable to create a static valuation model, then increase the sophistication of the model and introduce a scenario planning capacity.

This is the purpose of a dynamic brand valuation model: to incorporate causal relationships into a brand valuation model; use the model to carry out scenario planning in order to select the most appropriate strategy; and then to track the impact of the selected strategy. Such a model can be used for considering and comparing the level of marketing investment behind the brand in different segments. It can be used for flexing key assumptions on the basis of hypotheses and testing the value impact of changes to brand activities. It will show where brand and corporate value is being created and destroyed, together with the intermediate measures that cause the growth or decline.

Econometric modeling and BVA® research are used to identify historic and predictive cause-and-effect relationships between marketing inputs and sales volumes. Both these and market assumptions can be built into a dynamic brand evaluation model in such a way that the likely impact of marketing actions on short-term profitability and long-term value can be established.

Such a tool sounds like the marketing holy grail; however, it must be remembered that the predictive ability of the model will only be as good as the research that has been used to determine the causal relationships. Even in the absence of ideal research, we have found the process of estimating cause-and-effect relationships and assessing the sensitivity of the business model to changes in these assumptions to be an extremely useful process.

Case Study 29 illustrates how a major company uses brand valuation data to continuously track performance, and so give management strategic and operational control over the group's most valuable assets.

Case Study 29
DIAGEO
Performance tracking

Prior to its merger with Guinness to form Diageo, Grand Met had a portfolio of brands including names as prominent as Smirnoff, Baileys, Häagen-Dazs, Green Giant, and Burger King.

In 1988 Grand Met had shocked the financial world by including its acquired brands as intangible assets on its balance sheet. Being so rich in name brands, it was little surprise that senior management appreciated their importance to the long-term health of the organization and wished to reflect this in the company accounts. The 1988 balance sheet included brands with a cost of £608 million.

To the board of Grand Met, the fact that a series of expensive and high-profile acquisitions might not have been included in the accounts seemed an absurd contradiction and would have left the company perilously undervalued.

An anomaly remained. Only acquired brands were included on the balance sheet, despite the obvious value to Grand Met of its internally generated brands. Similarly, early valuations were based on historical earnings multiples, a method not currently seen as accurately reflecting the true worth of a brand.

Grand Met's response to this problem, and evidence of a real bridge being built between marketing and finance functions, was the introduction of its "brand equity monitor." The purpose of this wasn't to place a historical value on a brand, but to give management an idea of the performance of brands. The factors measured couldn't be measured in purely profit and loss terms, and the monitor included economic, consumer, and perceptual measures of performance, which together formed a subtle and responsive mechanism for tracking both brand health and, if necessary, financial brand value.

The process has been extended from its early beginnings, and Diageo now monitors a number of key financial and marketing drivers to establish the level of brand equity. These drivers focus management's attention on gaining customer awareness, loyalty, market share, and the brand's ability to charge a price premium. It is this premium which communicates the value of a brand to the company's stakeholders.

There are a number of checks used by Diageo staff to assess the trends in brand equity. A sample of these measures includes awareness, advertising spend, market penetration, and share of display. Management is able to gauge the relative health of brands from a flow of consistent and reliable data. The fact that the vast majority of this data will never be included in the company accounts is irrelevant; it provides, instead, a degree of strategic and operational control over the group's most valuable assets.

10

Conclusion

Throughout this book I have stressed that brands drive business in the new world. Only by allowing this to happen can companies achieve true consumer-centricity. The other side of this "coin" is that companies may initially create brands, but then brands are built and "owned" by customers, with companies having custody of them, and so the role of consumer insight becomes absolutely vital. Brand management has now changed in its emphasis, and isn't so much about persuading consumers to prefer your brand, but more about understanding consumers so well that you can give them a brand that really adds value to their lives. The brand has to become a part of them.

With this in mind, brand managers have to concentrate on things that move the souls of people, and these aren't found in the rational world. Emotion is the key to gaining consumer acceptance, friendship, and lasting loyalty, and yet so many companies still choose to ignore this fact. Simply put, rationally based branding doesn't work in a world where parity is the norm. Functional product differences, for example, will become even more trivial. This isn't to say that a brand's promise need not be based in quality, service, innovation, and ethics; on the contrary, all great brands must have these attributes. But it is more than that, and I guess it comes down to the fact that passion is playing a much more important role in consumer buying behavior than ever before. Brands must listen to, respond to, and support the changing needs of consumers, and they are changing fast. In fact, attitude is becoming a defining factor in brand performance.

Connected to this message is the debate as to whether brands are good for people and countries, and what the future looks like for branding. I believe the route to corporate success in the future will be found in developing brands that show more care. By this I mean that the "winning brands" in the foreseeable future will be those that demonstrate not just social responsibility, but a genuine willingness to care for people and the world in which we live. Some brands are already doing this, and are passionate about how they can contribute to the well-being of humanity. Some brands merely give lip service to this subject, and others don't bother at all.

This is what I mean by "winning brands." There needn't be a correlation between a powerful brand and an absence of "the human touch." The great brands of the future will be those that can demonstrate both market power and worldly compassion. Great brands will be like great people—those whom we respect for their humility, leadership, compassion, leading-edge thinking, and the trust they place in consumers. Brands that reach such heights will, in return, be a part of the lives of millions, admired for what they are and what they do. What brands actually do for people, and what people love and care for, will become a much more important determinant of success. Emotional proactivity will be a critical success factor for brand management.

This forecast, when taken together with all of the topics I have covered in this book, means that the role of brand management is huge and changing rapidly. The best brand managers of the future will be those that can run businesses, understand and care for consumers, constantly force innovation yet maintain top quality, balance profit with social responsibility, and motivate thousands of people to work for them happily. Indeed, this is why the world's top corporate executives are now those that are proficient in brand management and marketing skills.

The demand for additional skills in the repertoire of brand managers is going to increase significantly as a result. Professional knowledge and skills will no longer be enough. The top brand managers of the future will need to be special people, with a diverse array of knowledge, skills, and attitudes. The good news is that skilled brand managers are now in great demand all around the world, and there are many opportunities to work in this exciting and very dynamic field. One thing is for sure: you will never be bored when managing brands!

In the Toolkit that follows, I have compiled questions, lists, and thoughts that I hope will assist those given the responsibility for managing brands.

Good luck with all your branding initiatives, and keep in touch with our website for additional ideas: www.brandingasia.com.

Paul Temporal,
Singapore, January 2002
ptemporal@brandingasia.com

Appendix
Your Brand Management Toolkit

This toolkit is designed to help you with your overall brand management process. It is not exhaustive, but covers the following key areas:

1. Questions on the brand as a business
2. A general brand audit questionnaire
3. Building brand personality—creating a personality and test questions
4. A question guide to the brand positioning process
5. Customer relationship management—guidelines and benefits
6. An advertising diagnostics checklist
7. A sample statement on brand strategy for investor relations
8. A brand scorecard: The top 12 traits of the world's strongest brands—do you have them?

1. Questions on the brand as a business

The key questions you have to answer before you start to build and/or set plans for managing your brand are:

- What business is my brand in?
- What is the vision for my brand?
- What consumer insights can I use to help answer the first question?
- Has my brand business got its basis in the emotional sphere?
- What personality and attitude (character) does my brand have?
- Does the brand character match that of my target audience?

- How can I improve the emotional relationship between my consumers and my brand?
- What are the implications for the future development of my brand?
- Are projects and business activities that don't add value to the brand allowed or not?
- How does my company ensure that proper brand guardianship takes place?

2. A general brand audit questionnaire

This audit is a general one that is used merely to take a snapshot of what is happening in your brand world. It doesn't deal with specifics—those come in the following sections—but serves as a reminder of the things you have to keep an eye on. Such questions should be asked once or twice yearly. It also includes questions on OEM activities, as many companies get caught out, especially in recessionary times, because they have focused their efforts on building other people's brands and not their own.

A. Corporate brand questions

- When is the corporate brand name used?
- Where is it used?
- How is it used? On its own? With products? On what basis? Where are you on the continuum between true corporate branding and absolute product branding?
- What determines the usage of the corporate brand name when subsidiaries/alliance partners are involved?
- What is the vision of the company?
- Is this the same as, or different from, the brand vision? How do they relate?
- What are the core values of the company?
- What are the brand values?
- Do either sets of values conflict?
- Does the culture represent the values?
- What are the current consumer perceptions of the brand, and how do these differ by market/segment?

- What are your alliance partner's perceptions of the brand?
- Does the brand have a strategic competitive advantage compared to competitors?
- What are the current brand images (consumer perceptions) of the major competitors in each market/category/segment?
- What are the desired consumer perceptions of the brand? Do these vary by market/category/segment?
- What are the opportunities and threats facing the brand in each market/category/segment?
- Is there an obvious opportunity to stretch the brand into a different market/category/segment?

a. *Product/sub-brand questions*
- What is the current brand architecture, and is it appropriate?
- How do product and/or sub-brands relate, if at all, to the master brand?
- What are the strengths and weaknesses of each product/sub-brand?
- Do any of them have a strategic competitive advantage or a unique selling proposition?
- How do they compare against the main competitor brands in terms of brand image?
- Does this differ by market/segment? If so, how? How are categories changing, and what effects are these having on your brands?
- Is your emphasis on own brands or OEM?
- What determines whether a product is marketed as an OEM brand or not?
- How are new product brand names chosen?
- What is the decision-making procedure for bringing a new product to market?
- How are pricing decisions made?
- How well are your channels representing your brands?
- Are there any obvious gaps in the different categories that you could fill with a new or existing brand?
- Are you tempted to extend any of your brands?
- Have you pre-tested with consumers whether they will accept the extension?

- Is your brand still in touch with its target audience? Will it continue to be if you extend it?
- Has its image shifted negatively or positively? Will it shift with an extension?
- Are you evolving the brand in line with market changes while staying true to its personality?
- Is competition eroding its position?
- Does it need repositioning or revitalizing?
- Will consumers accept a new positioning?
- What investment do you need, and what returns can you expect from a revitalization process?
- If you need to "kill" a brand, can you cope with the fallout?
- Will you just reduce investment in the brand and let it die naturally, or will you need to delete it as quickly as possible?

b. *Marketing, advertising, and promotion questions*
- What percentage of turnover is spent on A&P?
- How is this split between advertising and promotion?
- How much goes on CRM?
- How does this compare to the main competitors?
- What determines how much is spent on each brand in each market/category/segment?
- Is there a corporate marketing communications plan?
- Are there marketing communications plans for each product/sub-brand?
- Are you providing your agency with proper positioning and communications briefs?
- Is the agency providing you with an integrated approach to brand communications?
- Have you tried co-branding, and has it been successful? Why or why not?

c. *Additional questions*
- What new joint ventures/strategic alliances/changes to current organizational structure are envisaged?

- How is the brand management function organized? Does it need strengthening?
- Is it intended to change the proportion of OEM business—if so, when, and by what proportion in which markets?
- What new products/brands are to be introduced in the short and longer term?
- What are the brand strengths and weaknesses of each subsidiary/ strategic alliance?
- List the brands in order of priority, from highest to lowest value in each market, taking into account gross profit and volume sales.

3. Building brand personality

A. Creating a personality

Your brand's personality can be created in two main ways:

- Create a list of personality characteristics, say 20 or 30, and then narrow these down to the three to seven most important ones you want your brand to have. These might include some that your brand already has or some you want it to have. In other words, some may already be brand strengths, and some weaker aspects of the brand you wish to be perceived as owning. This is a common way to create a personality for a brand that is being revitalized or repositioned. It needs consensus among all who can influence the brand inside your company, and you have to work very hard on the elements your brand doesn't yet possess—this may take time, but may be well worth the effort.
- Match the brand characteristics to those of your target audience. Here, you must rely on market research to tell you what these characteristics are.

B. Test questions

Test questions to gain agreement on how your brand might relate to people can include the following:

- What would your brand be if it were a holiday destination?
- What would it be if it were an animal? A film star? A car?

- What brands of clothing would it wear if it were an actual person?
- What kind of place would it live in?
- What would its lifestyle be like?
- What kind of friends would it have?
- If it went out to a restaurant, what food would your brand eat, in what kind of ambience?
- If you had to introduce your brand to a friend, what would you say?
- If you had to write an obituary for your brand, what would it say?

These questions are not only useful to test out the consistency of brand management thinking, but they can also be used within focus group discussions to see whether the personality is clear, and with agencies to determine what should and shouldn't appear in creative.

4. A question guide to the positioning process

This is a comprehensive set of questions to help you through all aspects of the positioning process.

Step 1: Taking a good look at the market

- How fast is the market growing?
- What level of competition is there, and where is it coming from?
- Who are our main competitors for each of our brands?
- What segments exist in the market we are interested in?
- Where are the growth opportunities? Which segments are growing faster than others, and why?
- Why do customers come to/leave us?
- Why do they go to each of our competitors?
- What are our priorities for business growth?

Step 2: Understanding our present image and position

- How do people (employees and customers) see us at present?
- What are the strengths and weaknesses of our current brand image?
- How does our image compare with those of our key competitors?

- What is our position relative to the competition on a consumer perceptual map?
- How close or far away from the consumer ideal preferences are we and the other players?
- What strategic opportunities are there to move into spaces or gaps that consumers would appreciate and yet haven't been filled?
- Can we do more research to add precision to these views of consumer perceptions?

Step 3: Developing positioning alternatives

- What is our desired position and image?
- What space do we want to move into in the mind map of consumers?
- What strategy, or combination of strategies, do we think are best suited to achieving our goal?
- How are we going to explain what we stand for in terms of our personality, and what makes us both different from and better than the main competitors?
- Are the options sustainable in the long run, or will they only afford us a short-term differential advantage?

Step 4: Creating the final positioning statement

Now it is time to write the final positioning statement, which is framed in consumer language as a statement of how precisely we want them to think about us.

- What business or product class are we in?
- Who is our target audience?
- What benefits are we offering them?
- Why are we better than and different from the competition?

Above all, this desired position and image we wish to create in people's minds must be credible, believable, relevant to them, and capable of being delivered.

Step 5: Adapting to the new position—delivering on the promise

- Do we have to develop a new product or adapt existing ones?
- Do we have to change our service standards?
- Do we have to change our visual identity or product packaging?
- Do we have to change our brand name(s)?
- Do we have to change our corporate culture?
- Do we have to adjust our pricing or distribution policies?
- What will be our communications strategy once all these things are in place?
- What is our communications plan?

Step 6: Monitoring success—have we achieved the brand image we want?

This last step is very important, as we may have to adjust what we offer, our communications, or even our position, if the market situation changes or the perceptions, needs, and wants of the consumers evolve. Monitoring image and positioning means constantly evaluating every one of the steps mentioned above. If this isn't done, there is a real danger that we will lose touch with the market and, importantly, consumer feelings and perceptions about us. Image building is a continuous process and requires continuous feedback from all quarters. There is no room for complacency, and corporate graveyards are littered with failed businesses that never understood the thoughts of those people who really counted. Images are fragile, delicate things that must be given care and attention. They exist only as thoughts and feelings, and temporarily occupy positions in people's minds. Without constant reinforcement and improvement, they will lose their importance and be replaced by other stronger images. The positioning process builds strong images, but it is careful management of the positions created that sustains them.

5. Customer relationship management—guidelines and benefits

A. *What is CRM?*

- CRM represents a fantastic opportunity for anyone wishing to build a corporate brand, because it helps the rapid build-up of both brand equity and brand value.
- Additionally, it creates differentiation and helps grow market share, and by so doing builds the financial value of the brand.
- CRM helps build brands *quickly*. It accelerates both the learning curve about the customer, and the development of the brand–customer relationship. It is the future of brand building.
- CRM is all about collaborating with your customer. It is concerned with creating the classic win–win situation, where you add value to your customer's daily life, and he or she gives you loyalty in return.
- Not all customers are equal. The Pareto principle (80:20 rule) nearly always applies to any business situation, where approximately 80% of your profits come from 20% of your customers.
- The purpose of a CRM program is to recognise the best customers and hold on to them. It also has the aim of transforming lower-value customers into higher-value ones.
- Effective CRM is about applying the knowledge you hold about your customer every time he or she interacts with you, in such a way that you add value to your product or service, strengthening the emotional bond between the customer, your brand, and your company.
- CRM isn't a fantastic new technique that has been created for the new millennium. It was being practiced way back in the days when Mom and Pop stores were everywhere.
- Many CRM programs take the form of points-based loyalty schemes, but generally speaking, points-based schemes do little to improve the loyalty of customers.
- CRM isn't something that can give impact to your business overnight. The real payback will come over time, but it will be real, and it will be permanent.
- I have yet to come across a single organization or business that wouldn't derive real benefits from CRM.

- CRM allows you do the unthinkable—to benefit your customer and yourself at the same time.

B. How CRM works

CRM works by:

- Creating a continuous communication loop between your organization and your customer.
- Getting to know the customer.
- Using existing customer data.
- Asking the customer what they want from you.
- Establishing the unlocked potential.
- Creating the knowledge.
- Reusing the knowledge time after time.
- Having CRM in your company will give you a large number of benefits, including:
  - Helping you to build your brand image.
  - Attracting new customers.
  - Selling more to your current customers.
  - Shielding your customers from approaches by your competitors.
  - Increased returns on brand investment.
  - Stronger and cheaper customer acquisition rates.
  - Increased customer referrals.
  - Lower rates of brand defection.
  - Expressing brand personality.
  - Increasing staff loyalty.
  - More effective use of A&P budgets.
  - Better understanding of the business cost drivers.
  - More effective, relevant product design.
  - Reduced research needs.
  - Increased profits and brand value.
  - Adding value to investor relations.
- Companies that focus on developing a strong relationship with their customers will obtain twice the sales growth of those that don't.
- Those same companies can expect to receive six times the return on equity of those that don't build a bond with their customers.

- Far and away the largest reason for customers leaving is that companies don't talk to them, and they feel unwanted or badly treated.

Adding value to your brand really means that it has to do one or all of the following:

- It saves customers money.
- It saves them time (time equals money).
- It saves them hassle (offers a quicker/more efficient service).
- It customizes products or services specifically to customer needs.

C. Implementation steps

- The key question for every manager every day is: What are you doing today to add value to your customers' lives?
- In the new-style company, it isn't the brand or product manager who is most important—it is the "customer manager."
- Segmentation has always been a key element of any marketing strategy and is vital to the branding process. The better-defined the target, the more effective your brand strategy is likely to be.
- Installing your CRM program is a great chance to "spring clean" your processes. Remove tasks being performed each day that add no real value to either your customers or your organization.
- Set up a pilot program and monitor its impact.
- Prepare for roadblocks to your CRM project in advance.
- Work through your financial justification for your project as soon as possible.
- Don't neglect your internal marketing.
- Reuse current initiatives wherever possible.
- Find a project champion.
- Make sensible use of outsourcing to speed up your project.
- Plan your migration strategy while your pilot is running.
- The three golden rules before starting your CRM program are:
  - Develop clear objectives.
  - Make things easy for the customer.
  - Be realistic about what you can achieve.

D. *Profitability of customers*

- You must establish the profitability of your customers.
- How does the Pareto principle apply to your customer base? Is it 80:20 or 90:10?
- Your money should be seeking out customers who:
  - buy from you regularly;
  - have bought from you recently;
  - are making a significant contribution to your company profits;
  - are recommending your product or service to friends and colleagues; and/or
  - have significant development potential.

You need to build a profile of your most profitable customers: who they are; where they live; what they do for a living; their family background; their lifestyle.

Your next priority is to look at the second most profitable group. Who is in this group and fits the profile of your most profitable customers? What are they doing differently which means they are not so profitable for you? How can you use your marketing skills via CRM to change their habits?

Plug your information gaps by talking to your customers by any means available to you.

The hub of any CRM initiative must be your marketing database. Without it, you cannot hope to harness the information you hold about your customers.

Look at the recency, frequency, and value of your interactions with your customers, and use this to prioritize your CRM activities.

When you build your program, include tiers to create recognition and to motivate customers within the program to perform in such a way that they reach the next level of value to your company.

6. An advertising diagnostics checklist

This is a basic framework for evaluating advertisements/storyboards put forward to you by agencies. Sometimes (in my experience, *always*) advertising agencies get carried away with their creative ideas. Some of these may be outstanding, but some may be way off strategy, and as a brand manager it's your call. You must be disciplined and tough to take on the pressure of agency persuasion. Here are some useful reminders of the kind of things you should be focusing on, instead of the "smoke and mirrors" the agencies sometimes produce in their efforts to gain revenue. Above all, try to be totally objective, even though your job and/or the brand's success depends on your judgment. Put yourself in the shoes of the target consumer. Have a mental picture of them, or some hard data that gives you an understanding of who they are and what they are like.

A. First reaction

- What is your immediate response to the agency's presentation?
- Is there a central message or idea?
- Will it be noticed?
- Will it be received and enjoyed?
- Is it entertaining?
- Is the idea capable of sustaining a long campaign?

B. Consumer response

- What will the consumer take out? (Not what the agency has put in.)
- What key messages are there from the brand's positioning?
- Does the brand personality come across adequately?

C. Visuals: Look at these very carefully with your colleagues

- What impact do the visuals have on you?
- As an entity, is it on brand or not?
- If you feel it is, does the opening shot set the stage and attract?
- Will consumers remember the brand and not the ad?
- Is the situation interesting to consumers?
- Can they identify with it—the style, story, mood, effects?
- Is it too gimmicky or quirky?
- Is there a story? Is the story believable?
- Is it simple and easy to understand?
- Will it stand out from the clutter?
- Is the tone right (e.g. not patronizing)?
- Is it durable, or will people tire of it very quickly?

D. Words: Read these two or three times

- Do the words support the pictures?
- Do they fit with the brand personality?
- Are they of interest to the consumer?

E.   Check for total understanding

- Does the whole represent your vision of the brand and the way it should relate to consumers?
- Does the advertisement attract the heart as well as the head?

7. A sample statement on brand strategy for investor relations

This statement is a typical media release intended for investors under circumstances when a company is either involved in a campaign for listing, or when trying to change the perceptions of investors in the light of repositioning activities. It is corporate by nature, for obvious reasons. It is fictitious and can be modified to suit different occasions and circumstances.

> Company X believes in the value of brands, and in their worth as strategic business assets. Developing and managing our brands is a business priority, and will fulfill our vision.
>
> In the industry we belong to, we believe that only the strong brands will survive in a profitable way. Whilst operational effectiveness is necessary, it does not serve to differentiate a company in a crowded market. We believe that competitive strategy is all about being different, and that branding brings about that difference.
>
> Company X has embarked on a program of activity to build a powerful corporate brand, and leverage on the significant competitive strengths that the company has. With a corporate reputation for being passionate, professional, innovative, and loving in the minds of consumers and partners, Company X intends to generate further brand awareness and loyalty at all levels of the value chain by enhancing the presence of the corporate brand in all market communications.

At present, a significant amount of our business has been created through the branding of our individual products as opposed to corporate branding, and we have done very well. However, a recent brand audit has revealed substantial opportunities to further enhance the image of the parent brand. While product branding is clearly an important feature of the overall business profile, a carefully introduced corporate master brand will add further consistency, trust, and confidence across all our offerings. It will add strength to individual brands and produce synergy across all our communications. Moreover, it will avoid the need for costly duplication of advertising and promotional resources, particularly when new brands are introduced, as they will be in the future.

The company believes that brands are strategic assets in their own right and is fully aware of the value that can be attached to brand names. Presently, a brand strategy project is nearing completion that will produce a "blueprint" guide to the building of Company X brand equity and value, both corporate and product.

8. A brand scorecard: The top 12 traits of the world's strongest brands—do you have them?

Throughout this book I have referred to best practices in brand management. These are now summarized in a brand scorecard. You will find it helpful to discuss and rate your brand(s) on these attributes, from both an internal and external perspective. Be honest, and *especially* look from the outside in—through the eyes of the consumer. Working hard on all of these attributes will ensure brand success. Ignoring any of them will leave your brand(s) with unfulfilled potential and a degree of vulnerability. It is also worth mentioning that the attributes are intertwined, and changes in one may bring about changes in others.

The world's most powerful brands have the following attributes in common:

1. They have a vision of their own.
2. They develop emotional capital.
3. They are well differentiated (positioned).
4. They are highly consistent in adherence to their values.

Index